# DB2 SQL PROCEDURAL LANGUAGE FOR LINUX, UNIX, AND WINDOWS

ISBN 013100772-6

# IBM DB2 Certification Guide Series

*DB2 SQL Procedural Language for Linux, UNIX, and Windows*
by Yip, Bradstock, Curtis, Gao, Janmohamed, Liu, and McArthur

*DB2 Universal Database for OS/390 v7.1 Application Certification Guide*
by Lawson

*DB2 Universal Database v7.1 Application Development Certification Guide*
by Sanyal, Martineau, Gashyna, and Kyprianou

*DB2 Universal Database v8 for UNIX, Linux, and Windows Administration Certification Guide, Fifth Edition*
by Baklarz and Wong

*DB2 Universal Database in Application Development Environments*
by Shirai, Barber, Saboji, Naick, and Wilkins

*DB2 Universal Database v6.1 Certification Guide, Third Edition*
by Cook, Harbus, and Shirai

*DB2 Universal Database in the Solaris Operating Environment*
by Shirai, Michel, Wilding, Logan, and Bauch

*DB2 Cluster Certification Guide*
by Cook, Janacek, and Snow

*DB2 Universal DRDA Certification Guide*
by Brandl, Bullock, Cook, Harbus, Janacek, and Le

*DB2 Replication Certification Guide*
by Cook and Harbus

*DB2 Universal Database and SAP R/3, Version 4*
by Bullock, Cook, Deedes-Vincke, Harbus, Nardone, and Neuhaus

*The Universal Guide to DB2 for Windows NT*
by Cook, Harbus, and Snow

# DB2® SQL Procedural Language for Linux, UNIX®, and Windows®

PAUL YIP ■ DREW BRADSTOCK ■ HANA CURTIS

MICHAEL X. GAO ■ ZAMIL JANMOHAMED

CLARA LIU ■ FRASER MCARTHUR

International Technical Support Organization
Austin, Texas 78758

PRENTICE HALL PROFESSIONAL TECHNICAL REFERENCE
UPPER SADDLE RIVER, NEW JERSEY 07458
www.phptr.com

Editorial/production supervision: *Mary Sudul*
Cover design director: *Jerry Votta*
Cover design: *Bruce Kenselaar*
Manufacturing manager: *Alexis Heydt-Long*
Acquisitions editor: *Jeff Pepper*
Editorial assistant: *Linda Ramagnano*
Marketing manager: *Debby vanDijk*

Published by Pearson Education, Inc.
Publishing as Prentice Hall Professional Technical Reference
Upper Saddle River, NJ 07458

Prentice Hall books are widely used by corporations and government agencies for training, marketing, and resale.

For information regarding corporate and government bulk discounts please contact:
Corporate and Government Sales (800) 382-3419 or corpsales@pearsontechgroup.com



Printed in the United States of America

10 9 8 7 6 5 4 3 2 1

ISBN 0-13-100772-6

Pearson Education LTD.
Pearson Education Australia PTY, Limited
Pearson Education Singapore, Pte. Ltd.
Pearson Education North Asia Ltd.
Pearson Education Canada, Ltd.
Pearson Educación de Mexico, S.A. de C.V.
Pearson Education — Japan
Pearson Education Malaysia, Pte. Ltd.

# CONTENTS

# About the Authors

This book was written by a team of DB2 UDB consultants from the IBM Toronto Software Laboratory, where the core of DB2 for Linux, UNIX and Windows is developed. The team has traveled all over North America, Asia Pacific, and Europe to help companies of all sizes to:

- Migrate applications and databases from other database management systems to DB2
- Perform application benchmarks
- Validate application architecture design
- Verify logical and physical database design
- Assist in critical application deployments
- Teach accelerated DB2 certification courses
- Teach experienced DBAs how to leverage their existing skills in DB2

As a group, the authors hold the following certifications:

- IBM Certified Solutions Expert - Database Administration (all)
- IBM Certified Solutions Expert - Family Application Development (all)
- IBM Advanced Technical Expert - DB2 Replication
- Sun Certified Java2 Programmer
- RedHat Linux Certified Engineer

They have published numerous articles and presented at technical conferences both externally and internally at IBM. Each author has his or her own unique specialties and experiences. The team has written or migrated thousands of stored procedures, triggers and user-defined functions for dozens of applications using DB2 SQL Procedural Language.

# ACKNOWLEDGMENTS

There are numerous people we'd like to thank for their contributions to this book.

We are grateful to Serge Rielau and Gustavo Arocena from DB2 development for not only assisting us in verifying the content and providing insight to version 8 SQL PL enhancements, but also for their technical guidance on SQL PL over the years (starting from well before the start of this project).

Mary Sudul and the entire book production team at Prentice Hall for working so hard to deliver the book to market.

James Huddleston, our editor, did an exceptional job in editing our book. The biggest challenge of writing a book with seven authors is consistency, and James helped us fill that need with both his technical expertise and editing skills.

Without the guidance of Susan Visser, Victoria Jones, and Jeffrey Pepper this book would never have been completed as smoothly as it has.

Special thanks to Kathryn Zeidenstein and Melinda Pfeiffer for designing and maintaining the official website for this book at DB2 Developer Domain. Without this site, we would have no way of providing errata and additional support material to our readers.

We are also indebted to Debra Eaton, Marina Greenstein, Brian Kalberer, Larry Menard, and Burt Vialpando, all of whom helped us review the book, made corrections for content and accuracy, and provided valuable feedback.

Finally, we'd like to thank the IBM International Technical Support Organization (ITSO) for allowing us to reprint SQL cross-platform compatibility charts of the Redbook, "Cross-Platform DB2 Stored Procedures: Building and Debugging".

Although many have helped us verify the contents of this book, any errors are our own. If you find an error, please contact us at db2sqlpl@ca.ibm.com so that we may correct it for the future.

# Support Materials

DB2 Developer Domain hosts the official website for this book at
**ibm.com**/software/data/developer/sqlplbook/

## DB2® Developer Domain

Your one-stop resource for technical information about IBM Data Management software: **ibm.com**/software/data/developer

*DB2 Developer Domain* is your online source for technical information about the DB2 and the IBM® data management development platform including DB2 Universal Database™, Informix®, and IBM Content Manager.

Find:

- Technical articles written by IBM developers, consultants, and other experts in the industry, including the authors of this book!
- Sample code and code downloads
- Hints and tips
- Links to fixes and product downloads

  ... and more

Find it here and find it ***fast.***

# Foreword

As I write this, we have recently delivered the newest version of DB2 to market, DB2 UDB version 8.1. This version represents the most significant release of DB2 since it was first introduced back in the early '90s. In version 8.1, we delivered over 400 new capabilities that serve to greatly advance the state of the art of modern database systems. Many of these features were designed to address the requirements of the developer and partner community and have helped solutions that are built atop DB2 to achieve new levels of performance, scalability and availability. One of these important development-oriented features is the very subject of this publication. Other abundant areas of technical leadership that have been introduced by DB2 in recent years, coupled with efficient pricing, unsurpassed quality, and leadership in technical support have all helped to propel DB2 to a market leadership position, growing much more quickly than other database systems available in the market today. We have grown from being one of the pack, to being the one to watch in database circles.

In keeping the tradition, with DB2 UDB version 8.1, we have delivered a breakthrough offering that incorporates world class scalability, reliability and high availability features, and at the same time we have greatly increased the ease of use, managability and simplicity of DB2. One of the areas that received a great deal of attention during our market introduction was our innovation to provide "Autonomic Computing" features as a base property of the database. "Autonomic Computing" can be roughly defined as an ability for a system to be self-tuning, self-diagnosing, and even self-healing. For DB2, our "Autonomic Computing" capabilities included, but are not limited to, the Configuration Advisor and Health Center, two facilities that help customers get up and running quickly with a more optimally tuned configuration, and to keep that configuration running with management by exception facilities that can detect problems and alert administrators proactively or even change dynamically. These features are delivering productivity boosts for administrators that work with DB2 and are serving to help eliminate outages or bottlenecks in production environments.

As I mentioned earlier, we also added many features which focus purely on the productivity of application developers who build solutions atop DB2 or want to migrate existing applications and/or business logic to DB2 in order to achieve better total cost of ownership and performance. The purpose of this book is to discuss one of the more important application development enhancements, the SQL Procedural Language for DB2.

Simply put, SQL PL for DB2 provides a high-level language to build portable application logic that has the potential for better performance and scalability by virtue of exploiting server-side resources and the eliminating client bottlenecks. In addition, exploiting SQL PL can serve to improve the managability and security of applications by providing a more modular structure. DB2 version 8.1 provides an added bonus with the Development Center which provides a graphical interface and facility for building, debugging and deploying SQL PL for DB2.

Knowing how and when to exploit the many capabilities of SQL PL for DB2 is an important skill to develop and the authors of this book have done a very nice job in laying out the many benefits in an efficient and consumable format for the reader. There are many good examples that will give the reader working samples of code to help get the ball rolling quickly. They include basic and advanced techniques and also cover tools such as the DB2 Development Center which will help in the creation and management of SQL PL for DB2. Furthermore, the authors represent true experts and practitioners in the field and have an impressive combined level of expertise for this domain. They practice "eating their own cooking" in many respects so their advice is well-grounded in fundamentals and experience.

We're proud of the success that we have had with DB2 and grateful to the many partners, developers and customers who have chosen to build and run their solutions with our database product. As always, our job is to listen intently to your requirements, and to respond by rapidly innovating solutions to address your needs. DB2 version 8.1 is the manifestation of addressing many such requirements. We trust that the skills that you are about to learn or hone for SQL PL for DB2 will serve you well and we look forward to a continuing relationship of delivering best of breed products to serve your needs.

Robert J. Picciano
Director of Database Technology
IBM Toronto Software Lab

CHAPTER 1

# Introduction

Welcome to DB2 SQL Procedural Language for Linux, UNIX and Windows (distributed platforms). Throughout this book you will learn how to use effectively the SQL Procedural Language (SQL PL) for IBM DB2 Universal Database (DB2 UDB). By the end of the book, you will have the skills and resources to create a wide variety of SQL procedures, triggers, and user-defined functions that use complex program and business logic.

Although this book focuses on SQL PL for distributed platforms, the language is fairly compatible across the DB2 family of products, including DB2 for OS/390 and AS400. To help with compatibility issues, a chart has been included in Appendix I - SQL PL Cross Platform Compatibility.

In addition to the language elements of SQL PL, this book will help you understand how stored procedures are implemented and how to best take advantage of the functionality available.

## 1.1 Intended Audience

This book is intended for any individual who works with databases such as database administrators (DBAs), application developers, technical consultants, and students. The reader is assumed to have worked with SQL and understand its purpose, syntax, and behavior. Instruction on using SQL is not provided, but because DB2 SQL PL has its roots in SQL, a working knowledge of SQL is essential to understanding the concepts discussed.

Knowledge of DB2 is not required for the reader to learn SQL PL, but it will help in understanding some of the more advanced topics in the book. For those who are new to DB2, Appendix A, "Getting Started with DB2" provides a quick tutorial with enough instruction on DB2 commands to get you started.

Since this book does not assume any previous knowledge of DB2, it is ideal for those who want to learn SQL PL, but do not have time to learn database administration details.

Finally, this book does not assume any programming experience in any language. A familiarity with fundamental programming concepts will give the reader a head start, but all programming concepts involved with SQL PL will be covered in detail.

The concepts and programs presented in this guide are all based on the SQL-99 standard. There are a number of excellent references available online that cover the standard in detail.

## 1.2 History of Stored Procedures

The use of databases has progressed rapidly in the last twenty years. As the amount of data collected by companies has increased, so have the demands on application developers to make use of it.

When databases were originally used, all of the processing was done on large mainframes with the output being sent to dumb terminals. There was no concern about where the application processed the data since the data always resided on the server. This changed when databases began to appear on midrange UNIX machines where the client and server were often separate. Stored procedures were created to allow data processing to occur on the much faster servers, to reduce the workload and CPU bottlenecks on the slower clients, and to reduce the amount of data sent across the network.

Originally in DB2, stored procedures were developed using the C programming language, which gave developers greater flexibility in how they could manipulate data. This flexibility, however, came with a price, since writing the procedures was a complicated and error-prone process. Developers had to be highly knowledgeable in both C and embedded SQL, which was often a difficult combination to find.

This created a demand for an easier method to write stored procedures. This led to the creation of a new third-generation (3GL) programming language. The language was based on the existing SQL syntax and used a simple structured programming language very similar to early BASIC™. This new language allowed programmers to quickly develop and build stored procedures without having to know any complex programming languages or data structures. The ease of development led to an explosion in the use of stored procedures, as both developers and database administrators learned how to work with this new simplified programming language.

Stored procedures have also improved the speed of the applications that use them. Using a stored procedure helps to reduce network traffic, since only the original request and the final output need to be transmitted between the client and the server. Using stored procedures also helps you to make better use of the larger number of CPUs and disks sitting on your database server as opposed to your client workstation. With the push for application interfaces running on the Web, it will become even more important to minimize the amount of work performed by the client.

Today's stored procedures are used in a range of applications, from small banking transactions to complex business logic that can be thousands of lines long.

## 1.3 DB2's SQL Procedural Language

The DB2 SQL Procedural Language (SQL PL) is a subset of the SQL Persistent Stored Modules (SQL/PSM) language standard. The specification of the current SQL/PSM standard can be found in ANSI/ISO/IEC 9075-4:1999 *Information Technology — Database Language SQL—Part 4: Persistent Stored Modules (SQL/PSM).* This standard is the basis for the structured programming languages used with SQL to write stored procedures and functions. The standard combines the ease of data access of SQL with the flow control structures of a simple programming language. It gives developers the ability to create compound SQL statements and procedures that only need to be coded once for multiple platforms. There are a great number of advantages to using stored procedures with your databases and applications. To name a few:

- All of the processing is done on the (typically) more powerful server side.
- Reduced network communication due to only the call and the results being transmitted across the network.
- They are modular and can be moved from database to database.
- Complex business and database logic can be hidden from application developers and reduced to a single procedure call.

With the vast number of web-based applications and the movement towards web services, it is important for developers to minimize the amount of work that is performed on the client. Running stored procedures on the server also allows database administrators to control what SQL is executed and tune performance for it.

Keeping complex business logic on the server in stored procedures will help improve the general performance of most data-driven applications. Instead of an application having to send data back and forth across a network for every SQL statement and cursor, a single call can be made with one result returned at the end. This makes the application more secure and also allows a network to handle more users without data transfers creating bottlenecks.

SQL procedures can be used to separate database access from application logic, which greatly reduces the complexity of application code. SQL procedures can be used to encapsulate all the complex logic and SQL operations while the applications remain lightweight, calling procedures as needed to do the database work on their behalf. Moreover, when using this model for development, applications can be more database independent and the SQL in stored procedures can be tuned for each database vendor.

Using SQL procedures also makes the code easier to test. Encapsulating business logic in SQL procedures allows developers to use procedures as modular units and even treat them as object-oriented programming units.

## 1.4 Introduction to the Development Center

Included with DB2 UDB V8 is an integrated SQL procedure development tool called the *Development Center*. This tool will allow you to build stored procedures and user-defined functions using SQL PL or Java. The Development Center can be run on its own or can be used as a component of IBM WebSphere Studio Application Developer (WSAD) or Microsoft Visual Studio. If the stored procedures are created using DB2 SQL PL, then you have a full range of debugging capabilities available to you that will, for example, allow you to step through SQL procedure execution line by line. An earlier version of the Development Center is available in DB2 UDB V7.2 but it has a different interface and is called the *Stored Procedure Builder*. It also allows you to build and debug stored procedures and can be used with the example code included with this guide. There are, however, some enhancements to SQL PL in Version 8 that will not work on DB2 UDB V7.2. A tutorial on how to use the Development Center is included in Appendix C - Using the DB2 Development Center.

## 1.5 Other Stored Procedure Languages

All of the major database vendors support their own versions of an SQL procedural language. Each language supports the same core SQL commands, but each has its own unique implementation. Microsoft's SQLServer and Sybase's procedural languages are quite similar and are called *T-SQL* (for *Transact-SQL*). Informix uses *Informix SPL* (stored procedure language), which is a 3GL similar to DB2 SQL PL. Oracle's procedural language is called PL/SQL. There are a number of references on the Web that can guide you in converting your stored procedures from other languages to stored procedures for DB2. A list of these references can be found in Appendix G, "Additional Resources."

## 1.6 Syntax Description

All SQL syntax diagrams throughout this book follow style that is consistent with DB2's official product documentation. The syntax diagrams are all read from left to right and top to bottom following the flow of the arrows at the end of each line. In all of the diagrams, all DB2 tokens are in uppercase and variable names are in italics.

**Example 1:**

```
>>---- Word1 --- Word2 -----------◊>
>>-------- Word3 ------ Word4 ----◊<

Output: Word1 Word2 Word3 Word4
```

All tokens that are in sequence must be included in the order in which they are listed.

**Example 2:**

```
                  ,--- optional Word ---,
>>-- Word1 ------------------------------------◊<

Output 1: Word1
Output 2: Word1 optionalWord
```

The *optional Word* token is optional and does not have to be included in the statement.

**Example 3:**

```
                     .---,------------.          .----- Word2 ---.
                     V                |          V               |
>>---  Word1   ----- host Variable --------------------------------◊>

Output 1: Word1
Output 2: Word1 hostVariable1, hostVariable2, hostVariable3
Output 3: Word1 Word2
Output 4: Word1 hostVariable1 Word2
```

Any tokens that have a flow arrow wrapping around are repeated zero or more times.

A common naming convention is used throughout the guide for all of the examples. You are not required to label your variables this way but it will make debugging and maintaining your code easier.

```
p_parameterName: SQL procedure input and output parameters
v_parameterName: SQL variables
c_cursorName: Cursors
```

## 1.7 Meanings of Style

There are a number of different styles used to indicate items of interest throughout the guide.

### 1.7.1 Code

```
CREATE PROCEDURE intro1 (OUT p_output INT)
LANGUAGE SQL
BEGIN
    SET p_output = 1;
END
```

### 1.7.2 Tip

This indicates an advanced tip in the context of the current topic.

## 1.8 Book Structure

Each successive chapter in the book is designed to be a prerequisite for the following chapters. At the beginning of every chapter there is a summary of the terms and subjects that will be covered. The summary allows experienced users to check if they already understand the material that will be covered in the chapter. If they feel that they already know the material they can quickly move on to other chapters.

# 1.9 Chapter Summaries

## 1.9.1 Chapter 1: Introduction

The introduction gives the reader a brief overview of DB2 SQL PL origins and the benefits of using SQL procedures. A detailed description of how to use this book and how it is laid out is also covered.

## 1.9.2 Chapter 2: Basic SQL Procedure Structure

The material in this chapter serves as a foundation for the remaining chapters. Topics covered in Chapter 2 include the CREATE PROCEDURE syntax, the structure of the SQL procedure program body, variable declaration and manipulation, and a discussion of what database commands are allowed in DB2 SQL procedures.

## 1.9.3 Chapter 3: Using Flow of Control Statements

This section explains how program flow and the sequence of execution are controlled in SQL procedures. Topics covered include labeling and creating compound statements, conditional statements (such as IF and CASE), looping statements (like FOR and WHILE), and branching and control statements.

## 1.9.4 Chapter 4: Understanding and Using Cursors and Result Sets

This chapter covers how cursors are created and used, at a series of levels that will help both beginners and experienced programmers alike. The topics covered include cursor concepts, creation, and various ways to use them.

## 1.9.5 Chapter 5: Condition Handling

This chapter explains how to handle warnings and exceptions properly to ensure stable and error-free programs. The topics covered include how to check and use the SQLCODE and SQLSTATE values, how and why you should create error and condition handlers, and advanced use of handlers to control program logic and behavior.

### 1.9.6 Chapter 6: Using Dynamic SQL

This chapter explains how to use dynamic SQL to increase the flexibility of SQL procedure code. The topics covered include a comparison of dynamic and static SQL, various forms of using dynamic SQL, parameter markers, and special considerations.

### 1.9.7 Chapter 7: Working with Nested SQL Procedures

The calling and nesting of SQL procedures is covered in this chapter. The ability to call SQL procedures from other SQL procedures allows much more flexibility for programming. The topics covered include passing of parameters between procedures, returning values, returning result sets and restrictions on nesting.

### 1.9.8 Chapter 8: Leveraging DB2 Advanced Features

This chapter covers the advanced application development features of DB2 and how to use them in SQL procedures. Previous chapters provided the foundations for creating SQL procedures, but this chapter gives both new and experienced programmers the tools to create even more complex and powerful procedures. The topics covered include working with sequences, identity columns, global temporary tables, savepoints and large objects.

### 1.9.9 Chapter 9: Deploying SQL Procedures

This chapter explains how to deploy SQL procedures in real-world situations, that is, to implement them in production environments. The topics covered include how to deploy SQL procedures using the GET and PUT ROUTINE commands, the GUI tools, and scripts. Security, schema, and codepage considerations are also discussed.

### 1.9.10 Chapter 10: Working with Triggers and User-Defined Functions

The last chapter of the book covers how the SQL Procedural Language is used in other areas of DB2. The topics include SQL PL usage in triggers and SQL user-defined functions.

### 1.9.11 Appendices

The appendices cover topics that are not directly related to the SQL Procedural Language itself, but will enhance your experience and understanding of it. Appendix A, "Getting Started with DB2," for example, is a quick tutorial for those who are new to DB2. A complete listing of the different topics covered in the appendices can be found in the table of contents.

## 1.10 The CD-ROM

Included with this book is a CD that contains a trial version of DB2 V8 Personal Edition for Windows. This software will allow you to have a working copy of DB2 installed and running on your machine. The Development Center is also part of the DB2 installation. All of the code samples listed in this book can be found on the CD in directories associated with each chapter. For example, the code snippets for Chapter 4 would be found on the CD-ROM in the directory '\samples\chapter4.' A simple naming convention for sample code is also used. For example, the name of the file containing code from Figure 6.4 will start with F6_4 followed by a short description.

## 1.11 Getting Started

The first thing that you will want to do is install DB2 on your system. If you are new to DB2, start by reading through Appendix A, "Getting Started with DB2." After you have installed DB2, you should create the DB2 sample database (as explained in Appendix A), as the examples presented in this book will make use of it. Depending on your development environment, it may be necessary to configure your environment to build SQL procedures. Please refer to Appendix B, "Setting Up the Build Environment."

## 1.12 Contacting the Authors

We are always looking for any feedback that you have both about this book and about DB2 SQL procedures. Please contact us with your opinions and inquiries at db2sqlpl@ca.ibm.com. Depending on the volume of inquires, we may be unable to respond to every technical question but we'll do our best. The DB2 newsgroup at comp.databases.ibm-db2 is another great way to get assistance from IBM employees and the DB2 user community.

Have fun!

CHAPTER 2

# Basic SQL Procedure Structure

## In this chapter, you will learn:

- the fundamental structure of an SQL procedure;
- how to define an SQL procedure in a DB2 database using the CREATE PROCEDURE statement;
- the various clauses for the CREATE PROCEDURE statement;
- the structure of the procedure body;
- the statements that can be coded in the procedure body.

SQL procedures are defined in a DB2 database using the CREATE PROCEDURE statement. The statement consists of various clauses as well as the procedure body. This chapter describes how to create simple SQL procedures.

## 2.1 The CREATE PROCEDURE Statement

The CREATE PROCEDURE statement defines a procedure in the database. The clauses define the name and parameters as well as the procedure body consisting of one or more SQL PL statements. Figure 2.1 describes the syntax of the CREATE PROCEDURE statement and the clauses that apply to SQL procedures.

**NOTE** There are many clauses available for the CREATE PROCEDURE statement, however it is often appropriate to just use the defaults.

**Figure 2.1** CREATE PROCEDURE Statement Syntax

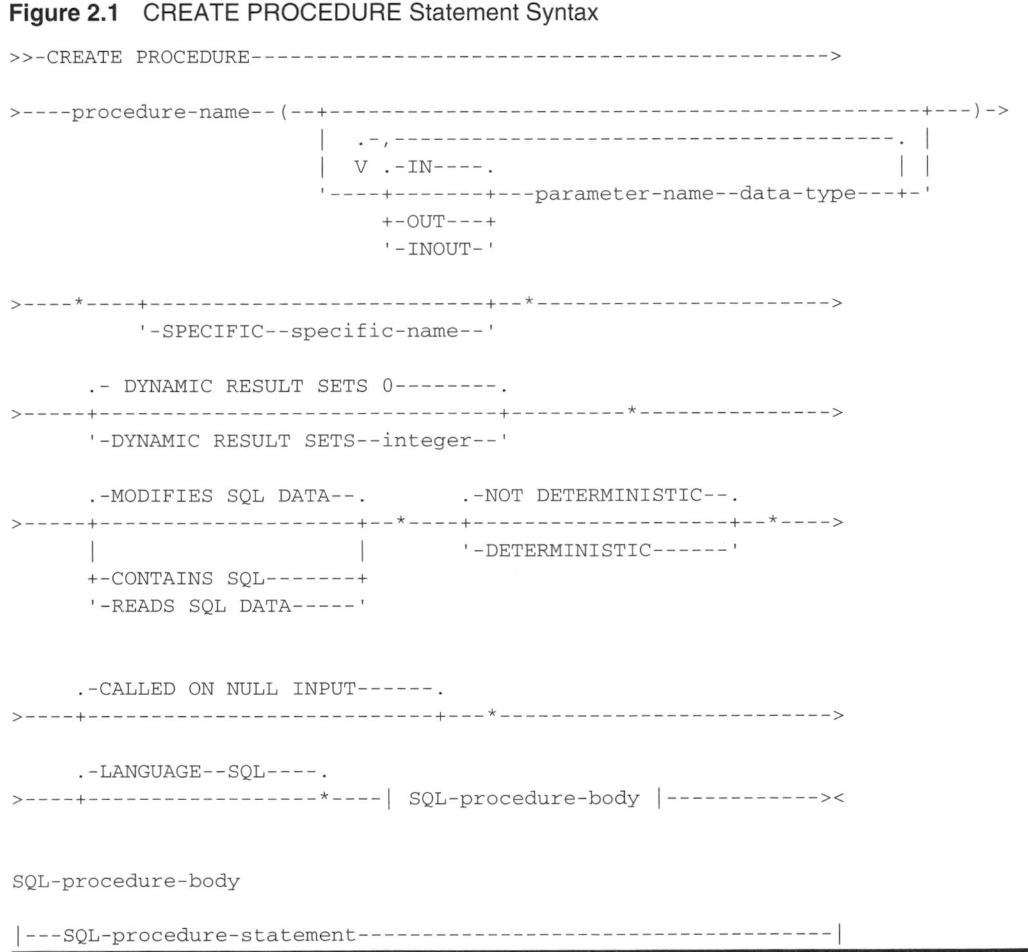

```
>>-CREATE PROCEDURE---------------------------------------------->

>----procedure-name--(--+-----------------------------------------------+---)->
                        |  .-,---------------------------------------.  |
                        |  V  .-IN----.                               | |
                        '----+-------+---parameter-name--data-type---+-'
                             +-OUT---+
                             '-INOUT-'

>----*----+--------------------------+--*----------------------->
          '-SPECIFIC--specific-name--'

      .- DYNAMIC RESULT SETS 0--------.
>-----+-------------------------------+---------*--------------->
      '-DYNAMIC RESULT SETS--integer--'

      .-MODIFIES SQL DATA--.        .-NOT DETERMINISTIC--.
>-----+--------------------+--*----+--------------------+--*---->
      |                    |        '-DETERMINISTIC------'
      +-CONTAINS SQL-------+
      '-READS SQL DATA-----'


     .-CALLED ON NULL INPUT------.
>----+---------------------------+---*-------------------------->

     .-LANGUAGE--SQL----.
>----+------------------*----| SQL-procedure-body |------------><


SQL-procedure-body

|---SQL-procedure-statement--------------------------------------|
```

When you issue the CREATE PROCEDURE statement, DB2 defines the procedure in the database. Entries are made in the catalog tables to record the existence of the procedure and other operations are performed by DB2 to make the procedure executable. (See Appendix D, "Security Considerations in SQL Procedures" for a detailed discussion of these steps.)

### 2.1.1 Procedure Name

The procedure name specifies the procedure being defined. The name is an SQL identifier that can be a maximum of 128 characters. It must begin with a letter and may be followed by additional letters, digits or the underscore character (_). You can define mixed case names by enclosing the name in quotation marks. However, the use of mixed case names is not encouraged because it adds complexity when calling these procedures as the names must be enclosed in quotation marks in the call as well.

These are examples of valid procedure names:

```
UPDATE_EMPLOYEE_SALARY
READEMP
```

These are unqualified procedure names. When a procedure name is unqualified, the procedure schema is determined by the CURRENT SCHEMA special register. By default, the CURRENT SCHEMA is the authorization ID of the current user. Procedure names may also be qualified by a schema name explicitly.

These are examples of valid qualified procedure names:

```
HRAPP.UPDATE_EMPLOYEE_SALARY
DB2ADMIN.READEMP
```

Similar to the procedure name, the schema name is an SQL identifier with a maximum of 128 characters. The schema name cannot begin with SYS.

The qualified procedure name does not necessarily need to be unique in the database. The combination of qualified procedure name and number of parameters (procedure signature), however, must uniquely identify a procedure. This will be discussed in more detail in the following section.

The SPECIFIC clause is important when there is a requirement to define procedures with the same name but with different parameters. To fully understand the purpose of this clause, parameters must be discussed.

### 2.1.2 Parameters

The parameters for a procedure are defined in the CREATE PROCEDURE statement. The definition of each parameter consists of three parts: mode, parameter name and data type.

- Mode defines whether the parameter is an input (IN), output (OUT) or both (INOUT).
- Parameter name specifies the name of the parameter. It is recommended that all parameter variables be pre-fixed with p_. This is discussed in detail in the "Variables" section of this chapter.
- Data type is the SQL data type and size, if applicable, for this parameter.

The list of parameters is enclosed in parentheses "()" and each parameter definition is delimited by a comma ",".

Figure 2.2 is an example of a partial CREATE PROCEDURE statement that defines the procedure and its parameters:

**Figure 2.2** CREATE PROCEDURE Statement Syntax Defining Procedure Parameters

```
CREATE PROCEDURE UPDATE_EMPLOYEE_SALARY (IN  P_EMPID INTEGER,
                                         IN  P_PERCENTINCR DECIMAL(4,2),
                                         OUT P_UPDATED_SALARY ) . . .
```

A procedure may be defined without any parameters. In DB2 V7, parentheses must still be coded in the CREATE PROCEDURE statement. For example:

```
CREATE PROCEDURE increase_salary() LANGUAGE SQL BEGIN …
```

However, in DB2 V8 the parentheses can be omitted. For example:

```
CREATE PROCEDURE increase_salary BEGIN …
```

It is possible to define multiple procedures with the same qualified name but different numbers of parameters. This is called overloading and the procedures are referred to as overloaded procedures. Figures 2.3 and 2.4 show examples of overloaded procedures.

DB2 does not allow you to define two procedures with the same name and same number of parameters even if the parameters are of different types. However, DB2 does allow User Defined Functions (UDFs) to be defined with the same name and same number of parameters. Refer to Chapter 10, "Working with Triggers and User-Defined Functions".

**Figure 2.3** Procedure Sum with Three Parameters

```
CREATE PROCEDURE sum(IN p_a INTEGER,IN p_b INTEGER,OUT p_s INTEGER)
SPECIFIC sum_ab
LANGUAGE SQL
    BEGIN
        SET p_s = p_a + p_b;
    END
```

**Figure 2.4** Procedure Sum with Four Parameters

```
CREATE PROCEDURE sum(IN p_a INTEGER,IN p_b INTEGER,IN p_c INTEGER,OUT p_s INTEGER)
SPECIFIC sum_abc
LANGUAGE SQL
    BEGIN
        SET p_s = p_a + p_b + p_c;
    END
```

In this example, two procedures have the same name, ***sum***. The first procedure has three parameters and the second has four parameters. When ***sum*** is called, DB2 will determine which version of the procedure to execute based on the number of parameters. Note that each procedure is defined with a unique specific name. Specific names will be discussed in the next section. To execute these procedures, enter the following:

```
CALL sum(100,200,?)
```

This call results in the first version of the ***sum*** procedure to be executed because there are three parameters. Note that since the third parameter is an output parameter, a '?' must be specified in its place.

Now, execute:

```
CALL sum(100,200,300,?)
```

This call results in the second version of the ***sum*** procedure to be executed because there are four parameters.

If you attempt to call a procedure where there is no procedure defined in the database with the same number of parameters, an error will occur. For example:

```
CALL sum(100,200,300,400,?)
```

This call will fail because a procedure named ***sum*** with five parameters does not exist.

### 2.1.3 Specific Name

SPECIFIC is an optional clause that defines a unique name for a procedure. Specific names are particularly useful when there are multiple procedures defined with the same name but have a different number of parameters (also known as overloaded procedures, as discussed in the previous section). In this case, each procedure would be given a different specific name which would be used to drop or comment on the stored procedure. Attempting to drop an overloaded procedure using only the procedure name would result in ambiguity and error.

**TIP** It is recommended that a specific name be used for a procedure as it makes managing them easier.

The following example illustrates the use of SPECIFIC name when two procedures with the same name are defined. Consider the two ***sum*** procedures defined in Figures 2.3 and 2.4.

To drop the procedure ***sum***, issue the following DROP PROCEDURE statement:

```
DROP PROCEDURE sum
```

This statement fails with SQLCODE -476 (SQLSTATE 42725) because the procedure is ambiguous. DB2 cannot determine which of the two procedures called ***sum*** should be dropped. To drop a particular version of the ***sum*** procedure, you must either specify the procedure parameters with the DROP PROCEDURE statement or use the DROP SPECIFIC PROCEDURE statement. These are valid statement that will drop the procedure:

```
DROP PROCEDURE sum(INTEGER,INTEGER,INTEGER)
DROP SPECIFIC PROCEDURE sum_ab
```

Using DROP SPECIFIC PROCEDURE, DB2 knows that it should drop the procedure with specific name ***sum_ab***.

The specific name can also be used with the COMMENT ON statement. For example:

```
COMMENT ON SPECIFIC PROCEDURE sum_abc IS 'THIS IS THE 3 PARM VERSION
OF THE PROCEDURE'
```

The specific name is an SQL identifier with a maximum length of 18 characters. The name can be unqualified or qualified by a schema-name. If it is qualified it must use the same schema-name as the procedure name. The specific name can be the same name as its procedure name. The qualified specific name must be unique among specific procedure names. The unqualified specific name can be the same as an existing procedure name.

If the specific name is not explicitly specified when creating a procedure, DB2 will generate a unique name for the procedure. The generated unique name consists of SQL and a character timestamp: SQLyymmddhhmmsshhn.

## 2.1.4 DYNAMIC RESULT SETS

DYNAMIC RESULT SETS clause specifies the maximum number of result sets you are returning.

For compatibility with past releases, DYNAMIC may be omitted. However, the standard defines that DYNAMIC be used.

Handling result sets is explained in detail in Chapter 4, "Understanding and Using Cursors and Result Sets," and Chapter 7, "Working with Nested SQL Procedures." Please refer to these chapters for information and examples.

## 2.1.5 CONTAINS SQL, READS SQL DATA, MODIFIES SQL DATA

The SQL-data access indication clause restricts the type of SQL statements that can be executed by the procedure. The default, MODIFIES SQL DATA, is the least restrictive and indicates that any supported SQL statements can be executed.

When CONTAINS SQL is specified, then only statements that do not read or modify data are allowed in the procedure. Examples of such statements are DECLARE GLOBAL TEMPORARY TABLE, PREPARE, SET special register and SQL control statements.

READS SQL DATA can be specified if the procedure contains only statements that do not modify SQL data.

Table 2.1 shows which SQL statements can be executed under the various data access indicators.

**Table 2.1** Using SQL Statements Under Various Data Access Indicators

| SQL Statement | CONTAINS SQL | READS SQL DATA | MODIFIES SQL DATA |
|---|---|---|---|
| ALTER... | N | N | Y |
| BEGIN DECLARE SECTION | Y | Y | Y |
| CALL | Y | Y | Y |

**Table 2.1** Using SQL Statements Under Various Data Access Indicators (continued)

| SQL Statement | CONTAINS SQL | READS SQL DATA | MODIFIES SQL DATA |
|---|---|---|---|
| CLOSE CURSOR | N | Y | Y |
| COMMENT ON | N | N | Y |
| COMMIT | N | N | N |
| COMPOUND SQL | Y | Y | Y |
| CONNECT(2) | N | N | N |
| CREATE | N | N | Y |
| DECLARE CURSOR | Y | Y | Y |
| DECLARE GLOBAL TEMPORARY TABLE | Y | Y | Y |
| DELETE | N | N | Y |
| DESCRIBE | N | Y | Y |
| DISCONNECT(2) | N | N | N |
| DROP ... | N | N | Y |
| END DECLARE SECTION | Y | Y | Y |
| EXECUTE | Y | Y | Y |
| EXECUTE IMMEDIATE | Y | Y | Y |
| EXPLAIN | N | N | Y |
| FETCH | N | Y | Y |
| FREE LOCATOR | Y | Y | Y |
| FLUSH EVENT MONITOR | N | N | Y |
| GRANT ... | N | N | Y |
| INCLUDE | Y | Y | Y |
| INSERT | N | N | Y |
| LOCK TABLE | Y | Y | Y |
| OPEN CURSOR | N | Y | Y |
| PREPARE | Y | Y | Y |
| REFRESH TABLE | N | N | Y |
| RELEASE CONNECTION(2) | N | N | N |
| RELEASE SAVEPOINT | N | N | Y |

**Table 2.1** Using SQL Statements Under Various Data Access Indicators (continued)

| SQL Statement | CONTAINS SQL | READS SQL DATA | MODIFIES SQL DATA |
|---|---|---|---|
| RENAME TABLE | N | N | Y |
| REVOKE ... | N | N | Y |
| ROLLBACK | Y | Y | Y |
| ROLLBACK TO SAVEPOINT | N | N | Y |
| SAVEPOINT | N | N | Y |
| SELECT INTO | N | Y | Y |
| SET CONNECTION(2) | N | N | N |
| SET INTEGRITY | N | N | Y |
| SET special register | Y | Y | Y |
| UPDATE | N | N | Y |
| VALUES INTO | N | Y | Y |
| WHENEVER | Y | Y | Y |

### 2.1.6 DETERMINISTIC or NOT DETERMINISTIC

This clause allows you to specify the procedure as DETERMINISTIC if it returns the same results for each invocation of identical input parameters or as NOT DETERMINISTIC if the results depend on the input values and/or other values which may change such as the current date or time. Identifying a procedure as DETERMINISTIC allows DB2 to perform additional optimizations to improve performance.

The default is NOT DETERMINISTIC and this is typically the desired behavior.

### 2.1.7 CALLED ON NULL INPUT

This clause indicates that the procedure will always be called even if its input parameters are null. This behavior is the default and the only value that can be specified. This clause is optional.

### 2.1.8 LANGUAGE SQL

LANGUAGE SQL identifies this procedure as an SQL procedure and indicates that the body of the procedure will be specified in the CREATE PROCEDURE statement body.

LANGUAGE SQL is a required clause in DB2 V7, however, it is optional in DB2 V8. In DB2 V8, the presence of the procedure body indicates to DB2 that this is an SQL procedure.

The LANGUAGE keyword is required when creating procedures in other languages such as Java and C.

## 2.2 SQL Procedure Body

For SQL procedures, the logic of the procedure is contained in the SQL procedure body of the CREATE PROCEDURE statement. The SQL procedure body can consist of a single SQL statement or several SQL statements in the form of a compound SQL statement. The next section explains the details of writing the SQL procedure body.

### 2.2.1 The SQL Procedure Body Structure

The SQL procedure body can consist of a single SQL statement or, more typically, a compound SQL statement consisting of a BEGIN/END block with multiple statements within it. The compound statement consists of various declarations followed by SQL procedure statements. All declarations must be specified first followed by SQL procedural statements. The syntax diagram in Figure 2.5 shows the required order of declarations.

**Figure 2.5** Compound Statement Syntax

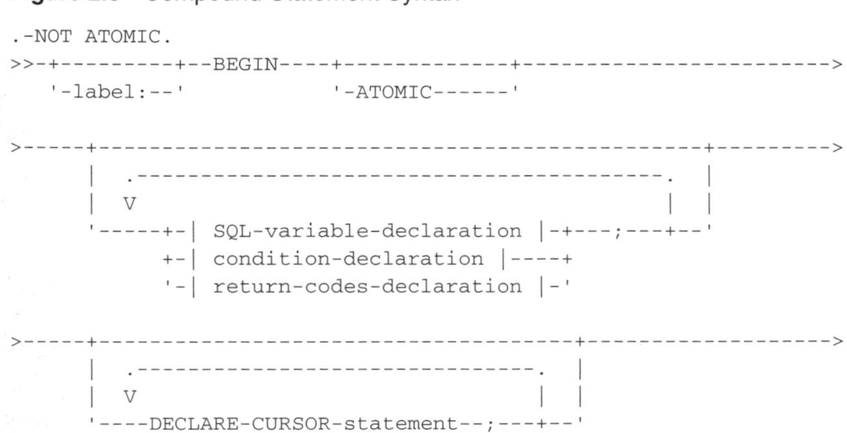

```
.-NOT ATOMIC.
>>-+---------+--BEGIN----+-------------+------------------------->
   '-label:--'           '-ATOMIC------'

>-----+-----------------------------------------------+--------->
      |  .-----------------------------------------.  |
      |  V                                          |  |
      '-----+-| SQL-variable-declaration |-+---;---+--'
            +-| condition-declaration |----+
            '-| return-codes-declaration |-'

>-----+-------------------------------------+------------------->
      |  .-------------------------------.  |
      |  V                               |  |
      '----DECLARE-CURSOR-statement--;---+--'
```

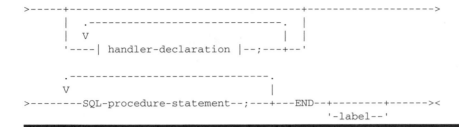

```
>-----+------------------------------------+-------------------->
      |  .-----------------------------.   |
      |  V                             |   |
      '----| handler-declaration |--;---+--'

      .------------------------------.
      V                              |
>--------SQL-procedure-statement--;---+---END--+--------+------><
                                                '-label--'
```

Variable declarations are discussed later in this chapter. Compound statements are discussed in Chapter 3, "Using Flow of Control Statements." Cursor declarations are discussed in Chapter 4, "Understanding and Using Cursors and Result Sets." Condition handlers are discussed in Chapter 5, "Condition Handling."

## 2.2.2 Comments

It is always good practice to include comments in programs. DB2 allows two styles of comments:

- -- When two dashes are specified, any text following them is treated as a comment. This style is typically used to comment on a specific variable declaration or statement. This comment style can be used on any line within the CREATE PROCEDURE statement.
- /* */ These are C style comments. The /* begins a comment and */ ends the comments. There may be multiple lines of comments between the delimiters. This style is typically used with multiple line comments. This comment style can only be used within the procedure body.

Figure 2.6 shows examples of comments used in an SQL procedure.

**Figure 2.6** Sample Comments

```
CREATE PROCEDURE proc_with_comments (IN aaa INTEGER, -- input var1
                        OUT bbb INTEGER ) -- output var1
SPECIFIC proc_with_comments
LANGUAGE SQL   -- creating SQL procedure
    BEGIN -- this is the beginning of the stored procedure
        /*
          Variables
        */
        DECLARE v_total INTEGET DEFAULT 0; -- amount total
         -- Procedural Logic
    END -- this is the end
```

### 2.2.3 Variables

The DECLARE statement is used to define variables within a compound SQL statement. Each variable declaration consists of a name for the variable, a DB2 data type and optionally a default value.

Variable declarations must be specified at the beginning of a BEGIN/END block before any SQL procedural statements are defined. The CREATE PROCEDURE statement will fail if a DECLARE is found anywhere else.

You must ensure that the variables defined in your procedure are different from the column names of tables that will be referenced in the procedure. Such a declaration is allowed but only causes confusion. It is recommended that you define a naming convention for your procedures that clearly differentiates variables and columns. In this book, as shown in Figure 2.7, we use the convention where variables are preceded with *v_* and procedures parameters are preceded with ***p_*** to differentiate them from possible column names.

**Figure 2.7** Defining Variables

```
CREATE PROCEDURE proc_with_variables (in p_empno char(4),…
    SPECIFIC proc_with_vars
    LANGUAGE SQL
    BEGIN
        DECLARE v_empno CHAR(4);
        DECLARE v_total, v_count INTEGER DEFAULT 0;
        SELECT empno INTO v_empno FROM employee WHERE empno = p_empno ;
    :
    :
    END
```

When variables are declared, they are initialized as null unless the DEFAULT clause is used to initialize the variable to a value. In Figure 2.7 the value of ***v_empno*** is null until it is set within the procedure body. The integer variables ***v_total*** and ***v_count*** are initialized to zero in the declaration.

### 2.2.4 Setting Variables

As in any programming language, you can initialize or set variables. There are several ways to set variables in SQL procedures and they are demonstrated in the sample code in Figure 2.8.

**Figure 2.8** Setting Variables

```
BEGIN
    DECLARE v_rcount INTEGER;
    DECLARE v_max INTEGER DEFAULT 0;
    DECLARE v_adate,v_another DATE;
    DECLARE v_total INTEGER DEFAULT 0;  -- (1)
    SET v_total = v_total + 1; -- (2)
    SELECT MAX(EMPNO) INTO v_max FROM PLAYERS; -- (3)
    VALUES CURRENT DATE INTO v_adate; -- (4)
    VALUES CURRENT DATE, CURRENT DATE INTO v_adate,v_another; (5)
    DELETE FROM EMPLOYEE WHERE ...
    GET DIAGNOSTICS rcount = ROW_COUNT; -- (6)
END
```

When declaring a variable, you can specify a default value using the DEFAULT clause as in (1).

Line (2) shows that a SET can be used to set a single variable.

Variables can also be set by executing a SELECT or FETCH statement in combination with INTO as shown in (3). Details on using FETCH can be found in Chapter 4, "Understanding and Using Cursors and Result Sets."

Lines (4 & 5) show how the VALUES statement can be used to evaluate a function or special register and assign the value to a variable. Special registers are discussed in more detail later in this chapter.

GET DIAGNOSTICS, on line (6), is used to initialize a variable with information related to the previous statement. In this example, GET DIAGNOSTICS retrieves the number of rows affected by the previous DELETE statement. More details on using GET DIAGNOSTICS can be found in Chapter 5, "Condition Handling."

## 2.3 SQL Statements

All SQL statements are allowed within the context of a procedure except for the following:

- CONNECT
- CREATE any object other than indexes, tables, or views
- DESCRIBE
- DISCONNECT
- DROP any object other than indexes, tables, or views

- FLUSH EVENT MONITOR
- REFRESH TABLE
- RELEASE (connection only)
- RENAME TABLE
- RENAME TABLESPACE
- REVOKE
- SET CONNECTION
- SET INTEGRITY

### 2.3.1 SQL Control Statements

SQL PL statements are used to write SQL procedures. The following lists the statements that are allowed and the chapter where you can find detailed information about them.

- ALLOCATE CURSOR statement – Chapter 7
- assignment statement – Chapter 2
- ASSOCIATE LOCATORS statement – Chapter 7
- CASE statement – Chapter 3
- compound statement - Chapter 3
- FOR statement - Chapter 3
- GET DIAGNOSTICS statement – Chapter 5
- GOTO statement – Chapter 5
- IF statement – Chapter 3
- ITERATE statement – Chapter 3
- LEAVE statement – Chapter 3
- LOOP statement – Chapter 3
- REPEAT statement - Chapter 3
- RESIGNAL statement - Chapter 5
- RETURN statement - Chapter 3
- SIGNAL statement - Chapter 5
- WHILE statement - Chapter 3

### 2.3.2 Special Registers

Special registers are memory registers that allow DB2 to provide information to an application about its environment. Special registers can be referenced in SQL statements. The most commonly used special registers are:

- CURRENT DATE – a date based on the time-of-day clock at the database server. If this register is referenced more than once in a single statement, the value returned will be the same for all references.
- CURRENT PATH – identifies the SQL path used to resolve function references and data type references for dynamically prepared SQL statements. The value of the CURRENT PATH special register is a list of one or more schema-names. This special register can be modified using the SET CURRENT PATH statement.
- CURRENT SCHEMA – identifies the schema name used to qualify unqualified database objects in dynamic SQL statements. The default value is the authorization ID of the current user. This special register can be modified using the SET CURRENT SCHEMA statement.
- CURRENT TIME – a time based on the time-of-day clock at the database server. If this register is referenced more than once is a single statement, the value returned will be the same for all references.
- CURRENT TIMESTAMP – a timestamp based on the time-of-day clock at the database server. If this register is referenced more than once in a single statement, the value returned will be the same for all references.
- USER – specifies the run-time authorization ID used to connect to the database.

Figure 2.9 shows the use of several special registers.

**Figure 2.9** Using Special Registers

```
CREATE PROCEDURE registersample (OUT p_start TIMESTAMP,
                                 OUT p_end TIMESTAMP,
                                 OUT p_c1 TIMESTAMP,
                                 OUT p_c2 TIME,
                                 OUT p_user CHAR(20))
    SPECIFIC registersample
    LANGUAGE SQL
P1: BEGIN
        CREATE TABLE DATETAB (C1 TIMESTAMP,C2 TIME,C3 DATE);

        VALUES CURRENT TIMESTAMP INTO p_start; -- (1)
        INSERT INTO DATETAB VALUES(CURRENT TIMESTAMP,
                                   CURRENT TIME,
                                   CURRENT DATE + 3 DAYS); -- (2)
        SELECT C1,C2 INTO p_c1,p_c2 FROM DATETAB;
        VALUES CURRENT TIMESTAMP INTO p_END;
        SET p_user = USER; -- (3)

        DROP TABLE DATETAB;
     END P1
```

The procedure ***registersample*** creates a table, ***datetab***, to demonstrate how special registers are used with SQL statements. This table is dropped at the end so that the procedure can be run repeatedly.

On line (1), the values statement is used to set the variable ***p_start*** to the current timestamp.

Line (2) shows several special registers being used within a single SQL statement to retrieve the date or time. Here, the time portion of the CURRENT TIMESTAMP special register will be the same as the value of the CURRENT TIME special register and the date portion of the CURRENT TIMESTAMP special register will be the same as the value of CURRENT DATE. This statement also demonstrates the use of built-in functions. Column ***C3*** will receive a date that is 3 days from the current date. More details on using built in DATE, TIME and TIMESTAMP functions can be found in the SQL Reference.

The ***p_user*** variable is set to the authorization ID of the currently connected user on line (3).

More information about special registers can be found in the SQL Reference. The following lists other special registers that are available.

- CURRENT DEFAULT TRANSFORM GROUP – identifies the name of a transform group used by dynamic SQL statements for exchanging user-defined structured type values with host programs.
- CURRENT DEGREE – specifies the degree of intra-partition parallelism for the execution of dynamic SQL statements.
- CURRENT EXPLAIN MODE – holds a value that controls the behavior of the explain facility.
- CURRENT EXPLAIN SNAPSHOT – holds a value that controls behavior of the explain snapshot facility.
- CURRENT NODE – in a DB2 EEE environment, identifies the coordinator node.
- CURRENT QUERY OPTIMIZATION – specifies the query optimization level used when binding dynamic SQL statements.
- CURRENT REFRESH AGE
- CURRENT SERVER – specifies the name of the database that the application is connected to.

### 2.3.3 Returning Values to Caller

SQL procedures allow a single integer value to be returned to the caller using the RETURN statement. If you need to return several values or values of other data types, then you must define output parameters for your procedure and set the output parameters before the procedure completes execution.

## 2.4 Bringing It All Together Example

Now, let us look at a detailed example demonstrating all the basic features discussed so far. The procedure in Figure 2.10 inserts a row into the *employee* table of the SAMPLE database. If you have not created the SAMPLE database, see Appendix A, "Getting Started with DB2." We recommend that you create this database as most examples in this book make use if it to demonstrate concepts.

**Figure 2.10** Using Special Registers

```
CREATE PROCEDURE add_new_employee (IN    p_empno CHAR(6),                 -- (1)
                                   IN    p_firstnme CHAR(12),
                                   IN    p_midinit CHAR(1),
                                   IN    p_lastname VARCHAR(15),
                                   IN    p_deptname VARCHAR(30),
                                   IN    p_edlevel SMALLINT,
                                   OUT   p_status VARCHAR(100),
                                   OUT   p_ts TIMESTAMP)
    SPECIFIC add_new_employee
    LANGUAGE SQL

P1: BEGIN
        DECLARE v_deptno CHAR(3) DEFAULT '   ';                                 -- (2)
        DECLARE v_create_ts TIMESTAMP;                                          -- (3)
        SET v_create_ts = CURRENT TIMESTAMP;
        /* Get the corresponding department number */
        SELECT deptno
          INTO v_deptno                                                         -- (4)
          FROM department
         WHERE deptname = p_deptname;


        /* Insert new employee into table */                                    -- (5)
        INSERT INTO employee (empno
                             ,firstnme
                             ,midinit
                             ,lastname
                             ,workdept
                             ,hiredate
                             ,edlevel)
```

```
            VALUES (p_empno
                   ,p_firstnme
                   ,p_midinit
                   ,p_lastname
                   ,v_deptno
                   ,DATE(v_create_ts) -- set hiredate to today's date
                   ,p_edlevel );
        SET p_status = 'Employee added';                            -- (6)
        SET p_ts = v_create_ts;                                     -- (7)
    END P1
```

The parameter list (1) defines input and output variables to the procedures. The input parameters represent column values that will be inserted into the ***employee*** table. Note that the ***p_*** prefix is used for each variable to differentiate variables from column names. The output parameters are used to return a status and the TIMESTAMP of the execution of the procedure.

Line (2) declares the ***v_deptno*** variable to hold the department number retrieved from the department table. ***v_deptno*** is initialized to ' '; .

Line (3) declares the ***v_create_ts*** variable to hold the TIMESTAMP of execution of the procedure. We want to use the same value for inserting the ***hiredate*** into the ***employee*** table. To ensure that these values are the same, we want to retrieve the CURRENT TIMESTAMP register only once in the procedure.

To look up the department number in the department table, a select statement (4) is used to retrieve ***deptno*** and save in ***v_deptno***.

Line (5) inserts a new employee into the ***employee*** table using parameter values ***v_deptno*** and ***v_create_ts***. The value of ***v_create_ts,*** which is of type TIMESTAMP, must be cast to DATE using the DATE casting function.

On lines (6) and (7), the output parameters, ***p_status*** and ***p_ts***, are set.

To execute the ***add_new_employee*** procedure, enter:

```
CALL add_new_employee('123456','ROBERT','K','ALEXANDER','PLANNING',1,?,?)
```

The output of this call is:

```
P_STATUS: Employee added
P_TS: 2002-09-29 17:19:10.927001

"ADD_NEW_EMPLOYEE" RETURN_STATUS: "0"
```

# 2.5 ROLLBACK and COMMIT

ROLLBACK and COMMIT statements can be used within the procedure body. These statements are introduced here but their use will be explained in detail in a later chapter.

## 2.5.1 ROLLBACK

The ROLLBACK statement is used to explicitly back out of any database changes that were made within the current unit of work (UOW). A unit of work is a sequence of SQL statements that are atomic for the purposes of recovery. Once the changes have been rolled back, a new unit of work is initiated.

DB2 also supports transaction SAVEPOINT and ROLLBACK TO SAVEPOINT. A ROLLBACK will cause the flow of control in your application to return to the previous SAVEPOINT declared within your unit of work.

**NOTE** You cannot issue a ROLLBACK or COMMIT from within an ATOMIC compound statement.

The syntax is shown in Figure 2.11.

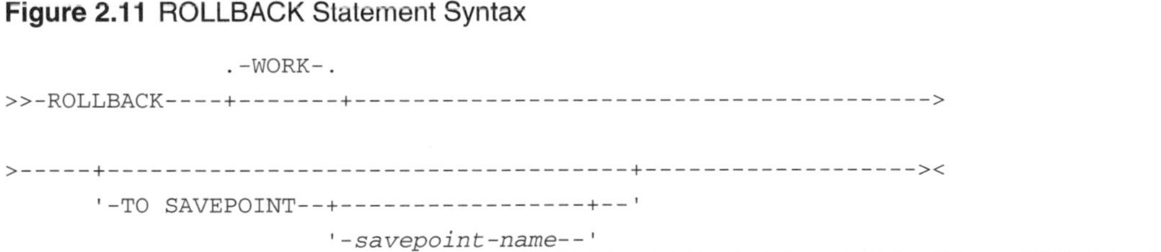


**Figure 2.11** ROLLBACK Statement Syntax

TO SAVEPOINT indicates that a partial rollback (ROLLBACK TO SAVEPOINT) is to be performed. If no savepoint is active, an SQL error is returned (SQLSTATE 3B502). After a successful ROLLBACK, the savepoint continues to exist. If a ***savepoint-name*** is not provided, rollback is to the most recently set savepoint.

If this clause is omitted, the ROLLBACK WORK statement rolls back the entire transaction. Furthermore, savepoints within the transaction are released.

The ***savepoint-name*** indicates the savepoint to which to rollback. After a successful ROLLBACK TO SAVEPOINT, the savepoint defined by ***savepoint-name*** continues to exist. If the savepoint name does not exist, an error is returned (SQLSTATE 3B001). Data and schema changes made since the savepoint was set are undone.

### 2.5.2 COMMIT

The COMMIT statement is used to complete the current unit of work and to permanently record any of the changes made inside it to the database.

The syntax shown in Figure 2.12 is trivial.

**Figure 2.12** COMMIT Statement Syntax

```
              .-WORK-.
>>-COMMIT----+-------+--------------------------------------><
```

## 2.6 Chapter Summary

SQL procedures are defined in a DB2 database using the CREATE PROCEDURE statement. The CREATE PROCEDURE statement defines the name, the parameters, and several other properties of the procedure. The combination of qualified procedure name and number of parameters uniquely identifies a procedure. The SPECIFIC clause can be used to uniquely identify a procedure when there are multiple procedures with the same name.

For SQL procedures, the procedure logic is defined in the procedure body of the CREATE PROCEDURE statement. The procedure body is typically a compound statement consisting of declarations followed by procedural statements. The DECLARE statement is used to declare variables, their data type and, optionally, a default value. The SET statement is typically used to assign values to variables. However, SELECT … INTO, VALUES, and GET DIAGNOSTICS statements can also be used. Most SQL statements can be used in the procedure body.

COMMIT and ROLLBACK statements can be used in the procedure body for transaction control.

This chapter covered some basic procedural statements required to create a simple procedure. Other SQL PL statements will be discussed in detail in the rest of this book.

CHAPTER 3

# Using Flow of Control Statements

## In this chapter, you will learn:

- how to use the compound statement;
- how to use labels in both compound statements and loops;
- how to use the two conditional statements (IF and CASE);
- how to use the four looping statements (FOR, WHILE, REPEAT, and LOOP);
- how to use the four transfer of control statements (GOTO, LEAVE, ITERATE and RETURN).

Sequential execution is the most basic path that program execution can take. With this method, the program starts execution at the first line of the code, followed by the next, and continues until the final statement in the code has been executed. This approach works fine for very simple tasks but tends to lack usefulness since it can only handle one situation. Like humans, most programs need to be able to decide what to do in response to changing circumstances. By controlling a code's execution path, a specific piece of code can then be used to handle intelligently more than one situation.

Flow of control statements are used to control the sequence of statement execution. Statements such as IF and CASE are used to conditionally execute blocks of SQL Procedural Language (SQL PL) statements, while other statements, such as WHILE and REPEAT, are typically used to execute a set of statements repetitively until a task is complete.

Although there are many flow of control statements to be discussed in this chapter, there are three main categories: conditional statements, loop statements, and transfer of control statements. Before jumping into a discussion on flow of control statements, it is important to first understand the use of compound statements.

## 3.1 Compound Statements

Of all the SQL control statements, the compound statement is the easiest to work with and understand. Compound statements are used to group together a set of related lines of code. You can declare variables, cursors, and condition handlers and use flow of control statements within a compound statement (cursors and condition handlers are discussed in later chapters).

BEGIN and END are keywords that define a compound statement. The BEGIN keyword defines the starting line of code for the compound statement, while the END keyword defines the final line of code. Compound statements are used to control variable scoping and for executing more than a single statement where a single statement is expected (such as within a condition handler, which will be discussed in Chapter 5, "Condition Handling").

Each compound statement has its own scope, where only variables and the like that have been declared within the same compound statement or within enclosing compound statements can be seen. That is, statements within one compound statement may not be able to refer to variables and values that are declared within another compound statement, even if both compound statements are part of the same SQL procedure body.

It is perfectly logical and, in most cases, completely valid to have the ability to define as many compound statements as needed within an SQL procedure (see ATOMIC for the exception). These compound statements are typically used to introduce scoping and a logical separation of related statements.

There is a specific order for declaring variables, conditions, cursors and handlers within a compound statement. Specifically, the order of declarations must proceed as follows:

```
BEGIN
   variable declarations
   condition declarations
   cursor declarations
   handler declarations
   assignment, flow of control, SQL statements, and other compound
   statements
END
```

Don't worry if you are not familiar with some of the above terms, as they will be discussed in greater detail later. Also, notice that one or several compound statements can be nested within other compound statements. In such cases, the same order of declarations continues to apply at each level.

It is important to understand the type of variable scoping (or visibility) that occurs when a compound statement has been defined. Specifically:

- Outer compound statements cannot see variables declared within inner compound statements.
- Inner compound statements can see variables that have been declared in outer compound statements.

Scoping is illustrated in Figure 3.1.

**Figure 3.1** Variable Scoping Example

```
BEGIN                           -- (1)
    DECLARE v_outer1 INT;
    DECLARE v_outer2 INT;

    BEGIN                       -- (2)
        DECLARE v_inner1 INT;
        DECLARE v_inner2 INT;

        SET v_outer1 = 100;     -- (3)
        SET v_inner1 = 200;     -- (4)
    END;                        -- (5)

    SET v_outer2 = 300;         -- (6)
    SET v_inner2 = 400;         -- (7)
END                             -- (8)
```

In the above, (1) and (8) define the outer compound statement, while (2) and (5) define the inner compound statement. All statements, except statement (7), will succeed. Statement (7) fails because an outer compound statement cannot see a variable declared within an inner compound statement. You will receive an SQLSTATE 42703 error with the message "'V_INNER2' is not valid in the context where it is used."

Scoping can be especially useful in the case of looping and exception handling, allowing the program flow to jump from one compound statement to another.

There are two distinct types of compound statements, which both serve a different purpose.

### 3.1.1 NOT ATOMIC Compound Statement

The previous example illustrated a NOT ATOMIC compound statement and is the default type used in SQL procedures. If an unhandled error (that is, no condition handler has been declared for the SQLSTATE raised) occurs within the compound statement, any work which is completed before the error will not be rolled back, but will not be committed either. The group of statements can only be rolled back if the unit of work is explicitly rolled back using ROLLBACK or ROLLBACK TO SAVEPOINT (the latter is discussed in Chapter 8, "Advanced Features"). You can also COMMIT successful statements if it makes sense to do so.

The syntax to for a NOT ATOMIC compound statement is shown in Figure 3.2.

**Figure 3.2** NOT ATOMIC Compound Statement Syntax Diagram

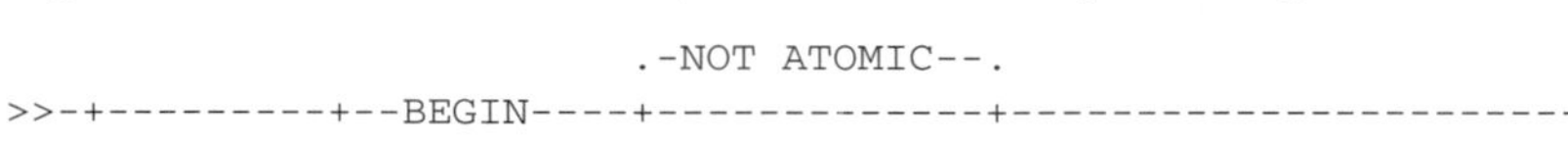

```
                                .-NOT ATOMIC--.
>>-+---------+--BEGIN----+-------------+----------------------->
   '-label:--'
...
Misc. Statements;
...
>-------------------------------------+---END--+--------+------><
                                               '-label--'
```

The optional *label* is used to define a name for the code block. The label can be used to qualify SQL variables declared within the compound statement. If the ending label is used, it must be the same as the beginning label. We will learn more about labels later in this chapter.

The use of the `NOT ATOMIC` keywords is optional, but usually suggested, as it reduces ambiguity of the code.

The SQL procedure illustrated in Figure 3.3 demonstrates the non-atomicity of NOT ATOMIC compound statements:

**Figure 3.3** NOT ATOMIC Compound Statement Example

```
CREATE PROCEDURE not_atomic_proc ()
    SPECIFIC not_atomic_proc
    LANGUAGE SQL
BEGIN NOT ATOMIC
   -- Declare variables
   DECLARE v_job VARCHAR(8);
   -- Procedure logic
   INSERT INTO atomic_test(proc, res)
          VALUES ('Not_Atomic_Proc','Before error test');
   SIGNAL SQLSTATE '70000';-- (1)
   INSERT INTO atomic_test(proc, res)
        VALUES ('Not_Atomic_Proc','After error test');
END
```

Right now, it is sufficient to understand that the SIGNAL statement at (1) is used to explicitly raise an error. Additionally, since this error is unhandled, the procedure will exit right after the error.

After calling this procedure, you will see that although an error has been raised halfway through execution, the first INSERT successfully inserted a row into the *atomic_test* table. It has not been committed or rolled back, however.

## 3.1.2 ATOMIC Compound Statement

The ATOMIC compound statement, as the name suggests, can be thought of as a singular whole—if any unhandled error conditions arise within it, all statements which have been executed up to that point are considered to have failed as well and are therefore rolled back. ATOMIC compound statements cannot be nested inside other ATOMIC compound statements.

In addition, you cannot use SAVEPOINTs or issue explicit COMMITs or ROLLBACKs from within an ATOMIC compound statement.

**NOTE** COMMIT, ROLLBACK, SAVEPOINTS and nested ATOMIC compound statements are not allowed within an ATOMIC compound statement.

The syntax to declare an ATOMIC compound statement is shown in Figure 3.4.

**Figure 3.4** ATOMIC Compound Statement Syntax Diagram

```
>>-+---------+--BEGIN ATOMIC------------------------------------>
   '-label:--'
...
Misc. Statements;
...
>--------------------------------------+---END--+--------+------><
                                                '-label--'
```

A label is used in the same way as with a NOT ATOMIC compound statement.

The example in Figure 3.5 illustrates the behavior of an ATOMIC compound statement. It is quite similar to the NOT ATOMIC example above, and only differs in name and the fact that it uses an ATOMIC compound statement.

**Figure 3.5** ATOMIC Compound Statement Example

```
CREATE PROCEDURE atomic_proc ()
    SPECIFIC atomic_proc
    LANGUAGE SQL
BEGIN ATOMIC
   -- Declare variables
   DECLARE v_job VARCHAR(8);
   -- Procedure logic
   INSERT INTO atomic_test(proc, res)
        VALUES ('Atomic_Proc','Before error test');
   SIGNAL SQLSTATE '70000';                                          -- (1)
   INSERT INTO atomic_test(proc, res)
        VALUES ('Atomic_Proc','After error test');
END
```

When the error condition of SQLSTATE 70000 is raised at (1), the unhandled error causes procedure execution to stop. Unlike the NOT ATOMIC example in Figure 3.3, the first INSERT statement will be rolled back, resulting in a table with no inserted rows from this procedure.

## 3.2 Using Labels

Labels can be used to name any executable statement, which includes compound statements and loops. By using labels, you can have the flow of execution either jump out of a compound statement or loop, or jump to the beginning of a compound statement or loop.

Optionally, you may supply a corresponding label for the END of a compound statement. If an ending label is supplied, it must be the same as the label used at its beginning.

Each label must be unique within the body of an SQL procedure.

Labels also help increase the readability of code. Try to label based on the purpose of the statement or code block.

A label can also be used to avoid ambiguity if a variable with the same name has been declared in more than one compound statement of the stored procedure. A label can be used to qualify the name of the SQL variable.

Figure 3.6 shows the use of a label to name a compound statement and also how to avoid ambiguous references to similarly named variables. It uses two variables of the same name (*v_ID*) defined in two differently labeled compound statements.

**Figure 3.6** Labeled Compound Statement Example

```
CREATE PROCEDURE show_label (OUT p_WorkerID INT)
    SPECIFIC show_label
    LANGUAGE SQL
-- Procedure logic
sl1: BEGIN
   -- Declare variables
   DECLARE v_ID INT;                                         -- (1)
   sl2: BEGIN
       DECLARE v_ID INT;                                     -- (2)
       SET sl1.v_ID = 1;                                     -- (3)
       SET sl2.v_ID = 2;                                     -- (4)
       SET v_ID = 3;                                         -- (5)
       SET p_WorkerID = sl2.v_ID;                            -- (6)
   END;
END sl1
```

You can see that, to avoid ambiguity, the two *v_ID* variables defined at (1) and (2) are qualified with the label of the compound statement that they were defined in at (3), (4), and (6). When qualification is not used, as in (5), the variable will be qualified with the label of the compound statement from which it is being referenced. So the value assignment at (5) will actually assign a value of 3 to *sl2.v_ID*, which means that *p_WorkerID* at (6) will also be assigned a value of 3.

It is always good programming practice not to declare multiple variables of the same name, regardless of the fact that they can be referenced as *label.variable_name*.

Additionally, the label of the compound statement or loop can be used with the LEAVE statement to exit the labeled compound statement or loop. Labels can also be used with the ITERATE statement to jump back to the labeled beginning of a LOOP. These SQL PL statements are covered in greater detail further on in this chapter.

## 3.3 Conditional Statements

Conditional statements allow stored procedures to make decisions. They are used to define multiple branches of execution based on whether or not a condition was met.

A commonly used conditional statement is the IF statement, where a branch of execution can be taken if a specific condition is satisfied. IF statements can also define a branch of execution for when a condition is not met.

Another conditional statement in SQL PL is the CASE statement, which is similar to an IF statement, but the branching decision can be based on the value of a single variable.

### 3.3.1 The IF Statement

The most commonly used approach for conditional execution is the IF statement. There are essentially three different types of IF statements.

The simplest form of the IF statement does something if a condition is true, and nothing otherwise.

But what happens if you want to do one thing if a condition is true and something else if it is false? This is where the ELSE clause comes in handy. When used in conjunction with an IF statement, you can do something IF a condition is true and something ELSE if the condition is false.

Thirdly, ELSEIF is used to branch to multiple code paths based on mutually exclusive conditions in the same manner as an IF statement. You can make use of an ELSEIF statement to rewrite a ladder of nested IF … ELSE statements for readability. Your procedure can specify an unlimited number of ELSEIF statements.

The syntax of an IF statement is depicted in Figure 3.7.

**Figure 3.7** IF Syntax Diagram

```
>>-IF--search-condition--THEN------------------------------------>

         .-------------------------------.
         V                               |
>--------SQL-procedure-statement--;---+------------------------>

         .----------------------------------------------------------------------.
         V                                                                      |
>--------+----------------------------------------------------------------------+--+>
         |                                    .------------------------------.  |
         |                                    V                              |  |
         '-ELSEIF--search-condition--THEN-----SQL-procedure-statement--;---+--'

>-----+------------------------------------------+--END IF----><
      |       .------------------------------.   |
      |       V                              |   |
      '-ELSE-----SQL-procedure-statement--;---+--'
```

The *search-condition* specifies the condition for which an SQL statement should be invoked. If the condition is false, processing continues to the next *search-condition,* until either a condition is true or processing reaches the ELSE clause.

SQL-procedure-statement specifies the statements to be invoked if the preceding search-condition is true. If no search-condition evaluates to true, then the SQL-procedure-statement following the ELSE keyword is invoked.

The snippet of an SQL procedure shown in Figure 3.8 demonstrates how the rating of an employee determines the raise in salary and bonus that he or she will receive.

**Figure 3.8** **Figure 3.8** IF Statement Example

```
IF rating = 1 THEN                                                  -- (1)
   UPDATE employee
       SET salary = salary * 1.10, bonus = 1000
       WHERE empno = employee_number;
ELSEIF rating = 2 THEN                                              -- (2)
   UPDATE employee
       SET salary = salary * 1.05, bonus = 500
       WHERE empno = employee_number;
ELSE                                                                -- (3)
   UPDATE employee
       SET salary = salary * 1.03, bonus = 0
       WHERE empno = employee_number;
END IF;
```

SQL PL does not require the use of a compound statement to execute more than one statement in a branch of a conditional statement.

Indent statements within the body of IF, ELSEIF, and ELSE statements in order to improve readability. If there are several levels of nesting, indent code at each level to reflect their level of nesting.

At (1), an employee with a 1 rating can expect a raise of 10% and a bonus of $1000. At (2), an employee with a 2 rating earns a 5% raise with a $500 bonus. At (3), all other employees can expect a 3% pay hike with no bonus.

You are not simply limited to mathematical operators such as equals (=) and greater than (>). You can also use the SQL keywords NOT, AND, and OR to build conditions in your IF statements.

**NOTE** An IF or ELSEIF condition must involve an operator. It is not sufficient to merely specify a variable (as can be done in some other programming languages), as SQL PL does not support the notion of a negative value meaning false and a positive value meaning true.

Your stored procedure can also make use of nested IF statements. There is no limit imposed by DB2 on the number of nested levels, though it is best not to get too carried away as it takes away from the readability of your code. Now if that's not enough, you can also nest IF statements inside of loops and loops inside of IF statements. When nesting IFs, a common problem is inadvertently matching an ELSE with the wrong IF. Beware.

## 3.3.2 The CASE Statement

The CASE statement provides the ability to evaluate a list of options based on the value of a single variable. You would most likely choose to use a CASE statement if you have a large decision tree and all branches depend on the value of the same variable. Otherwise you would be better off using a series of IF, ELSEIF, and ELSE statements. The syntax diagram for the CASE statement is shown in Figure 3.9.

**Figure 3.9** CASE Statement Syntax Diagram

```
>>-CASE----+-| searched-case-statement-when-clause |-+---------->
           '-| simple-case-statement-when-clause |---'

>----END CASE------------------------------------------------><

simple-case-statement-when-clause

|---expression----------------------------------------------->
```

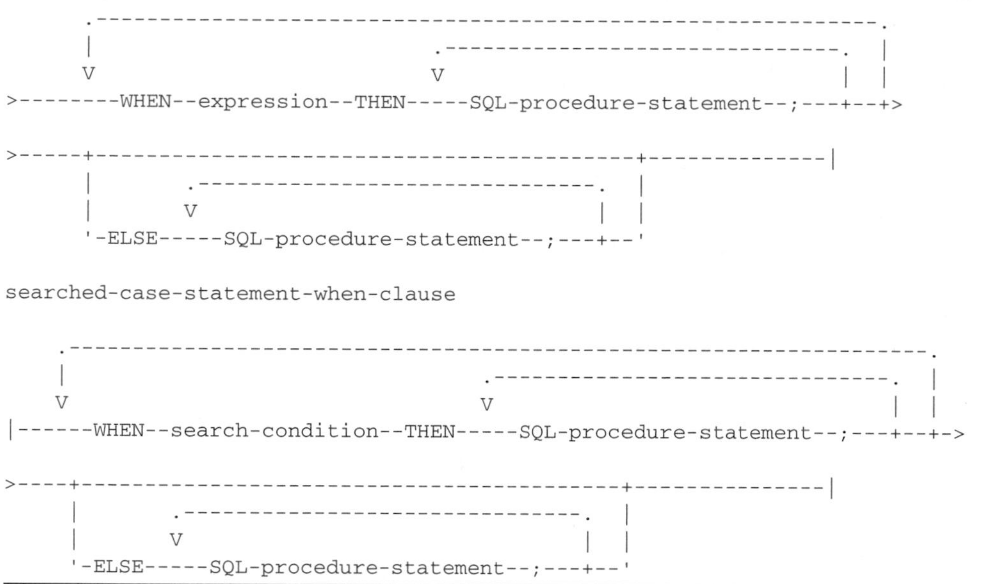

>--------WHEN--expression--THEN-----SQL-procedure-statement--;---+--+>
>-----+---------------------------------------+--------------|
'-ELSE-----SQL-procedure-statement--;---+--'
searched-case-statement-when-clause
|------WHEN--search-condition--THEN-----SQL-procedure-statement--;---+--+->
>----+----------------------------------------+---------------|
'-ELSE-----SQL-procedure-statement--;---+--'


The CASE statement has two general forms: one that uses a *simple-case-statement-when-clause*, and one that uses a *searched-case-statement-when-clause*.

In the *simple-case-statement-when-clause*, the *expression* prior to the first WHEN keyword is tested for equality with the value of each *expression* that follows the WHEN keyword. If the expressions result in the same value, the *SQL procedure-statement* following the THEN keyword is executed. Otherwise, comparisons are continued between the first *expression* and the *expression* following the next WHEN clause. If the result does not match any of the search conditions, and an ELSE clause is present, the statements in the ELSE clause are processed.

In a *searched-case-statement-when-clause*, the *search-condition* following each WHEN keyword is evaluated. If *search-condition* evaluates to true, the statements in the associated THEN clause are processed. If it evaluates to false, the next *search-condition* is evaluated. If no *search-condition* evaluates to true and an ELSE clause is present, the statements in the ELSE clause are processed.

Both forms of the CASE statement require END CASE to denote the end of the statement. It is possible to use a CASE statement without an ELSE clause. However, if none of the conditions specified in the `WHEN` clause are true at run-time, an error will result(SQLSTATE 20000).

The example that you have already seen in Figure 3.8 could be rewritten as shown in Figure 3.10 using the *simple-case-statement-when-clause*.

**Figure 3.10** Simple CASE Example

```
CASE rating
   WHEN 1 THEN                                    -- (1) Note: WHEN argument is a value
      UPDATE EMPLOYEE
         SET SALARY = SALARY *1.10, BONUS = 1000
         WHERE EMPNO = employee_num;
   WHEN 2 THEN                                                               -- (2)
      UPDATE EMPLOYEE
         SET SALARY = SALARY *1.05, BONUS = 500
         WHERE EMPNO = employee_num;
   ELSE
      UPDATE EMPLOYEE                                                        -- (3)
         SET SALARY = SALARY *1.03, BONUS = 0
         WHERE EMPNO = employee_num;
END CASE;
```

Once again, at (1), an employee with a rating of 1 can expect a raise of 10% and a bonus of $1000. At (2), an employee with a rating of 2 earns a 5% raise and a bonus of $500, while at (3), all other employees can simply expect a raise of 3% and no bonus.

Perhaps there have been some recent changes to the rating system, and there is now a wider range of ratings that employees can receive. Now, two employees with slightly different ratings can earn the same raise and bonus. Obviously, our code needs to be updated.

Figure 3.11 reflects the changes to the rating system and shows how to handle this using a *searched-case-statement-when-clause*. Note that the WHEN clause now contains a condition.

**Figure 3.11** Searched CASE Example

```
CASE
   WHEN rating >= 1 AND rating < 4 THEN                                      -- (1)
      UPDATE EMPLOYEE
         SET SALARY = SALARY *1.10, BONUS = 1000
         WHERE EMPNO = employee_num;
   WHEN rating >= 4 AND rating < 8 THEN
      UPDATE EMPLOYEE
         SET SALARY = SALARY *1.05, BONUS = 500
         WHERE EMPNO = employee_num;
   ELSE
      UPDATE EMPLOYEE
         SET SALARY = SALARY *1.03, BONUS = 0
         WHERE EMPNO = employee_num;
END CASE;
```

As you can see, our code now handles a range of ratings for each condition of the CASE statement. For example, at (1), an employee with a rating that falls between 1 and 3 inclusive will receive a raise of 10% and a bonus of $1000.

## 3.4 Looping Statements

Loops allow you to execute a set of statements repeatedly until a certain condition is reached. The loop terminating condition may be defined at the beginning, in the middle, or at the end of the loop using the WHILE, LOOP, and REPEAT statements, respectively. Also, a FOR loop is available for iterating over a read-only result set and its terminating condition is when no more rows are left to read. Once the loop terminating condition has been met, looping ceases and the flow of control continues on the line directly following the loop. Variables cannot be declared within loops.

For readability, it is best to indent the loop body relative to the loop statement.

The WHILE and REPEAT loops are typically used when you do not know how many times to iterate through the loop prior to entering it. You should use the WHILE loop when you may not want to execute the loop even once, and the REPEAT loop when you want to ensure that the statements within the loop are executed at least once. The FOR loop is used for situations where you need to iterate over a read-only result set, using result set values for some purpose such as defining the value of a variable. LOOP is generally used for all other cases.

### 3.4.1 FOR Loop

The FOR loop is used to iterate over a read-only result set that is defined by its ***select-statement***. Looping will cease when there are no rows left in the result set. Positioned updates and deletes are not supported in the FOR loop. However, searched updates and deletes are allowed.

The syntax is depicted in Figure 3.12.

**Figure 3.12** FOR Statement Syntax Diagram

```
>>-+---------+---FOR--for-loop-name--AS------------------------>
   '-label:--'

>-----+-------------------------+--select-statement---DO------->
      '-cursor-name--CURSOR FOR--'

      .------------------------------.
      V                              |
>--------SQL-procedure-statement--;---+--END FOR----+--------+-><
                                                    '-label--'
```

The *for-loop-name* specifies a label for the implicit compound statement generated to implement the FOR statement. It follows the rules for the label of a compound statement except that it cannot be used with ITERATE or LEAVE (which are described later). The *for-loop-name* can be used to qualify the column names in the result set as returned by the select-statement.

The *cursor-name* simply names the cursor that is used to select rows from the result set. If not specified, DB2 will automatically generate a unique cursor name internally.

The column names of the *select-statement* must be unique and a FROM clause specifying a table (or multiple tables if doing some kind of JOIN or UNION) is required. The table(s) and column(s) referenced must exist prior to the loop being executed. This allows you to iterate over result sets that are formed from tables that exist prior to invoking the stored procedure, or tables that have been created by a previous SQL PL statement (such as declared user-temporary tables, which are discussed in Chapter 8, "Advanced Features").

The FOR loop is essentially a CURSOR defined by the *select-statement*. This CURSOR cannot be referenced outside of the FOR loop, however, so OPEN, FETCH, and CLOSE statements will result in error.

In Figure 3.13, the FOR loop is used to iterate over all rows of the employee table (since no WHERE clause is being used).

**Figure 3.13** FOR Loop Example

```
FOR v_row AS SELECT firstnme, midinit, lastname                        -- (1)
    FROM employee
    DO
        SET v_fullname = v_row.lastname || ', ' || v_row.firstnme || ' ' ||
           v_row.midinit;                                              -- (2)
    INSERT INTO tname VALUES (v_fullname);                             -- (3)
END FOR
```

You can see the defining ***select-statement*** at (1) and where the columns of the result set are being concatenated together to form the ***v_fullname*** at (2). Finally, this newly formed ***v_fullname*** is inserted into a table called ***tname*** at (3).

## 3.4.2 WHILE Loop

The defining feature of a WHILE loop is that its looping condition is evaluated prior to initial loop execution and all following loop iterations. The WHILE loop will continue to execute until the looping condition evaluates to false. Be sure not to define a condition that always evaluates to true, or you will get caught in an infinite loop.

When defining the looping condition, be sure to specify a full conditional statement (which includes operators). Otherwise, your SQL procedure will not build. For example:

```
WHILE (variable) DO
  statement1;
  statement2;
END WHILE;
```

is not enough. You need to use an operator, as in:

```
WHILE (variable = 1) DO
  statement1;
  statement2;
END WHILE;
```

The syntax for the WHILE loop is illustrated in Figure 3.14.

**Figure 3.14** WHILE Loop Syntax Diagram

```
>>-+---------+--WHILE--search-condition--DO-------------------->
   '-:label--'

       .-------------------------------.
       V                               |
>--------SQL-procedure-statement--;---+--END WHILE-------------->

>-----+--------+----------------------------------------------><
      '-label--'
```

The *search-condition* specifies a condition that is evaluated before each execution of the loop. If the condition is true, the *SQL-procedure-statements* in the loop are processed.

Figure 3.15 illustrates how to use a WHILE loop to sum all integer values between ***n*** and ***m*** (which are assumed to be positive and provided by input parameters to the procedure).

**Figure 3.15** Simple WHILE Loop Example

```
CREATE PROCEDURE sum_mn (IN p_start INT
                        ,IN p_end INT
                        ,OUT p_sum INT)
SPECIFIC sum_mn
LANGUAGE SQL
smn: BEGIN
   DECLARE v_temp INTEGER DEFAULT 0;
   DECLARE v_current INTEGER;
```

```
    SET v_current = p_start;

    WHILE (v_current <= p_end) DO
        SET v_temp = v_temp + v_current;
        SET v_current = v_current + 1;
    END WHILE;

    SET p_sum = v_temp;

END smn
```

The above example is fairly simple and is intended to show you how the WHILE loop works using as little code as possible. More commonly, however, a WHILE loop is used to repeatedly perform SQL procedure statements, such as FETCH (for retrieving row values from a cursor). For examples of using WHILE loops with cursor operations such as OPEN, FETCH and CLOSE, see Chapter 4, "Understanding and Using Cursors and Result Sets."

## 3.4.3 REPEAT

In the WHILE loop, you saw that the looping condition is evaluated at the very beginning of the loop. If the looping condition evaluates to false at this first examination, then the loop body will not execute at all.

In some cases, however, it may be necessary that the loop be executed at least once.

This is where the REPEAT loop is useful. A REPEAT loop ensures that at least one iteration of the loop is completed. This is the case because the looping condition is not evaluated until the final line of code in the loop.

The syntax for the REPEAT loop is shown in Figure 3.16.

**Figure 3.16** REPEAT Loop Syntax Diagram

```
                                .-----------------------------.
                                V                             |
>>-+---------+--REPEAT-------SQL-procedure-statement--;---+----->
   '-label:--'

>----UNTIL--search-condition---END REPEAT----+--------+--------><
                                             '-label--'
```

In Figure 3.17, the procedure from Figure 3.15 is re-implemented using REPEAT.

**Figure 3.17** REPEAT Loop Example

```
CREATE PROCEDURE sum_mn2 (IN p_start INT
                         ,IN p_end INT
                         ,OUT p_sum INT)
SPECIFIC sum_mn2
LANGUAGE SQL
smn2: BEGIN
   DECLARE v_temp INTEGER DEFAULT 0;
   DECLARE v_current INTEGER;

   SET v_current = p_start;

   REPEAT
       SET v_temp = v_temp + v_current;
       SET v_current = v_current + 1;
   UNTIL (v_current > p_end)
   END REPEAT;

   SET p_sum = v_temp;

END smn2
```

## 3.4.4 LOOP

The LOOP statement is somewhat different from the other types of loops that we have looked at thus far. The LOOP does not have a terminating condition clause that is part of its declaration statement. It will continue to loop until some other piece of code inside it explicitly forces the flow of control to jump to some point outside of the loop.

LOOP will commonly have some logic that eventually branches to a LEAVE statement. You can also use a GOTO statement instead of a LEAVE, but the use of GOTO is discouraged. Ensure that some action within the loop eventually invokes a LEAVE or GOTO statement. Otherwise, your code can get caught in an infinite loop.

The LOOP syntax is illustrated in Figure 3.18.

**Figure 3.18** LOOP Syntax Diagram

```
                                .-------------------------------.
                                V                               |
>>-+----------+--LOOP-------SQL-procedure-statement--;---+------->
   '-label:--'

>----END LOOP----+--------+------------------------------------><
                 '-label--'
```

There is no terminating condition defined within the LOOP syntax itself.

An example of using LOOP is deferred until the discussion on LEAVE in the next section.

## 3.5 Transfer of Control Statements

Transfer of control statements are used to specifically tell the SQL procedure where to continue execution. This unconditional branching can be used to cause the flow of control to jump from one point to another point, which can either precede or follow the transfer of control statement.

SQL PL supports four such statements: GOTO, LEAVE, ITERATE, and RETURN. Each will be discussed in detail in the following sections.

### 3.5.1 GOTO

GOTO is a straightforward and basic flow of control statement that causes an unconditional change in the flow of control. It is used to branch to a specific user-defined location using labels defined in the procedure.

Usage of the GOTO statement is generally considered to be poor programming practice and is not recommended. Extensive use of GOTO tends to lead to unreadable code especially when procedures get long. Besides, GOTO is not necessary since there are better statements available to control the execution path. There are no specific situations that require the use of GOTO; instead, it is more often used for convenience (or lack of effort).

The GOTO syntax is shown in Figure 3.19.

**Figure 3.19** GOTO Syntax Diagram

```
>>-GOTO--label-----------------------------------------------><
```

There are a few additional scope considerations to be aware of:

- If the GOTO statement is defined in a FOR statement, *label* must be defined inside the same FOR statement, *excluding* a nested FOR statement or nested compound statement.

- If the GOTO statement is defined in a compound statement, *label* must be defined inside the same compound statement, *excluding* a nested FOR statement or nested compound statement.
- If the GOTO statement is defined in a handler, *label* must be defined in the same handler, following the other scope rules.
- If the GOTO statement is defined outside of a handler, *label* must not be defined within a handler.
- If *label* is not defined within a scope that the GOTO statement can reach, an error is returned (SQLSTATE 42736).

Good programming practice should limit the use of the GOTO statement in your stored procedure. The use of GOTO decreases the readability of your code since it causes execution to jump to a new line contained anywhere within the procedure body. This "spaghetti" code can be difficult to understand, debug, and maintain.

If you must use GOTO, then try to use it to skip to the end of the stored procedure or loop.

The GOTO statement is local to the stored procedure that declares it. The label that a GOTO statement could jump to must be defined within the same stored procedure as the GOTO statement, and don't forget that scoping rules still apply.

In Figure 3.20, a stored procedure is used to increase the salary of those employees who have been with the company for over 1 year. The employee's serial number and rating are passed into the stored procedure, which then returns an output parameter of the newly calculated salary. The employee's salary is increased based on the rating.

This stored procedure makes use of the GOTO statement at (1) to avoid increasing the salary of those employees who have not yet been with the company for over a year.

**Figure 3.20** GOTO Example

```
CREATE PROCEDURE adjust_salary ( IN p_empno CHAR(6)
            ,IN p_rating INTEGER
            ,OUT p_adjusted_salary DECIMAL (8,2) )
    SPECIFIC adjust_salary
    LANGUAGE SQL
as: BEGIN
   -- Declare variables
   DECLARE v_new_salary DECIMAL (9,2);
   DECLARE v_service DATE;
   -- Procedure logic
   SELECT salary, hiredate
     INTO v_new_salary, v_service
     FROM employee
     WHERE empno = p_empno;

   IF v_service > (CURRENT DATE - 1 year) THEN
      GOTO exit;                                                          -- (1)
   END IF;

   IF p_rating = 1 THEN
      SET v_new_salary = v_new_salary + (v_new_salary * .10);             -- (2)
   ELSEIF p_rating = 2 THEN
      SET v_new_salary = v_new_salary + (v_new_salary * .05);             -- (3)
   END IF;

   UPDATE employee                                                        -- (4)
      SET salary = v_new_salary
      WHERE empno = p_empno;

exit:                                                                     -- (5)
   SET p_adjusted_salary = v_new_salary;
END as
```

If the employee has worked for the company for more than a year, he or she is given a 5% or 10% raise if he or she received a rating of 2 or 1, respectively at (1) and (3), and the ***employee*** table is updated to reflect the new salary (4).

If it is discovered that the employee has not yet worked with the company for a year, the GOTO ***exit*** statement causes execution to jump to the second last line of code at (5) in the procedure. The ***p_adjusted_salary*** is simply set to the original salary and no changes are made to the ***employee*** table.

## 3.5.2 LEAVE

The LEAVE statement is used to transfer the flow of control out of a loop or compound statement. The syntax for the command, shown in Figure 3.21, is trivial.

**Figure 3.21** LEAVE Syntax Diagram

```
>>-LEAVE--label----------------------------------------------><
```

Figure 3.22 illustrates how to use LOOP and LEAVE.

**Figure 3.22** Example of LOOP and LEAVE

```
CREATE PROCEDURE verify_ids (IN p_id_list VARCHAR(100)
                            ,OUT p_status INT)
SPECIFIC verify_ids
LANGUAGE SQL
vid: BEGIN

DECLARE v_current_id VARCHAR(10);
DECLARE v_position INT;
DECLARE v_remaining_ids VARCHAR(100);
DECLARE v_tmp INT;
DECLARE SQLCODE INT DEFAULT 0;

SET v_remaining_ids = p_id_list;
SET p_status = 0;

L1: LOOP
        SET v_position = LOCATE (':',v_remaining_ids);                    --(1)

        -- take off the first id from the list
        SET v_current_id = SUBSTR (v_remaining_ids, 1, v_position);       --(2)

        IF LENGTH(v_remaining_ids) - v_position > 0 THEN                  --(3)
        SET v_remaining_ids = SUBSTR (v_remaining_ids, v_position+1);
        ELSE
            SET v_remaining_ids = '';
        END IF;

        -- take off the colon in last position of the current token
        SET v_current_id = SUBSTR (v_current_id, 1, v_position-1);        --(4)

        -- determine if employee exists
        SELECT 1 INTO v_tmp FROM employee where empno = v_current_id;     --(5)

        IF (SQLCODE <> 0) THEN
            -- employee id does not exist
        SET p_status=-1;
        LEAVE L1;                                                         --(6)
        END IF;


        IF length(v_remaining_ids) = 0 THEN
           leave L1;
```

```
      END IF;

END LOOP;

END vid
```

The SQL procedure in Figure 3.22 takes a colon separated list of employee IDs as input. For example, this input might look like:

```
000310:000320:000330:
```

The list is then parsed (lines (1) through (4)) to determine if all employee IDs are valid by verifying if the employee exists at (5). If any IDs in the list are not valid, the LOOP immediately exists using LEAVE at (6). If all employee IDs in the list are valid, the result of ***p_status*** is 0. Otherwise, the result of ***p_status*** is -1 to indicate an error.

## 3.5.3 ITERATE

The ITERATE statement is used to cause the flow of control to return to the beginning of a labeled LOOP. The syntax for ITERATE, depicted in Figure 3.23, is simple:

**Figure 3.23** ITERATE Syntax Diagram

```
>>-ITERATE--label----------------------------------------------><
```

The example in Figure 3.24 is similar to the example in Figure 3.22, except that instead of exiting on the first invalid employee ID, the procedure returns the number of valid IDs found. ITERATE at (1) is used to return to the top of the LOOP whenever an invalid ID is encountered so that it is not counted.

**Figure 3.24** ITERATE Example

```
CREATE PROCEDURE verify_ids (IN p_id_list VARCHAR(100)
                            ,OUT p_status INT)
SPECIFIC verify_ids
LANGUAGE SQL
vid: BEGIN

   DECLARE v_current_id VARCHAR(10);
   DECLARE v_position INT;
   DECLARE v_remaining_ids VARCHAR(100);
   DECLARE v_tmp INT;
   DECLARE SQLCODE INT DEFAULT 0;

   SET v_remaining_ids = p_id_list;
```

```
   SET p_status = 0;

   L1: LOOP
           SET v_position = LOCATE (':',v_remaining_ids);

           -- take off the first id from the list
           SET v_current_id = SUBSTR (v_remaining_ids, 1, v_position);

           IF LENGTH(v_remaining_ids) - v_position > 0 THEN
           SET v_remaining_ids = SUBSTR (v_remaining_ids, v_position+1);
           ELSE
               SET v_remaining_ids = '';
           END IF;

           -- take off the colon in last position of the current token
           SET v_current_id = SUBSTR (v_current_id, 1, v_position-1);

           -- determine if employee exists
           SELECT 1 INTO v_tmp FROM employee where empno = v_current_id;

           IF (SQLCODE <> 0) THEN
              -- employee id does not exist
              IF length(v_remaining_ids) > 0 THEN
                   ITERATE L1;--(1)
              ELSE
                 LEAVE L1;
              END IF;
           END IF;

           SET p_status = p_status + 1;
       IF length(v_remaining_ids) = 0 THEN
   leave L1;
       END IF;

   END LOOP;

END vid
```

## 3.5.4 RETURN

RETURN is used to unconditionally and immediately terminate a stored procedure by returning the flow of control to the caller of the stored procedure.

It is mandatory when RETURN is issued that it return an integer value. The value returned is typically used to indicate success or failure of the stored procedure's execution. This value can be a literal, variable, or an expression as long as it is an integer or evaluates to an integer. In order for an OUT parameter to return a value, it must be set prior to the RETURN statement being invoked.

You can make use of more than one RETURN statement in a stored procedure. RETURN can be used anywhere within the SQL procedure body.

The syntax for RETURN is illustrated in Figure 3.25.

**Figure 3.25** RETURN Syntax Diagram

```
>>-RETURN--+------------+------------------------------------><
           '-expression-'
```

Figure 3.26 uses the employee serial number (*p_empno*) to check if an employee's last name, as stored in the database, matches the last name passed in as an input parameter (*p_emplastname*).

**Figure 3.26** RETURN example

```
CREATE PROCEDURE return_test ( IN p_empno CHAR(6)
            ,IN p_emplastname VARCHAR(15) )
    SPECIFIC return_test
    LANGUAGE SQL
rt: BEGIN
    -- Declare variables
    DECLARE v_lastname VARCHAR(15);
    -- Procedure logic
    SELECT lastname
       INTO v_lastname
       FROM EMPLOYEE
       WHERE empno = p_empno;
    IF v_lastname = p_emplastname THEN                                      -- (1)
       RETURN 1;                                                            -- (2)
    ELSE                                                                    -- (3)
       RETURN -1;                                                           -- (4)
    END IF;
END rt
```

This procedure receives two input parameters: *p_emplastname* and *p_empno*. If *p_emplastname* matches the lastname in the ***employee*** table identified by the employee number (*p_empno*) at (1), then the procedure exits with a return value of 1 at (2) implying success. If there is no match (3), then the stored procedure returns with a failure indicated by a -1 return code at (4).

## 3.6 Chapter Summary

This chapter discussed all SQL PL elements related to flow of control. It included discussions and examples of:

- compound statements and scope, which can be defined as ATOMIC or NOT ATOMIC to suit your needs,
- labels and the various ways in which they are used,
- IF and CASE conditional statements (and their various forms) for more intelligent SQL procedures,
- Looping statements FOR, WHILE, REPEAT and LOOP to perform repetitive sets of SQL statements, and
- GOTO, LEAVE, ITERATE and RETURN transfer of control statements.

With these flow of control statements at your disposal, you can write powerful and robust SQL stored procedures.

CHAPTER 4

# Understanding and Using Cursors and Result Sets

## In this chapter, you will learn:

- what a cursor is;
- how to use cursors inside SQL procedures;
- how to perform positioned deletes and positioned updates;
- about cursor behavior on commit and rollback;
- how cursors are used to return result sets to applications.

In previous chapters, you have seen how SQL procedures can manipulate table data by directly executing INSERT, UPDATE and DELETE statements. SQL used in this manner, however, means that operations must be applied to the entire set of data defined by the WHERE clause of the statement. In SQL procedures, it is possible to define a set of data rows (which we will call a result set from here on) and then to perform complex logic on a row-by-row basis. Using the same mechanics, an SQL procedure can also define a result set and return it directly to another program for processing. To take advantage of these features, the concept of cursors must be introduced.

A cursor can be viewed as a pointer to one row in a set of rows. The cursor can reference only one row at any given time, but can move to other rows of the result set as needed. For example, if a cursor is defined as:

```
SELECT * FROM employees WHERE sex='M'
```

the result set will be all employees who are male. The cursor will be positioned just before the first row of the result set initially. To position the cursor onto the first row, you execute a FETCH operation. Once positioned onto a row, the data can be processed. To retrieve the next row, FETCH can be executed again. This can be repeated until all rows of the result set have been processed.

In this chapter, only returning result sets from SQL procedures will be covered. Chapter 7, "Nested SQL Procedures," covers receiving result sets in another SQL procedure program. Examples of receiving result sets in Java or C client programs will be presented in Appendix H, "Sample Application Code for Chapter 4."

## 4.1 Using Cursors in SQL Procedures

In order to use cursors inside SQL procedures, you need to:

- declare the cursor
- open the cursor to establish the result set
- fetch the data into local variables as needed from the cursor, one row at a time
- close the cursor when done.

The simplified syntax of the DECLARE CURSOR and FETCH statements are shown in Figures 4.1 and 4.2 respectively. The syntax of the OPEN cursor and CLOSE cursor statements is very straightforward and no syntax diagram is required. They will be illustrated by example.

**Figure 4.1** Simplified DECLARE CURSOR Syntax

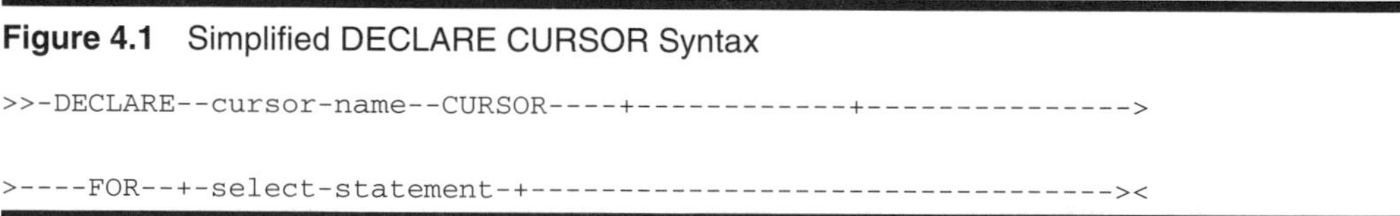

```
>>-DECLARE--cursor-name--CURSOR----+------------+-------------->

>----FOR--+-select-statement-+--------------------------------><
```

**Figure 4.2** Simplified FETCH Syntax

```
>>-FETCH--+-------+---cursor-name------------------------------>
          '-FROM--'

              .-,---------------.
              V                 |
>-----+-INTO-----host-variable---+---------+------------------><
```

The `FETCH` statement positions the cursor at the next row of the result set and assigns values from the current row of the cursor to procedure variables.

Figure 4.3 demonstrates the use of a cursor inside an SQL procedure to access data one row at a time. The procedure calculates the cost of giving raises to the employees of a company based on the following rules:

- The company has decided that everyone in the company except for the president will get at least the minimum raise, which is defined by the input parameter *p_min*.
- Any employee with a bonus over $600 will get an extra 4% raise.
- Employees with higher commissions will get a smaller raise. Employees with commissions of less than $2000 will get an extra 3% raise, while those with commissions between $2000 and $3000 will get an extra 2% raise.
- Anyone with commissions of over $3000 will receive an extra 1% raise only.
- Finally, no matter how much of a raise an employee might get, the total amount cannot be higher than a maximum limit, which is provided by the other input parameter, *p_max*.

Given the complexity of these rules, it is ideal to use a cursor in this situation.

**Figure 4.3** Example of Simple Cursor Usage

```
CREATE PROCEDURE total_raise
    ( IN  p_min    DEC(4,2)
     ,IN  p_max    DEC(4,2)
     ,OUT p_total  DEC(9,2) )
SPECIFIC total_raise
LANGUAGE SQL
tr: BEGIN
    -- Declare variables
    DECLARE v_salary DEC(9,2);
    DECLARE v_bonus  DEC(9,2);
    DECLARE v_comm   DEC(9,2);
    DECLARE v_raise  DEC(4,2);
```

```
    DECLARE v_job    VARCHAR(15) DEFAULT 'PRES';
    -- Declare returncode
    DECLARE SQLSTATE CHAR(5);

    -- Procedure logic
    DECLARE c_emp CURSOR FOR
        SELECT salary, bonus, comm
        FROM   employee
        WHERE  job != v_job;                                  -- (1)

    OPEN c_emp;                                               -- (2)

    SET p_total = 0;

    FETCH FROM c_emp INTO v_salary, v_bonus, v_comm;          -- (3)

    WHILE ( SQLSTATE = '00000' ) DO
        SET v_raise = p_min;

        IF ( v_bonus >= 600 ) THEN
            SET v_raise = v_raise + 0.04;
        END IF;

        IF ( v_comm < 2000 ) THEN
            SET v_raise = v_raise + 0.03;
        ELSEIF ( v_comm < 3000 ) THEN
            SET v_raise = v_raise + 0.02;
        ELSE
            SET v_raise = v_raise + 0.01;
        END IF;

        IF ( v_raise > p_max ) THEN
            SET v_raise = p_max;
        END IF;

        SET p_total = p_total + v_salary * v_raise;
        FETCH FROM c_emp INTO v_salary, v_bonus, v_comm;
    END WHILE;

    CLOSE c_emp;                                              -- (4)
END tr
```

This procedure works on the employee table of the SAMPLE database. The SELECT statement (1) within the DECLARE CURSOR statement defines the columns and rows that make the result set. Once declared, the cursor needs to be opened using the OPEN cursor statement (2). The FETCH cursor statement (3) is then used to retrieve data into local variables. As a good programming practice, the CLOSE cursor statement (4) should be issued once the cursor is no longer needed.

If you choose to rely on DB2 to close cursors for you, a CLOSE cursor statement will be executed as the last statement, even after your explicit RETURN statement. This can overwrite the return code of the procedure.

Normally the FETCH cursor statements are used in conjunction with loops to step through all rows of the result set. The SQLSTATE can be used to check if the last line is reached.

Once the data are fetched into local variables, you can perform logic as needed.

If the SELECT statement of the cursor declaration contains CURRENT DATE, CURRENT TIME, or CURRENT TIMESTAMP, all FETCH statements will return the same value. The value for these special registers is determined at the time of OPEN CURSOR.

In DB2 SQL procedures, the SET parameter statement below will fail if more than one row is returned. DB2 will not simply assign the first value to the local variable for you.

```
SET v_c1 = (SELECT c1 FROM t1);
```

Creating a cursor solely for the purpose of fetching the first value to a local variable as in Figure 4.4 is highly inefficient and is not recommended. Opening a cursor is an expensive operation for a database.

**Figure 4.4** Improper Use of Cursor to Fetch the First Row Only

```
DECLARE c_tmp CURSOR FOR
    SELECT c1
    FROM t1;

OPEN c_emp;

FETCH FROM c_emp INTO v_c1;

CLOSE c_emp;
```

The proper way of handling this situation is to use FETCH FIRST 1 ROW ONLY clause.

```
SET v_c1 = (SELECT c1 FROM t1 FETCH FIRST 1 ROW ONLY);
```

This statement will set the local variable to the value in the first row should more than one row be returned.

# 4.2 Positioned Delete

The previous example demonstrated a read-only cursor, which is the cursor used to read the data from the result set, but not to change the underlying data. Cursors can be used to delete data at the current cursor position as long as it is deletable.

A cursor is deletable if all of the following are true:

- Each FROM clause of the outer fullselect identifies only one base table or deletable view (it cannot identify a nested or common table expression or a nickname) without use of the OUTER clause.
- The outer fullselect does not include a VALUES, GROUP BY or HAVING clause and does not include column functions, DISTINCT in the select list.
- The outer fullselect does not include SET operations (UNION, EXCEPT, or INTERSECT) with the exception of UNION ALL.
- The select-statement does not include an ORDER BY or FOR READ ONLY clause.
- The cursor is statically defined or the FOR UPDATE clause is specified.

Using a cursor to delete the row on which it is currently positioned is known as a positioned delete. The syntax diagram for positioned delete is shown in Figure 4.5. You need to declare the cursor using the FOR UPDATE clause before it can be used in a positioned delete.

**Figure 4.5** Positioned DELETE Syntax

```
>>-DELETE FROM----+-table-name-------------------+-------------->
                  +-view-name--------------------+
                  '-ONLY--(--+-table-name-+---)--'
                             '-view-name--'

>----WHERE CURRENT OF--cursor-name------------------------------><
```

The example in Figure 4.6 demonstrates how to use a cursor for positioned delete.

**Figure 4.6** Example of Positioned Delete

```
CREATE PROCEDURE cleanup_act
    ( IN  p_date     DATE
     ,OUT p_deleted INT )
SPECIFIC cleanup_act
LANGUAGE SQL
ca: BEGIN
    -- Declare variable
    DECLARE v_date  DATE;
    -- Declare returncode
```

```
    DECLARE SQLSTATE CHAR(5);

    -- Procedure logic

    DECLARE c_emp CURSOR FOR                          -- (1)
        SELECT emendate
        FROM   emp_act
    FOR UPDATE;

    OPEN c_emp;

    FETCH FROM c_emp INTO v_date;
    SET p_deleted = 0;

    WHILE ( SQLSTATE = '00000' ) DO

        IF ( v_date < p_date ) THEN
            DELETE FROM emp_act
            WHERE CURRENT OF c_emp;                   -- (2)

            SET p_deleted = p_deleted + 1;
        END IF;

        FETCH FROM c_emp INTO v_date;
    END WHILE;

    CLOSE c_emp;
END ca
```

This procedure removes old records from the *emp_act* table in the SAMPLE database. It takes a cut-off date as the input parameter to delete all records in the *emp_act* table prior to that date and returns the number of rows deleted as the output parameter. This is a simple example to show how to use positioned delete. In the real world, a searched delete (that is, a direct DELETE statement without using a cursor) would perform much better for a simple operation like this. However, with positioned delete, you will be able to implement much more complicated logic on the data retrieved before deciding if you want to delete the current row.

The DECLARE CURSOR statement (1) is similar to the read-only cursor except for the FOR UPDATE clause. The FOR UPDATE clause is required if you intend to perform positioned deletes (you will run into compilation errors without it).

In SQL procedures, if the FOR UPDATE clause is not specified, the cursor will be considered a read-only cursor even if the cursor meets the criteria of a deletable or updatable cursor.

The WHERE CURRENT OF clause in the DELETE statement at line (2) indicates that the row to be deleted is the row where the cursor is currently positioned. When the positioned delete is executed, the cursor must be positioned on a row. That is, if you want to delete the first row in a result set, you must execute FETCH to properly position the cursor.

## 4.3 Positioned Update

Positioned update works similar to a positioned delete, except that the cursor has to meet requirements for being updatable.

A cursor is updatable if all of the following are true:

- The cursor is deletable (defined above).
- The column resolves to a column of the base table.
- Select-statement includes the FOR UPDATE clause (the column must be specified explicitly or implicitly in the FOR UPDATE clause).

If a positioned update is attempted on a cursor which does not meet all above requirements, SQLSTATE 42829 will be raised.

The syntax diagram for positioned update is shown in Figure 4.7:

**Figure 4.7** Positioned UPDATE Syntax

```
>>-UPDATE----+-table-name------------------+------------------->
             +-view-name-------------------+
             '-ONLY--(--+-table-name-+---)--'
                        '-view-name--'

>-----SET--| assignment-clause |-------------------------------->

>-----WHERE CURRENT OF--cursor-name---------------------------><
```

The example in Figure 4.8 is similar to the *total_raise()* procedure in Figure 4.3. Instead of calculating the total cost of issuing a raise, the *upd_raise()* procedure applies the raise by directly updating the salary field of the employee record.

**Figure 4.8** Example of Positioned Update

```
CREATE PROCEDURE upd_raise
    ( IN  p_min   DEC(4,2)
     ,IN  p_max   DEC(4,2) )
SPECIFIC upd_raise
LANGUAGE SQL
ur: BEGIN
    -- Declare variables
    DECLARE v_salary DEC(9,2);
    DECLARE v_bonus  DEC(9,2);
    DECLARE v_comm   DEC(9,2);
    DECLARE v_raise  DEC(4,2);
    -- Declare returncode
    DECLARE SQLSTATE CHAR(5);

    -- Procedure logic
    DECLARE c_emp CURSOR FOR
        SELECT salary, bonus, comm
        FROM   employee
        WHERE  job!='PRES'
    FOR UPDATE OF salary;

    OPEN c_emp;

    FETCH FROM c_emp INTO v_salary, v_bonus, v_comm;

    WHILE ( SQLSTATE = '00000' ) DO
        SET v_raise = p_min;

        IF ( v_bonus >= 600 ) THEN
            SET v_raise = v_raise + 0.04;
        END IF;

        IF ( v_comm < 2000 ) THEN
            SET v_raise = v_raise + 0.03;
        ELSEIF ( v_comm < 3000 ) THEN
            SET v_raise = v_raise + 0.02;
        ELSE
            SET v_raise = v_raise + 0.01;
        END IF;

        IF ( v_raise > p_max ) THEN
            SET v_raise = p_max;
        END IF;

        UPDATE employee                                    -- (1)
        SET    salary = v_salary * (1 + v_raise)
        WHERE CURRENT OF c_emp;

        FETCH FROM c_emp INTO v_salary, v_bonus, v_comm;
    END WHILE;
```

```
    CLOSE c_emp;
END ur
```

The logic used to determine the appropriate raise amount is the same as in the *total_raise()* procedure of Figure 4.3. After the raise amount is calculated for the current employee, the salary is updated right away using a positioned update (1) before the cursor moves forward. The WHERE CURRENT OF clause indicates that the update should occur on the row where the cursor is currently positioned. In our case, the cursor is still positioned at the employee whose information was just fetched.

## 4.4 Cursor Behavior with COMMIT/ROLLBACK

One of the most important concepts in database programming is the transaction or the unit-of-work. A transaction or a unit-of-work is a set of one or more SQL statements that execute as a single operation. Proper transaction control using COMMIT and/or ROLLBACK is critical for guaranteeing data integrity.

In DB2, the COMMIT and ROLLBACK statements are supported inside SQL procedures. When you use COMMIT or ROLLBACK statements with cursors, the behavior of the cursor depends on whether or not it is declared using the WITH HOLD clause. Figure 4.9 is an enhanced version of the syntax diagram presented in Figure 4.1 for DECLARE CURSOR which includes the WITH HOLD clause. The WITH RETURN clause is used to pass the result set defined by the cursor to an application or another procedure and is discussed later in this chapter. The TO CALLER and TO CLIENT clauses are meaningful only in the context of nested SQL procedures and are discussed in Chapter 7, "Nested SQL Procedures."

**Figure 4.9** Syntax Diagram for DECLARE CURSOR

```
>>-DECLARE--cursor-name--CURSOR----+-----------+-------------->
                                   '-WITH HOLD--'

>-----+-----------------------------+------------------------->
      |              .-TO CALLER--.  |
      '-WITH RETURN--+------------+--'
                     '-TO CLIENT--'

>----FOR--+-select-statement-+------------------------------><
          '-statement-name---'
```

If the cursor is not declared using the WITH HOLD clause, all resources (cursor, locks and LOB locators) are released upon either COMMIT or ROLLBACK. Therefore, if you wanted to still use the cursor after a COMMIT or ROLLBACK statement, you will have to re-open the cursor and traverse it from the first row. Defining a cursor using WITH HOLD will cause the cursor to maintain its position, locks and LOB locators across transactions.

A lock is a database object that is used to control how different applications can access the same resource. A LOB locator is a four-byte value stored in a host variable that a program can use to refer to a LOB value held in the database system.

For cursors defined WITH HOLD after COMMIT:

- the cursor will remain open.
- the cursor will be positioned before the next logical row.
- the only permitted operations on cursors immediately after the COMMIT statement are FETCH and CLOSE.
- positioned delete and positioned update are valid only for rows that are fetched within the same unit of work.
- all LOB locators will be released.

For cursors defined WITH HOLD after ROLLBACK:

- all cursors will be closed.
- all locks will be released.
- all LOB locators will be released.

To better explain WITH HOLD behavior, let's look at the example in Figure 4.10.

**Figure 4.10** Example of the Cursor Behavior on COMMIT/ROLLBACK

```
CREATE PROCEDURE update_department
    ( )
SPECIFIC upd_dept
LANGUAGE SQL
ud: BEGIN
    -- Declare variable
    DECLARE v_deptno CHAR(3);
    -- Declare returncode
    DECLARE SQLSTATE CHAR(5);

    DECLARE c_dept CURSOR WITH HOLD FOR
        SELECT deptno
        FROM   department
```

```
    FOR UPDATE OF location;

    -- Declare condition handler
    DECLARE CONTINUE HANDLER FOR SQLSTATE '24504', SQLSTATE '24501'
    BEGIN
    END;

    -- Procedure logic
    OPEN c_dept;

    FETCH FROM c_dept INTO v_deptno;                                       -- (01)
    UPDATE department SET location='FLOOR1' WHERE CURRENT OF c_dept;       -- (02)
    COMMIT;                                                                -- (03)

    FETCH FROM c_dept INTO v_deptno;                                       -- (04)
    COMMIT;                                                                -- (05)
    UPDATE department SET location='FLOOR2' WHERE CURRENT OF c_dept;       -- (06)

    FETCH FROM c_dept INTO v_deptno;                                       -- (07)
    UPDATE department SET location='FLOOR3' WHERE CURRENT OF c_dept;       -- (08)
    COMMIT;                                                                -- (09)

    FETCH FROM c_dept INTO v_deptno;                                       -- (10)
    UPDATE department SET location='FLOOR4' WHERE CURRENT OF c_dept;       -- (11)
    ROLLBACK;                                                              -- (12)

    FETCH FROM c_dept INTO v_deptno;                                       -- (13)
    UPDATE department SET location='FLOOR5' WHERE CURRENT OF c_dept;       -- (14)

    CLOSE c_dept;

    RETURN 0;
END ud
```

The *update_department()* procedure mixes five fetch/update blocks with COMMIT and ROLLBACK statements to show their effect on transactions. It accesses and updates the DEPARTMENT table in the sample database. Figure 4.11 shows the first five rows of the two relevant columns in the DEPARTMENT table, before the execution of the procedure.

**Figure 4.11** Partial Table DEPARTMENT Before the Execution of update_department()

```
DEPTNO LOCATION
------ --------
A00      -
B01      -
C01      -
D01      -
D11      -
```

Figure 4.12 shows the same five rows, after the *update_department()* procedure has completed. Only two rows have been updated.

**Figure 4.12** Partial Table DEPARTMENT After the Execution of update_department()

```
DEPTNO LOCATION
------ --------
A00    FLOOR1
B01    -
C01    FLOOR3
D01    -
D11    -
```

Here is an analysis of the sequence of execution. After the cursor was declared as FOR UPDATE and opened, it was positioned before the first row. The first block of FETCH and UPDATE on lines (1) and (2) ran without a problem. Line (3) is a COMMIT statement. Because the cursor was declared using the WITH HOLD clause, it remained open and was positioned before the second row for the next unit of work, line (4) and line (5). The lock on the first row has been released and the location field in the first row has been updated to *"FLOOR1".*

The FETCH statement on line (4) was successful. However, because of the COMMIT statement on line (5), the cursor was no longer positioned at the second row, it was positioned before the third row, which has not been FETCHED at this point. The UPDATE statement on line (6) failed because the cursor was not positioned on any rows. The cursor was between the second and third rows. It would have generated the following SQL error if the error had not been caught in the error handling block.

```
SQL0508N  The cursor specified in the UPDATE or DELETE statement is
not positioned on a row.  SQLSTATE=24504
```

Even though error handling has not yet been covered, (see Chapter 5, "Condition Handling"), the example uses it to allow all the procedures to run through to the end. If the handler did not exist, the procedure would terminate at the first error and roll back changes to the last COMMIT point.

The next two sets of FETCH and UPDATE statements on line (7), (8) and line (10), (11) ran successfully and the third and fourth rows were updated.

Line (12) is a ROLLBACK statement. It can only rollback changes made since the last COMMIT statement. So the change made to the location field on the fourth row was set back to the original null value. But the change to the third row was not affected because of the COMMIT statement on line (9).

After the ROLLBACK statement, the cursor was closed and all locks were released. The FETCH statement on line (13) would have caused the following error, which was also caught by the error-handling block. The UPDATE statement on line (14) failed as well.

```
SQL0501N  The cursor specified in a FETCH or CLOSE statement is not
open.  SQLSTATE=24501
```

If the cursor had not been declared using the WITH HOLD clause, all the fetch and update statements from line (4) through to line (14) would have failed with the SQL error above because the cursor would be closed implicitly by either COMMIT or ROLLBACK statement.

## 4.5 Using Cursors to Return Result Sets

Besides using cursors to process data within the SQL procedure, you can also use cursors to return result sets to the calling program for processing. To contrast these two cursor usage scenarios, the *total_raise()* procedure in Figure 4.3 is rewritten as an SQL procedure which returns all qualifying employees' salary, bonus and commission fields as a result set, in conjunction with a client program which receives the result set. The total raise, then, is calculated at the client. The SQL procedure called *read_emp()* is shown in Figure 4.13.

The result sets can be received by either SQL procedures or client programs developed in programming languages such as Java or C. Receiving result sets from another SQL procedure will be covered in Chapter 7, "Nested SQL Procedures." The Java and C client program used to receive this result set is provided in Appendix H, "Sample Application Code for Chapter 4."

**Figure 4.13** Example of Using Cursor to Return Single Result Set

```
CREATE PROCEDURE read_emp
    (  )
SPECIFIC read_emp
DYNAMIC RESULT SETS 1                                    --(1)
LANGUAGE SQL
re: BEGIN
    -- Procedure logic
    DECLARE c_emp CURSOR WITH RETURN FOR                 --(2)
        SELECT salary, bonus, comm
        FROM   employee
        WHERE  job!='PRES';

    OPEN c_emp;                                          --(3)
END re
```

When using a cursor to return the result set to a calling application, you need to:

- specify DYNAMIC RESULT SETS clause in CREATE PROCEDURE statement (1).
- declare the cursor using the WITH RETURN clause (2).
- keep the cursor open for the client application (3).

This example is quite straightforward. Let's look at another, more interesting example.

In DB2 SQL procedures, besides DML statements such as SELECT, DELETE and UPDATE, you can also use DDL statements, such as the CREATE TABLE statement. You can create a table, populate it and then use a cursor to return the result set from the same table. The tricky part is that the DECLARE CURSOR statement has to be at the beginning of the BEGIN...END block. The table creation has to be in the body of the block. If you put the DECLARE CURSOR statement at the beginning, the table is not created yet. You will get a compile-time error complaining the table is not found. If you put the CURSOR statement after the CREATE TABLE statement, you will run into another compile-time error indicating your DECLARE CURSOR statement is not supposed to be there. What should you do now?

The solution to this dilemma requires understanding the concept of scope. In DB2, the BEGIN...END blocks can be nested. The scope of any declarations within a BEGIN/END block is the block itself. The DECLARE CURSOR statement is required to be at the beginning of a BEGIN/END block, before any SELECT, DELETE, UPDATE or CREATE TABLE statements in that block. Hence, you can use a nested BEGIN...END block to declare a cursor at the end of procedure. Figure 4.14 illustrates this.

In order to return result sets from a table created in the same BEGIN...END block, you need to declare cursors inside a nested BEGIN...END block.

**Figure 4.14** Example of Using Cursor on Newly Created Table

```
CREATE PROCEDURE create_and_return
    ( )
SPECIFIC create_and_return
DYNAMIC RESULT SETS 1
LANGUAGE SQL
cr: BEGIN
    -- Procedure logic
    CREATE TABLE mytable (sid INT);
```

```
    INSERT INTO mytable VALUES (1);
    INSERT INTO mytable VALUES (2);

    BEGIN                                         --(1)
    DECLARE c_cur CURSOR WITH RETURN
        FOR SELECT *
            FROM mytable;
    OPEN c_cur;                                   --(2)
    END;                                          --(3)
END cr
```

You can see from the example in Figure 4.14 how a new BEGIN...END block from lines (1) to (3) allows us to declare the cursor for the table created in the same procedure. The OPEN CURSOR statement at line (2) must also be inside the new BEGIN...END block as the cursor *c_cur* is only valid in the inner BEGIN...END block. It is not visible outside the block.

A very practical usage of this scheme is when you need a temporary table in your SQL procedure. You can either use a permanent table for temporary purpose or create a real DB2 user temporary table. For more information on DB2 user temporary tables, please refer to Chapter 8, "Advanced Features."

Another approach to solve the above dilemma is to use dynamic SQL, which will be covered in Chapter 6, "Dynamic SQL."

## 4.6 Returning Multiple Result Sets

So far, the examples presented have returned a single result set to the calling application. It is also possible to define multiple cursors and return multiple result sets to the caller. To do this, the following are required:

- Specify DYNAMIC RESULT SETS clause in the CREATE PROCEDURE statement corresponding to the number of result sets you intend to return.
- Declare the cursors for each result set using the WITH RETURN clause.
- Keep all cursors to be returned open for the client application.

Figure 4.15 shows a procedure that returns multiple result sets. To demonstrate the use of multiple result sets, the procedure *read_emp()* from Figure 4.13 is re-written to return each of the columns via three separate cursors, instead of one cursor with three columns. An example of a Java and C program used to receive multiple result sets has been provided in Appendix H, "Sample Application Code for Chapter 4."

**Figure 4.15** Example of Returning Multiple Result Sets

```
CREATE PROCEDURE read_emp_multi
    ( )
SPECIFIC read_emp_multi
DYNAMIC RESULT SETS 3                                       --(1)
LANGUAGE SQL
re: BEGIN
    -- Procedure logic
    DECLARE c_salary CURSOR WITH RETURN FOR
        SELECT salary
        FROM   employee;

    DECLARE c_bonus CURSOR WITH RETURN FOR
        SELECT bonus
        FROM   employee;

    DECLARE c_comm CURSOR WITH RETURN FOR
        SELECT comm
        FROM   employee;

    OPEN c_salary;
    OPEN c_bonus;
    OPEN c_comm;
END re
```

Because three result sets are returned, the DYNAMIC RESULT SETS value is set to three (1). Each cursor is declared and left open for the client application. The order in which the cursors are opened reflects the order in which the result sets are returned to the client. In this example, the first result set your client code can access is the salary result set, followed by the bonus and commission result sets.

## 4.7 Chapter Summary

In this chapter, you have seen the usage of the cursors in SQL procedures. Cursors allow you to access and process data one row at a time, giving you the opportunity to implement much more complex logic that would otherwise be impossible or difficult to carry out. When using cursors to process data, you can perform reads and positioned deletes/updates. You can use the cursor either to process the data within the SQL procedure, or to return result sets to the client program.

C H A P T E R 5

# Condition Handling

## In this chapter, you will learn:

- what SQLCODE and SQLSTATE are, and the difference between them;
- what a condition handler is, how and when to best use it, its range and scope, and how to work with multiple handlers;
- how to force an application or user-defined exception, and set the appropriate message tag to go along with it;
- about various ways of returning errors, and how to check the success and/or failure of a stored procedure call.

Any textbook that deals with the subject of writing code is not complete without a discussion of how to process errors and other conditions. Anticipating and handling conditions is part and parcel of good, robust programming style. With DB2 SQL procedures, this is accomplished through the use of condition handlers. In fact, it is also desirable to be able to check for and act on warnings that may be encountered. With DB2 SQL procedures, warnings are also a type of condition, and thus warnings and errors are handled in a very similar fashion. This chapter will describe the various types of condition handlers and techniques of how and when to use them.

## 5.1 Basic Error Checking: SQLCODE and SQLSTATE

A stored procedure can be written without any error checking at all. In this case, if an error is encountered, execution stops and the procedure will terminate. In order to write SQL procedures responsibly, you need to learn how errors can best be handled within procedures.

SQLSTATE and SQLCODE are two values within DB2's communications area that are populated each time an SQL statement is executed. These values can be accessed within a stored procedure to determine the state, such as success or failure, of the previously executed statement. They are identifiers that can be used to get more detailed information about the state of the statement.

SQLSTATE is a five-digit numeric string that conforms to the ISO/ANSI SQL92 standard. This is a code that is common across the DB2 family of products. For example, if you were trying to drop a table that did not exist, you would get an SQLSTATE 42704, which would be the same SQLSTATE regardless of whether the statement was issued against any DB2 product. The first two characters of SQLSTATE are known as the SQLSTATE class code. A class code of 00 means successful completion. Thus an SQLSTATE beginning with 00 implies a successful completion of the previous statement. Similarly, a class code of 01 implies a warning and a class code of 02 implies a *not found* condition. All other class codes are considered errors. Messages associated with SQLSTATEs are general in nature. For example the message associated with SQLSTATE 42704 is, "An undefined object or constraint name was detected."

SQLCODE is an integer status code. It is a database vendor specific code. There are some SQLCODEs that are common across database vendors, such as +100, (which means "NOT FOUND"), but the vast majority of codes do not overlap across the various database products. There are some simple rules that can be followed when working with SQLCODEs. A value of 0 for SQLCODE means that the statement executed successfully, a positive value implies successful completion but with a warning message, and a negative value indicates an error occurred. Messages associated with an SQLCODE are specific in nature. Using the same example of dropping a table that does not exist, the SQLCODE returned is -204 and the associated message is ""<name>" is an undefined name", where <name> would be the name of the table.

So how are SQLSTATE and SQLCODE used in a DB2 SQL procedure? Each statement in an SQL procedure is an SQL statement. Therefore, after the execution of each statement, the value of SQLCODE and SQLSTATE are implicitly set. To access these values, you need to explicitly declare the variables SQLCODE and SQLSTATE.

SQLCODE and SQLSTATE are reserved variable names and can only be declared at the outermost scope of a procedure, meaning they can only be declared at the start of the procedure.

SQLCODE and SQLSTATE can only be accessed in the first statement after a statement has been executed, since they are set after every statement execution.

To make your code more portable, use SQLSTATE for exception handling instead of SQLCODE. In addition to being standard across the DB2 family of products, a large proportion of SQLSTATEs are also standard across database vendors.

It's probably a good time to look at some code snippets to elaborate on what has been presented so far. Consider the example in Figure 5.1.

**Figure 5.1** (Incorrect) Example of Simple ErrorChecking

```
CREATE PROCEDURE simple_error (IN p_midinit CHAR
                              ,IN p_empno CHAR(6) )
SPECIFIC simple_error
LANGUAGE SQL
se: BEGIN
   DECLARE SQLSTATE CHAR(5) DEFAULT '00000';
   DECLARE SQLCODE INT DEFAULT 0;
   UPDATE employee                                   -- (1)
      SET midinit = p_midinit
    WHERE empno = p_empno;
   IF SUBSTR(SQLSTATE,2) NOT IN ('00','01','02') THEN  -- (2)
       ... ... ... ;
   END IF;
END se
```

The IF statement at (2) will evaluate to true if an error condition exists. Recall that SQLSTATEs not beginning with 00, 01 or 02 are considered errors. We could have also checked for SQLCODE being less than zero.

At first glance, you may think that this is a reasonable example of exception handling but it will not perform as expected. If the UPDATE statement at (1) is successful, the procedure will run as expected. If the UPDATE statement is unsuccessful, however, it will never get to the IF at (2). Remember that whenever an error is encountered, the stored procedure terminates and control is transferred to the calling application.

So, is this a Catch-22? Not really. This is where the concept of condition handlers can be introduced—the subject of the next section.

## 5.2 Condition Handlers

A condition handler is basically an SQL statement that is executed when a specified condition is encountered by a statement within the procedure body. The handler is declared within a compound statement, and its scope is limited to the compound statement in which it is declared. The body of an SQL procedure is always enclosed within a BEGIN and END block and hence, by definition, an SQL procedure is a compound statement. The scope for a handler declared at the start of a procedure is the whole stored procedure.

There are two things required to declare a condition handler. First you need to determine under which condition the handler will be invoked, and second, you need to decide which type of handler to declare. The type of handler is used to indicate where control is passed after the handler completes execution.

DB2 SQL PL provides some general conditions: SQLEXCEPTION, SQLWARNING, and NOT FOUND.

SQLEXCEPTION covers all conditions where the execution of an SQL procedure body statement results in an error, represented by an SQLSTATE value whose first two characters are not 00, 01, or 02, or a SQLCODE whose value is a negative integer. SQLWARNING and NOT FOUND will be discussed later in this section.

### 5.2.1 Types of Handlers

There are three handler types that you can declare: EXIT, CONTINUE, and UNDO.

An EXIT handler will execute the SQL statement in the handler, and continue execution at the end of the compound statement in which it was declared. Thus an EXIT handler declared at the start of a procedure would EXIT the procedure upon completion.

In contrast, a CONTINUE handler will continue execution at the statement following the one that raised the exception.

UNDO handlers are similar to EXIT handlers, in that execution will continue at the end of the compound statement in which it was declared. Any statements that were successfully executed within the compound statement will be rolled back with an UNDO handler, however. UNDO handlers can only be declared within ATOMIC compound statements.

Figure 5.2 shows the syntax diagram for declaring handlers.

**Figure 5.2** Abbreviated Syntax Diagram for Condition Handler Declaration

```
---DECLARE----+-CONTINUE-+---HANDLER--FOR-----condition-------->
              +-EXIT-----+
              '-UNDO-----'

>----SQL-procedure-statement-----------------------------------|
```

You can see from the syntax diagram that the handler declaration is very simple. The variable *condition* refers to a specific condition described using a keyword for a general condition, an SQLSTATE or a previously declared condition. The examples in the next few sections will explain handler declarations in detail.

## 5.2.2 Compound Statements

Within compound statements, a condition handler declaration follows all other types of declarations, such as variable declarations and cursor declarations.

If you require multiple statements to be executed within a condition handler, use a compound statement (BEGIN and END block).

Figure 5.3 expands on the example presented earlier and shows how it can be corrected using a condition handler.

**Figure 5.3** Example of Simple Error Checking

```
CREATE PROCEDURE simple_error ( IN p_midinit CHAR
                              ,IN p_empno CHAR(6) )
    SPECIFIC simple_error
    LANGUAGE SQL
se: BEGIN
   -- Declare variables
   DECLARE v_sqlstate_test CHAR(5);                          -- (1)
   DECLARE v_sqlcode_test INT;                               -- (2)
   -- Declare return codes
   DECLARE SQLSTATE CHAR(5) DEFAULT '00000';
   DECLARE SQLCODE INT DEFAULT 0;
   -- Declare condition handlers
   DECLARE CONTINUE HANDLER FOR SQLEXCEPTION                 -- (3)
        SELECT SQLSTATE
              ,SQLCODE
          INTO v_sqlstate_test
```

```
                ,v_sqlcode_test
            FROM sysibm.sysdummy1;
    -- Procedure logic
    UPDATE employee                                     -- (4)
       SET midinit = p_midinit
     WHERE empno = p_empno;
    IF SUBSTR(SQLSTATE,2) NOT IN ('00','01','02') THEN  -- (5)

       … … …;
    END IF;
END se
```

As you can see, two variables *v_sqlstate_test* and *v_sqlcode_test,* have been added at (1) and (2), as well as a CONTINUE handler at (3). The handler sets the values of SQLCODE and SQLSTATE raised by the error condition to the variables *v_sqlcode_test* and *v_sqlstate_test*. The other change made was the test condition at (5), to test for the variable set in the handler as opposed to the actual SQLCODE.

Note that SQLCODE and SQLSTATE from the statement that raised the condition are only accessible in the first statement of the handler. That is the reason a SELECT INTO statement is used to capture both simultaneously, so that both variables (*v_sqlcode_test* and *v_sqlstate_test*) can be assigned properly. The table, *sysibm.sysdummy1*, referenced in the FROM clause is a DB2 special, built-in catalog view that contains one row only.

The example in Figure 5.3 works, but it seems like a very cumbersome way to do any error checking. It forces you to check for an error after each and every execution of a statement. In fact, it is only presented for demonstration purposes. Creating a handler, just to set SQLCODE and SQLSTATE, defeats its intended purpose. The real value in creating handlers is to group errors into classes for which similar action can be taken.

To elaborate, if you were to rethink the example above, what you would really want to do is to return SQLCODE and SQLSTATE as output parameters to the calling application. This can be accomplished by writing an EXIT handler instead of a CONTINUE handler. Figure 5.4 shows the previous example rewritten, with a more appropriate use of the condition handler.

**Figure 5.4** Revised Example of Simple Error Checking

```
CREATE PROCEDURE simple_error ( IN p_midinit CHAR
                              ,IN p_empno CHAR(6)
                              ,OUT p_sqlstate_out CHAR(5)
                              ,OUT p_sqlcode_out INT )
    SPECIFIC simple_error
    LANGUAGE SQL
```

```
se: BEGIN
   -- Declare return codes
   DECLARE SQLSTATE CHAR(5) DEFAULT '00000';
   DECLARE SQLCODE INT DEFAULT 0;
   -- Declare condition handlers
   DECLARE EXIT HANDLER FOR SQLEXCEPTION
        SELECT SQLSTATE
              ,SQLCODE
          INTO p_sqlstate_out
              ,p_sqlcode_out
          FROM sysibm.sysdummy1;
   -- Procedure logic
   -- Initialize output parameters with defaults
   VALUES (SQLSTATE, SQLCODE)
     INTO p_sqlstate_out
         ,p_sqlcode_out;
   UPDATE employee                                    -- (1)
      SET midinit = p_midinit
    WHERE empno = p_empno;
END se
```

As soon as an error is encountered, the handler is invoked. It sets the values for the output parameters, *p_sqlcode* and *p_sqlstate*. Once the handler completes, the procedure exits. Since the procedure terminates on error, there is no need to check for an error condition after the UPDATE statement at (1).

In addition to SQLEXCEPTION, there are two other general conditions for handlers available to you, namely SQLWARNING and NOT FOUND.

SQLWARNING covers all conditions where the execution of an SQL statement completed successfully, but a warning was issued. That is, an SQLSTATE value whose first two characters are 01, or an SQLCODE value that is a positive integer, not including +100.

NOT FOUND condition represents the case where the execution of an SQL statement returns an SQLSTATE value whose first two characters are 02, or an SQLCODE value of +100.

## 5.2.3 Naming Specific Conditions

It is also possible to declare handlers for specific conditions, rather than one of the general conditions, by declaring a handler for a specific SQLSTATE. This can be done in two ways. One is through the declaration of the condition handler, as in

```
DECLARE EXIT HANDLER FOR SQLSTATE '23503' ...;
```

While the statement above will work, it does not make the code in the procedure very readable or intuitive. The SQL PL allows you to declare condition names for specific SQLSTATEs to make the code clearer. Consider the following code snippet:

```
DECLARE FOREIGN_KEY_VIOLATION CONDITION FOR SQLSTATE '23503';
DECLARE EXIT HANDLER FOR FOREIGN_KEY_VIOLATION ...;
```

This makes your code more readable and easier to understand. Consider two syntax diagrams, one for the condition declaration (Figure 5.5), and the other for the more complete handler declaration (Figure 5.6).

**Figure 5.5** Syntax Diagram for Condition Declaration

```
|---DECLARE--condition-name--CONDITION--FOR--------------------->

                  .-VALUE-.
     .-SQLSTATE--+-------+---.
>----+-----------------------+---string-constant---------------|
```

**Figure 5.6** Complete Syntax Diagram for Condition Handler Declaration

```
---DECLARE----+-CONTINUE-+---HANDLER--FOR---------------------->
              +-EXIT-----+
              '-UNDO-----'

        .-,----------------------------------.
        V                .-VALUE-.           |
>---------+-SQLSTATE--+-------+--string--+--+------------------->
          +-condition-name---------------+
          +-SQLEXCEPTION-----------------+
          +-SQLWARNING-------------------+
          '-NOT FOUND--------------------'

>----SQL-procedure-statement-----------------------------------|
```

## 5.2.4 Working with Multiple Handlers

For any given procedure, you can declare multiple handlers, for different conditions. For example, you can declare an EXIT handler for SQLEXCEPTION and another EXIT handler for SQLSTATE 23503. This can introduce some ambiguity since SQLSTATE 23503 is also a SQLEXCEPTION. In cases where more than one condition handler might fit the bill, the handler for the more specific condition is invoked. So in a situation where handlers for both SQLEXCEPTION and SQLSTATE 23503 are declared, a statement that results in a foreign key violation would invoke the condition handler declared for SQLSTATE 23503 and the SQLEXCEPTION condition handler is ignored.

Several concepts have been introduced in the last section. It's time now to look at a more comprehensive example, with multiple handlers, to bring some of these ideas together.

The example in Figure 5.7 is a procedure that inserts into the *department* table. If the insert fails because of a duplicate row error, then an update is performed. It takes the column values for *department* as input and returns SQLCODE and SQLSTATE as output parameters.

**Figure 5.7** Example of Named Condition and Multiple Handlers

```
CREATE PROCEDURE insert_update_department ( IN p_deptno CHAR(3)
                                           ,IN p_deptname VARCHAR(29)
                                           ,IN p_mgrno CHAR(6)
                                           ,IN p_admrdept CHAR(3)
                                           ,IN p_location CHAR(16)
                                           ,OUT p_sqlstate_out CHAR(5)
                                           ,OUT p_sqlcode_out INT )
    SPECIFIC ins_upd_dept
    LANGUAGE SQL
iud: BEGIN
    -- Declare variables
    DECLARE SQLSTATE CHAR(5) DEFAULT '00000';
    DECLARE SQLCODE INT DEFAULT 0;
    DECLARE v_duplicate INT DEFAULT 0;
    -- Declare condition
    DECLARE c_duplicate CONDITION FOR SQLSTATE '23505';                -- (1)
    -- Declare handlers
    DECLARE EXIT HANDLER FOR SQLEXCEPTION
        SELECT SQLSTATE                                                 -- (2)
              ,SQLCODE
          INTO p_sqlstate_out
              ,p_sqlcode_out
          FROM sysibm.sysdummy1;
    -- Handler for duplicate condition
    DECLARE CONTINUE HANDLER FOR c_duplicate                            -- (3)
        SET v_duplicate = 1;
    -- Initialize output parms
    VALUES (SQLSTATE, SQLCODE)                                          -- (4)
      INTO p_sqlstate_out
          ,p_sqlcode_out;

    -- Try insert, if duplicate, then update
    INSERT INTO department ( deptno
                            ,deptname
                            ,mgrno
                            ,admrdept
```

```
                              ,location )
                    VALUES ( p_deptno
                              ,p_deptname
                              ,p_mgrno
                              ,p_admrdept
                              ,p_location);
    IF v_duplicate = 1 THEN
        -- only update if non-null value provided as input parameter
        UPDATE department
           SET deptname = coalesce(p_deptname, deptname)
              ,mgrno    = coalesce(p_mgrno, mgrno)
              ,admrdept = coalesce(p_admrdept, admrdept)
              ,location = coalesce(p_location, location)
         WHERE deptno = p_deptno;
    END IF;
END iud
```

A condition is declared at (1) for SQLSTATE 23505, which is the SQLSTATE for duplicate rows. A handler is then declared at (3) for the specific condition that sets the variable indicating a duplicate condition.

Observe the VALUES statement at (4). This is an alternative to issuing two SET statements, or a statement such as *SELECT ... FROM sysibm.sysdummy1* as at (2). The VALUES INTO is more efficient than two SET statements because the variables are assigned in parallel. Additionally, each statement has some overhead associated with it, for example condition checking at the end of each statement. Therefore, reducing the number of statements also reduces the processing cost.

# 5.3 Advanced Error Handling—Custom Errors and Error Messages

## 5.3.1 Using SIGNAL to Force the Invocation of a Handler

So far, you've only seen examples where condition handlers are automatically invoked for a specific SQLSTATE. What if you want to force the invocation of a handler? For example, a column value returned from a select statement may indicate an application error for which you may want to invoke a handler.

The SIGNAL statement allows you to do just that. It forces an error or warning through the setting of SQLSTATE. You also have the option of customizing a message associated with the SQLSTATE. If a handler is declared for that SQLSTATE, it will be invoked. If no handler is declared for that SQLSTATE, then the handler for SQLEX-

CEPTION or SQLWARNING is invoked as necessary. If no handlers are declared at all, the exception is returned to the application as a database exception.

SQLSTATEs beginning with the characters 01 or 02 are warnings and not found conditions, respectively. All other SQLSTATEs (not beginning with the characters 00) are considered exceptions. Any warnings and not found conditions issued via a SIGNAL statement will be assigned an SQLCODE of +438, and any exceptions will be assigned an SQLCODE of -438.

In fact the SIGNAL statement even allows you to issue a customized condition or SQLSTATE. If a condition for an SQLSTATE, customized or otherwise, is declared, then it can be referenced in a SIGNAL statement. Figure 5.8 shows the syntax diagram for the SIGNAL statement.

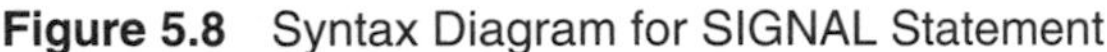
**Figure 5.8** Syntax Diagram for SIGNAL Statement

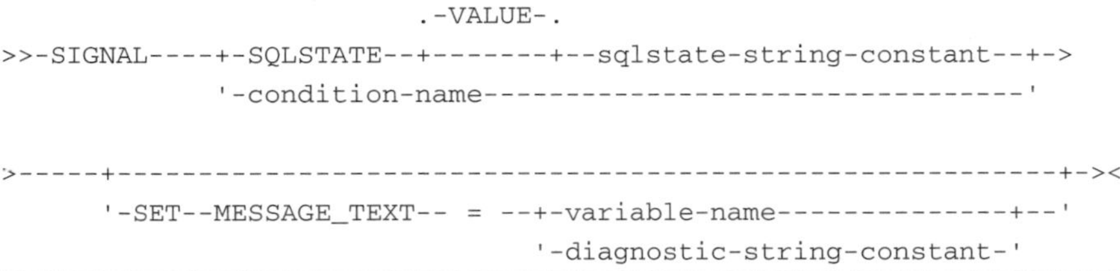

```
                          .-VALUE-.
>>-SIGNAL----+-SQLSTATE--+-------+--sqlstate-string-constant--+->
             '-condition-name--------------------------------'

>-----+-----------------------------------------------------+-><
      '-SET--MESSAGE_TEXT-- = --+-variable-name-------------+--'
                                '-diagnostic-string-constant-'
```

There are some rules that need to be followed when defining your own SQLSTATE. The following excerpt is from the DB2 SQL Reference(Chapter 6, "SQL Control Statements," section on SIGNAL statement) pertaining to custom SQLSTATEs:

> SQLSTATE values are comprised of a two-character class code value, followed by a three-character subclass code value. Class code values represent classes of successful and unsuccessful execution conditions. Any valid SQLSTATE value can be used in the SIGNAL statement. However, it is recommended that programmers define new SQLSTATEs based on ranges reserved for applications. This prevents the unintentional use of an SQLSTATE value that might be defined by the database manager in a future release.
>
> - SQLSTATE classes that begin with the characters '7' through '9', or 'I' through 'Z' may be defined. Within these classes, any subclass may be defined.
> - SQLSTATE classes that begin with the characters '0' through '6', or 'A' through 'H' are reserved for the database manager. Within these classes, subclasses that begin with the characters '0' through 'H' are reserved for the database manager. Subclasses that begin with the characters 'I' through 'Z' may be defined.

Figure 5.9 shows an example that employs the SIGNAL statement. To illustrate, the previous example from Figure 5.7 is expanded to declare a condition for a customized SQLSTATE. The logic is changed such that if more than ten rows are found in the DEPARTMENT table, an exception is raised.

**Figure 5.9** Example of SIGNAL Statement

```
CREATE PROCEDURE insert_update_department ( IN p_deptno CHAR(3)
                                           ,IN p_deptname VARCHAR(29)
                                           ,IN p_mgrno CHAR(6)
                                           ,IN p_admrdept CHAR(3)
                                           ,IN p_location CHAR(16)
                                           ,OUT p_sqlstate_out CHAR(5)
                                           ,OUT p_sqlcode_out INT )
    SPECIFIC ins_upd_dept
    LANGUAGE SQL
iud: BEGIN
    -- Declare variables
    DECLARE SQLSTATE CHAR(5) DEFAULT '00000';
    DECLARE SQLCODE INT DEFAULT 0;
    DECLARE v_duplicate INT DEFAULT 0;
    DECLARE v_num_rows INT DEFAULT 0;
    -- Declare condition
    DECLARE c_duplicate CONDITION FOR SQLSTATE '23505';
    DECLARE c_too_many_rows CONDITION FOR SQLSTATE '99001';
    -- Declare handlers
    DECLARE EXIT HANDLER FOR SQLEXCEPTION
        SELECT SQLSTATE
              ,SQLCODE
          INTO p_sqlstate_out
              ,p_sqlcode_out
          FROM sysibm.sysdummy1;
    DECLARE CONTINUE HANDLER FOR c_duplicate
        SET v_duplicate = 1;

    -- Initialize output parms
    VALUES (SQLSTATE, SQLCODE)
      INTO p_sqlstate_out
          ,p_sqlcode_out;

    -- See how many rows are already in the DEPARTMENT table
    SELECT COUNT(1)
      INTO v_num_rows
      FROM department;

    -- Signal an error if more than 10 rows exist
    IF v_num_rows > 10 THEN
        SIGNAL c_too_many_rows
           SET MESSAGE_TEXT = 'Too many rows in table DEPARTMENT'; -- (1)
    END IF;
```

```
    -- Try insert, if duplicate, then update
    INSERT INTO department ( deptno
                           ,deptname
                           ,mgrno
                           ,admrdept
                           ,location )
                    VALUES ( p_deptno
                           ,p_deptname
                           ,p_mgrno
                           ,p_admrdept
                           ,p_location);
    IF v_duplicate = 1 THEN
        -- only update if non-null value provided as input parameter
        UPDATE department
           SET deptname = coalesce(p_deptname, deptname)
              ,mgrno = coalesce(p_mgrno, mgrno)
              ,admrdept = coalesce(p_admrdept, admrdept)
              ,location = coalesce(p_location, location)
         WHERE deptno = p_deptno;
    END IF;

END iud
```

If you examine the example in Figure 5.9, you will sec that if less than eleven rows exist in the DEPARTMENT table, the procedure will function as it did in Figure 5.7. However, if more than ten rows are encountered, an exception with an SQLSTATE of 99001 is raised by the SIGNAL statement at (1). Since there is no specific handler for the specified SQLSTATE, the EXIT handler for the SQLEXCEPTION is invoked. The control returns to the caller after the handler finishes execution. In this case, 99001 will be returned as the SQLSTATE value and -438 will be returned as the SQLCODE.

### 5.3.2 Using RESIGNAL to Force the Invocation of a Handler

Along the same lines as the SIGNAL statement, there is a similar statement, RESIGNAL, which warrants some discussion. The RESIGNAL statement can only be invoked from inside a condition handler. It is used for one of two things. It can be used to issue a warning or error in the same way as the SIGNAL statement, but from within a handler. The SQLSTATE and SQLCODE that caused the handler to be invoked are overridden. Alternatively, it can be used to reissue the same condition that caused the handler to be invoked. The reason for the latter case will become more apparent in the next section.

Figure 5.10 shows the syntax diagram for the RESIGNAL statement.

**Figure 5.10** Syntax Diagram for RESIGNAL Statement

```
>>-RESIGNAL----+---------------------------------------+------><
               '-| signal-value |--+------------------+--'
                                   '-| signal-info |-'

signal-value

                .-VALUE-.
|---+-SQLSTATE--+-------+--sqlstate-string-constant--+---------|
    '-condition-name---------------------------------'

signal-info

|---+-----------------------------------------------------+-|
    '-SET--MESSAGE_TEXT-- = --+-variable-name-------------+--'
                              '-diagnostic-string-constant-'
```

As you can see, the *signal-value* and *signal-info* specifications are optional. If they are omitted, the statement will reissue the same SQLSTATE and SQLCODE that caused the handler to be invoked.

This is a good time for another example. Again, this example is for illustration purposes only to show a crude way to override the SQLSTATE that invoked the handler. In Figure 5.11, the example in Figure 5.9 is expanded to contain a handler for the condition forced by the SIGNAL statement. The handler in turn issues a RESIGNAL statement.

**Figure 5.11** Example of RESIGNAL Statement

```
CREATE PROCEDURE insert_update_department ( IN p_deptno CHAR(3)
                                          ,IN p_deptname VARCHAR(29)
                                          ,IN p_mgrno CHAR(6)
                                          ,IN p_admrdept CHAR(3)
                                          ,IN p_location CHAR(16)
                                          ,OUT p_sqlstate_out CHAR(5)
                                          ,OUT p_sqlcode_out INT )
    SPECIFIC ins_upd_dept
    LANGUAGE SQL
------------------------------------------------------------------------
-- SQL Stored Procedure
------------------------------------------------------------------------
iud: BEGIN
    -- Declare variables
    DECLARE SQLSTATE CHAR(5) DEFAULT '00000';
    DECLARE SQLCODE INT DEFAULT 0;
    DECLARE v_duplicate INT DEFAULT 0;
    DECLARE v_num_rows INT DEFAULT 0;
```

```
    -- Declare condition
    DECLARE c_duplicate CONDITION FOR SQLSTATE '23505';
    DECLARE c_too_many_rows CONDITION FOR SQLSTATE '99001';
    DECLARE c_error CONDITION FOR SQLSTATE '99999';
    -- Declare handlers
    DECLARE EXIT HANDLER FOR SQLEXCEPTION
        SELECT SQLSTATE, SQLCODE
          INTO p_sqlstate_out
              ,p_sqlcode_out
          FROM sysibm.sysdummy1;
    -- Handler with RESIGNAL
    DECLARE CONTINUE HANDLER FOR c_too_many_rows                        -- (1)
        RESIGNAL c_error SET MESSAGE_TEXT = 'Too many rows in table DEPARTMENT';
    DECLARE CONTINUE HANDLER FOR c_duplicate
        SET v_duplicate = 1;
    -- Initialize output parms
    VALUES (SQLSTATE, SQLCODE)
      INTO p_sqlstate_out
          ,p_sqlcode_out;

    -- See how many rows are already in the DEPARTMENT table
    SELECT COUNT(1)
      INTO v_num_rows
      FROM department;
    -- Signal an error if more than 10 rows exist
    IF v_num_rows > 10 THEN
        SIGNAL c_too_many_rows;
    END IF;

    -- Try insert, if duplicate, then update
    INSERT INTO department ( deptno
                           ,deptname
                           ,mgrno
                           ,admrdept
                           ,location )
                    VALUES ( p_deptno
                           ,p_deptname
                           ,p_mgrno
                           ,p_admrdept
                           ,p_location);
    IF v_duplicate = 1 THEN
        -- only update if non-null value provided as input parameter
        UPDATE department
           SET deptname = coalesce(p_deptname, deptname)
              ,mgrno    = coalesce(p_mgrno, mgrno)
              ,admrdept = coalesce(p_admrdept, admrdept)
              ,location = coalesce(p_location, location)
         WHERE deptno = p_deptno;
    END IF;

END iud
```

The example shows that when more than ten rows exist in the DEPARTMENT table, an error is SIGNALed with an SQLSTATE of 99001. The condition handler for this condition RESIGNALs with an SQLSTATE of 99999. Thus, when there are too many rows in the department table, the calling application will receive an SQLSTATE of 99999, not 99001 as in the example from Figure 5.9.

The real value of the RESIGNAL statement is seen when you have multiple handlers with multiple levels of compound statements, which you will see in the next section.

### 5.3.3 Scope of Handlers

So far, all the examples we have seen have been fairly simple. The logic in the procedures has also been simple. Simple examples are a good way to learn new concepts, but it is sometimes necessary to show more complex examples to demonstrate some of the more advanced topics.

Recall that condition handlers are declared within a compound statement. An SQL procedure by definition is a compound statement, which can contain other compound statements, and so on. Hence, it follows that each of these nested compound statements can contain condition handlers as well. What is the behavior of the stored procedure when nested compound statements with multiple handlers are used?

Figure 5.12 shows some pseudocode to help paint a scenario for discussion.

**Figure 5.12** Pseudocode for Nested Handlers

```
CREATE PROCEDURE
s: BEGIN
    s1: DECLARE EXIT HANDLER FOR SQLEXCEPTION RESIGNAL
    s2: SQL Procedure Statement
    s3: SQL Procedure Statement
    s4: BEGIN
        s4-1: DECLARE EXIT HANDLER FOR SQLEXCEPTION RESIGNAL
        s4-2: DECLARE EXIT HANDLER FOR '99999' BEGIN END
        s4-3: SQL Procedure Statement
        s4-4: SQL Procedure Statement
        s4-5: BEGIN
            s4-5-1: DECLARE EXIT HANDLER FOR SQLSTATE '23503'
                            RESIGNAL SQLSTATE '99999'
            s4-5-2: SQL Procedure Statement
            s4-5-3: SQL Procedure Statement
            s4-5-4: IF <cond> THEN SIGNAL SQLSTATE '23503' END IF
        END s4-5
        s4-6:  BEGIN
            s4-6-1: DECLARE UNDO HANDLER FOR SQLSTATE '23503'
                            RESIGNAL SQLSTATE '99998'
```

```
            s4-6-2: SQL Procedure Statement
            s4-6-3: SQL Procedure Statement
            s4-6-4: IF <cond> THEN SIGNAL SQLSTATE '23503' END IF
        END s4-6
        s4-7: IF <cond> THEN SIGNAL SQLSTATE '23503' END IF
    END s4
    s5: SQL Procedure Statement
END s
```

Based on this example, the scope of each of the handlers is the compound statement in which they are declared. Specifically:

- The scope of the handler declared in line *s1* is the *s* compound statement (lines *s1* through line *s5*).
- The scope of the handler declared in line *s4-1* is the *s4* compound statement (lines *s4-1* through *s4-7*).
- The scope of the handler declared in line *s4-2* is also the *s4* compound statement (lines *s4-1* through *s4-7*).
- The scope of the handler declared in line *s4-5-1* is the *s4-5* compound statement (lines *s4-5-2* through *s4-5-4*).
- The scope of the handler declared in line *s4-6-1* is the *s4-6* compound statement (lines *s4-6-2* through *s4-6-4*).

So it follows that if an exception is encountered or SIGNALed in line:

- *s4-5-4*, then the procedure continues execution after executing a couple of handlers. First, the EXIT handler declared at line *s4-5-1* is invoked with SQLSTATE 23503 and SQLCODE -438. It RESIGNALs an exception with SQLSTATE 99999 and SQLCODE –438 and EXITs the *s4-5* compound statement. At this point, the EXIT handler declared at line *s4-2* is invoked. This handler executes and EXITs the *s4* compound statement upon completion and continues to execute line *s5*. Note that compound statement *s4-6* is skipped. Since the EXIT handler *s4-2* did not RESIGNAL a condition, the *s1* handler was not invoked upon EXIT of the *s4* compound statement.
- *s4-6-4*, then the procedure continues execution after executing a couple of handlers. First, the UNDO handler declared at line *s4-6-1* is invoked with SQLSTATE 23503 and SQLCODE -438. Any statements within the *s4-6* compound statement are rolled back. Thus, statements *s4-6-2* and *s4-6-3* are rolled back. The UNDO handler RESIGNALs an exception with SQLSTATE 99998 and SQLCODE –438 and EXITs the *s4-6* compound statement. At this

point, the EXIT handler declared at line *s4-1* is invoked, since there is no specific handler declared for SQLSTATE 99998. This handler RESIGNALs with the same SQLSTATE and SQLCODE and EXITs the *s4* compound statement. Here the handler declared at line s1 takes over, and the handler RESIGNALs the same SQLSTATE and SQLCODE and EXITs the procedure.

- *s4-7*, then SQLSTATE 23503 and SQLCODE –438 is returned to the calling application. First, the EXIT handler declared at line *s4-1* is invoked with SQLSTATE 23503 and SQLCODE -438. This handler RESIGNALs with the same SQLSTATE and SQLCODE and EXITs the *s4* compound statement. Here, the handler declared at line *s1* takes over, and this handler RESIGNALs the same SQLSTATE and SQLCODE and EXITs the procedure.
- *s4-5-3*, then the SQLSTATE and SQLCODE causing the exception is returned to the calling program. In this case, there is no handler within the *s4-5* compound statement to handle this exception, so a handler in the outer scope is invoked, namely the handler declared at line *s4-1*. Handler *s4-1* RESIGNALs with the same SQLSTATE and SQLCODE and EXITs the *s4* compound statement. Here, the handler declared at line *s1* takes over, and this handler RESIGNALs the same SQLSTATE and SQLCODE and EXITs the procedure.

Note the use of the RESIGNAL statement in the scenario described. It is sometimes useful to have a handler that executes some SQL statements, and then reissue the same condition. This is especially useful when nested scoping is used. In Figure 5.12, the handler in line *s4-5-1* could easily be modified to contain one or more SQL statements prior to the RESIGNAL statement, (as long as they are enclosed with a BEGIN and END).

The pseudocode in Figure 5.12 is not a working example, but does serve to show you the flow of logic under some of the more complex situations. Section 5.4, "Bringing It All Together," will build a working example of such a scenario.

## 5.3.4 GET DIAGNOSTICS

When presenting scenarios for condition handling, it is necessary to introduce (or reiterate, if you've seen this topic in another chapter) the use of the GET DIAGNOSTICS statement. The GET DIAGNOSTICS statement is used to obtain information relating to the statement that was just executed. For example, many tests for error conditions rely on knowing how many rows are affected as a result of an INSERT, UPDATE or DELETE statement. The GET DIAGNOSTICS statement helps you get this information. The syntax diagram for this statement is shown in Figure 5.13.

**Figure 5.13** Syntax Diagram for GET DIAGNOSTICS Statement

```
>>-GET DIAGNOSTICS-+-SQL-variable-name--=----+-ROW_COUNT-----+--+-><
                   |                         '-RETURN_STATUS-'  |
                   '-condition-information----------------------'

condition-information
               .-,-------------------------------------------.
               V                                             |
|-EXCEPTION-1-+--SQL-variable-name--=--+--MESSAGE_TEXT-------+--+---|
                                       '--DB2_MESSAGE_TOKEN--'
```

You will notice that it has three alternatives. When invoked as the first statement after an INSERT, UPDATE or DELETE statement, ROW_COUNT will retrieve the number of rows that were affected by the previous statement. If this statement follows a PREPARE statement, then ROW_COUNT will return the number of estimated rows expected as a result of the PREPAREd statement. It is a common misconception that the GET DIAGNOSTICS statement will also give the number of rows retrieved by a SELECT. This is not true.

Figure 5.14 shows a simple example of using the statement with the ROW_COUNT option. It deletes from the *employee* table rows that have values of *empno* beginning with the parameter value passed in, and returns the number of rows deleted.

**Figure 5.14** Example of GET DIAGNOSTICS with ROW_COUNT

```
CREATE PROCEDURE get_diag ( IN p_empno CHAR(6)
                           ,OUT p_rows INT )
    SPECIFIC get_diag
    LANGUAGE SQL
gd: BEGIN
    DECLARE v_rows INT DEFAULT -1;
    DELETE FROM employee
     WHERE empno like p_empno || '%';
    GET DIAGNOSTICS v_rows = ROW_COUNT;
    SET p_rows = v_rows;
END gd
```

Another alternative to GET DIAGNOSTICS, RETURN_STATUS, is used after a CALL statement to another procedure. It returns the value specified in the RETURN statement of the called procedure. The RETURN statement and working with results from called procedures is the subject of the next section (*Processing Results from Called Procedures*).

The *condition-information* clause allows the retrieval of error or warning information related to the SQL statement that just executed. The MESSAGE_TEXT keyword will retrieve the actual error or warning message associated with the SQL statement, or a blank or empty string if the statement completed successfully without warnings. This is useful in cases where you would like to return an error message from the procedure instead of just the SQLSTATE and/or SQLCODE.

The example in Figure 5.15 shows the *simple_error()* procedure from Figure 5.4 changed to return a message instead of SQLCODE and SQLSTATE.

**Figure 5.15** Revised Example of Simple Error Checking with MESSAGE_TEXT

```
CREATE PROCEDURE simple_error_message ( IN p_midinit CHAR
                                      ,IN p_empno CHAR(6)
                                      ,OUT p_error_message VARCHAR(300) )
    SPECIFIC simple_error_msg
    LANGUAGE SQL
sem: BEGIN
   -- Declare condition handlers
   DECLARE EXIT HANDLER FOR SQLEXCEPTION
        GET DIAGNOSTICS EXCEPTION 1 p_error_message = MESSAGE_TEXT;
   -- Procedure logic
   SET p_error_message = '';
   UPDATE employee                                    -- (1)
      SET midinit = p_midinit
    WHERE empno = p_empno;
END sem
```

The procedure in Figure 5.15 will return a message when an exception occurs, instead of SQLCODE and SQLSTATE as shown in Figure 5.4. The error message will contain both the SQLCODE and SQLSTATE inside it.

To see an example of an error message, assume that the *employee* table is dropped after the procedure in Figure 5.15 is created. A subsequent execution of the stored procedure would result in the message shown in Figure 5.16 being passed in the output parameter:

**Figure 5.16** Example of an Error Message

```
SQL0727N  An error occurred during implicit system action type "1".  Information
returned for the error includes SQLCODE "-204", SQLSTATE "42704" and message
tokens "DB2ADMIN.EMPLOYEE".  SQLSTATE=56098
```

The message starts with a message identifier and ends with the SQLSTATE. The message identifier for SQL messages begins with a prefix ('SQL') followed by a message number. The message number can be easily translated to a SQLCODE. It contains an unsigned number representing the SQLCODE and one of three letters, "N", "W," or "C", indicating notifications, warnings or critical errors, respectively. For the SQL-CODE translation, warnings imply that the sign of the SQLCODE is positive, and notifications and critical errors imply the sign of the SQLCODE is negative. The rest of the message is informative and may contain one or more tokens which are enclosed in double quotes ("). Not all messages will contain tokens.

The DB2_TOKEN_STRING keyword of the *condition-information* clause in the GET DIAGNOSTICS statement can be used to retrieve just the string of tokens, without the error message. Why would you want to do this? Well, in some cases, you may know what the message is and the action you need to take in a handler is based on the value of one of the tokens. Thus getting just the tokens would be sufficient. Alternatively, you may just want to return the SQLCODE or SQLSTATE and the string of tokens to your calling application and have your calling application's error handling process use the DB2 APIs (*sqlaintp()*, *sqlogstt()*) to get the error message. In this case, when the calling application retrieves the error message, the message will have placeholders for the tokens, since the context of the original message is no longer known. This is where the string of tokens can be used for a manual substitution. This second approach seems like a lot of work for the calling application, but is often desired to limit the size of the parameter being passed back.

It may not be obvious, but being able to return both the SQLCODE or SQLSTATE and the DB2_TOKEN_STRING presents a dilemma. Recall that if you want to retrieve the SQLCODE or SQLSTATE, it needs to be accessed on the first statement after an SQL statement is executed, or be the first statement in a handler. The same rules apply for the GET DIAGNOSTICS statement. So how can we get both values related to a single statement? The answer is to use nested handlers and the RESIGNAL statement.

The example in Figure 5.17 will show the procedure from Figure 5.15 rewritten to return SQLCODE, SQLSTATE and the string of message tokens.

**Figure 5.17** Example of Simple Error Checking with DB2_TOKEN_STRING and Nested Handlers

```
CREATE PROCEDURE simple_error_token ( IN p_midinit CHAR
                                     ,IN p_empno CHAR(6)
                                     ,OUT p_sqlcode_out int
                                     ,OUT p_sqlstate_out char(5)
                                     ,OUT p_token_string VARCHAR(100) )

    SPECIFIC simple_error_token
    LANGUAGE SQL
setk: BEGIN
```

```
    -- Declare variables
    DECLARE SQLSTATE CHAR(5) DEFAULT '00000';
    DECLARE SQLCODE INT DEFAULT 0;
   -- Declare condition handlers
   DECLARE EXIT HANDLER FOR SQLEXCEPTION                              -- (1)
      BEGIN
        DECLARE CONTINUE HANDLER FOR SQLEXCEPTION                     -- (4)
           GET DIAGNOSTICS EXCEPTION 1 p_token_string = DB2_TOKEN_STRING;
        SELECT SQLCODE                                                -- (2)
              ,SQLSTATE
          INTO p_sqlcode_out
              ,p_sqlstate_out
          FROM sysibm.sysdummy1;
        RESIGNAL;                                                     -- (3)
      END;
   -- Procedure logic
   SET p_token_string =  '';
   VALUES (SQLCODE, SQLSTATE)
     INTO p_sqlcode_out
         ,p_sqlstate_out;
   UPDATE employee
      SET midinit = p_midinit
    WHERE empno = p_empno;
END setk
```

Notice the EXIT handler at (1) contains a CONTINUE handler within it. If an error occurred, the first statement to execute within the handler, at (2), will get the SQL-CODE and SQLSTATE values. The next statement to execute, at (3), will reissue the same error. At this point the nested handler at (4) will kick in to retrieve the DB2_TOKEN_STRING. Since this handler is a CONTINUE handler, execution will continue after the RESIGNAL statement at (3), which is the end of the EXIT handler, thus control is returned to the calling program.

Again, to see an example of DB2_TOKEN_STRING, assume that the EMPLOYEE table is dropped, after the procedure in Figure 5.17 is created. A subsequent execution of the procedure would result in the following string being passed in the *p_token_string* parameter:

```
1ÿ-204ÿ42704ÿDB2ADMIN.EMPLOYEE
```

The tokens in the string are delimited by the 'ÿ' character, 0xFF in hexadecimal or ASCII character code 255. It contains four tokens that are substitution values for the corresponding message. The actual message was shown in Figure 5.15 with the tokens substituted. Note the order of the tokens is the substitution order.

## 5.4 Processing Results from Called Procedures

So far, you've seen examples of passing values back to the calling program through OUT parameters in the SQL procedure declaration. You can also return values using the RETURN statement. Figure 5.18 shows the syntax diagram for the return statement within a procedure.

**Figure 5.18** Syntax Diagram for RETURN Statement

```
>>-RETURN--+------------+--------------------------------------><
           '-expression-'
```

The expression in this case must be an INTEGER, and therefore, you are quite limited in what you can RETURN through this statement. The calling procedure issues GET DIAGNOSTICS with RETURN_STATUS to get the returned value. The GET DIAGNOSTICS must be issued immediately after the CALL to a procedure.

Careful consideration must be given when using this method for returning parameters. Typical use for this statement would be to RETURN 0 upon success and -1 on failure. In order to ensure a -1 on failure, your first instinct would be to write a handler to catch exceptions and issue a RETURN -1 from the handler. This cannot be done, however, because RETURN statements are not allowed within handlers. To get around such situations, you would have to use a nested compound statement, as in the code snippet in Figure 5.19.

**Figure 5.19** Example of RETURN with a Compound Statement

```
CREATE PROCEDURE ret_value (  )
    SPECIFIC ret_value
    LANGUAGE SQL
rv: BEGIN
    DECLARE v_ret_value INT DEFAULT 0;

    body: BEGIN
        DECLARE EXIT HANDLER FOR SQLEXCEPTION
            SET v_ret_value = -1;
        <body of procedure>;
    END body;

    RETURN v_ret_value;
END rv
```

It is often not enough for an application to just see a return value. The application may need more information if an error occurred. The additional information can be passed back using an OUT parameter. This is shown in Figure 5.21.

The body of the procedure is within a compound statement that has a handler that sets the return value on an exception. Note that there are limitations even with this solution. For example, if you wanted to RESIGNAL an SQLSTATE to the calling program, you would not be able to do so because you cannot have a handler declared at the outermost compound statement in the procedure and still RETURN a value.

The alternative to the RETURN statement is the passing of OUT parameters in the procedure declaration, for which you've already seen many examples. What you haven't seen is an example of a CALL to another procedure, and checking the output parameters and/or return codes, as in Figure 5.20.

**Figure 5.20** Example of a Stored Procedure Call with Checking for Parameters

```
CREATE PROCEDURE call_procs (  )
    SPECIFIC call_procs
    LANGUAGE SQL
-------------------------------------------------------------------------
-- SQL Stored Procedure
-------------------------------------------------------------------------
cp: BEGIN

    DECLARE v_empno CHAR(6) DEFAULT 'A'; -- Input to get_diag()
    DECLARE v_num_rows INT;              -- Output from get_diag()
    DECLARE v_ret_value INT;             -- Return value from ret_value()

    -- Example of a call to a procedure where a parameter is passed back in the
    --  argument list as an OUT parameter
    CALL get_diag( v_empno, v_num_rows );
    IF v_num_rows = 0 THEN
        <statements>
    END IF;

    -- Example of a call to a procedure where the RETURN statement is used to
    --   to return the value to the caller
    CALL ret_value();
    GET DIAGNOSTICS v_ret_value = RETURN_STATUS;

    RETURN v_ret_value;

END cp
```

The example above makes two calls to other procedures. The first CALL statement is a call to the *get_diag()* procedure (Figure 5.14), which passes back return values in the argument list. The second call is a call to the *ret_value()* procedure (Figure 5.19), which uses a RETURN statement to pass back a value to the calling program.

## 5.5 Bringing It All Together

To summarize the concepts that have been introduced in this chapter, this section presents an example that incorporates many of these concepts.

The sample procedure in Figure 5.21 shows an example of a procedure that is used to delete a row from the *department* table. It takes the department number to be deleted as an input parameter and returns a message as an output parameter. The row is only deleted if none of the child tables below it contain the department number that is to be deleted. A return value of -1 is returned if an error is encountered, 0 upon successful completion, and 1 if successful but no rows were deleted because none existed.

**Figure 5.21** Example for Delete Department

```
CREATE PROCEDURE delete_dept (  IN p_deptno CHAR(3)
                               ,OUT p_message VARCHAR(100) )
    SPECIFIC delete_dept
    LANGUAGE SQL
------------------------------------------------------------------------
-- Procedure Description
--
-- Deletes a department, as long as there are no rows with the input
--    department number in any child tables (EMPLOYEE and PROJECT).
--
-- RETURNS:  1 if successful, but now rows existed for deletion
--           0 on successful completion
--          -1 on un-successful complete
--    SETS: Appropriate message in output parameter 'p_message'
------------------------------------------------------------------------
dd: BEGIN
    -- Declare variables
    DECLARE SQLCODE INT DEFAULT 0;                                       -- (1)
    DECLARE SQLSTATE CHAR(5) DEFAULT '00000';
    DECLARE v_ret_value INT DEFAULT 0;
    -- In order to return a value to the calling program, the value
    --   to be returned is set in the compound statement, and possibly
    --   in a handler within the compound statement.
    body:BEGIN                                                           -- (2)
        -- Declare variables within compound statement
        DECLARE v_num_rows INT DEFAULT 0;
        -- Declare conditions                                            -- (3)
        DECLARE c_EMP_child_rows_exist  CONDITION FOR SQLSTATE '99001';
```

```
        DECLARE c_PROJ_child_rows_exist CONDITION FOR SQLSTATE '99002';
        -- Declare handlers
        DECLARE EXIT HANDLER FOR SQLEXCEPTION
        BEGIN
            SET p_message = 'Unknown error, SQLSTATE: "' || SQLSTATE ||
                            '", SQLCODE=' || CHAR(SQLCODE);              -- (4)
            SET v_ret_value = -1;
        END;
        -- Declare handlers for custom conditions                         -- (5)
        DECLARE EXIT HANDLER FOR c_EMP_child_rows_exist
        BEGIN
            SET p_message = 'Cannot delete, child EMPLOYEE rows exist.';
            SET v_ret_value = -1;
        END;
        DECLARE EXIT HANDLER FOR c_PROJ_child_rows_exist
        BEGIN
            SET p_message = 'Cannot delete, child PROJECT rows exist.';
            SET v_ret_value = -1;
        END;

        -- Child table: EMPLOYEE
        SELECT COUNT(1)
          INTO v_num_rows
          FROM employee
         WHERE workdept = p_deptno;
        IF v_num_rows <> 0 THEN
            SIGNAL c_EMP_child_rows_exist;                                 -- (6)
        END IF;

        --Child table: PROJECT
        SELECT COUNT(1)
          INTO v_num_rows
          FROM project
         WHERE deptno = p_deptno;
        IF v_num_rows <> 0 THEN
            SIGNAL c_PROJ_child_rows_exist;                                -- (7)
        END IF;

        -- No rows in dependant tables, delete department
        DELETE FROM department
        WHERE deptno = p_deptno;
        GET DIAGNOSTICS v_num_rows = ROW_COUNT;                            -- (8)

        -- Set the appropriate return message
        IF v_num_rows = 0 THEN
        BEGIN
            SET v_ret_value = 1;
            SET p_message = 'No rows exist for deletion of department ' ||
p_deptno || '.';
        END;
        ELSE
            SET p_message = 'Department ' || p_deptno || ' successfully
deleted.';
```

```
        END IF;
    END body;

    RETURN v_ret_value;                                                   -- (9)

END dd
```

The following notes correspond to the location numbers shown in Figure 5.21:

1. SQLCODE and SQLSTATE need to be declared, since they will be accessed in the EXIT handler at (4).
2. Since the procedure returns a return value (in addition to an output parameter), the main logic of the procedure is within a nested compound statement. This way, the nested statement can set the appropriate return value in an EXIT handler. The EXIT handler will continue execution at the end of the compound statement. This will then execute the RETURN statement with the appropriate value.
3. Conditions are named for customized SQLSTATEs. These conditions will be used to set the appropriate error message within the handler declared at (5).
4. The message for non-handled conditions is constructed using SQLCODE and SQLSTATE, so the calling program can have access to it.
5. Handlers for the named conditions SET the appropriate message for the output parameter.
6. The SIGNAL statement is used to invoke the handler if child rows in the *employee* table are found.
7. The SIGNAL statement is used to invoke the handler if child rows in the PROJECT table are found.
8. The GET DIAGNOSTICS statement is used to determine if any rows were deleted. If no rows were deleted, then an appropriate message is sent back to the calling application.
9. The RETURN statement is used to send the return value to the calling application. At this point, the appropriate return value has been set, along with the output parameter, so all that is required is to execute the RETURN statement.

## 5.6 Chapter Summary

This chapter has shown some techniques for handling exceptions and completion conditions within DB2 SQL procedures. Basic definitions of SQLCODE and SQLSTATE were provided, followed by a description of how to use them in conjunction with condition handlers. Three different types of handlers can be declared, namely EXIT, CONTINUE and UNDO handlers. The scope of a condition handler is the compound statement in which the handler is declared.

The concept of naming specific conditions was also described. In addition to making the stored procedure code more readable, the ability to name conditions is useful for specifying user-defined conditions. Additionally, the SIGNAL and RESIGNAL statements were discussed to show how you could force a condition in the SQL procedure body by specifying an SQLSTATE or a named condition.

Finally, passing parameters back to calling procedures and retrieving return values from called procedures were considered. The RETURN statement can be used for returning values, and the GET DIAGNOSTICS statement is used to receive the returned value. If non-integer or multiple values need to be passed back to a calling application, OUT parameters can always be used.

CHAPTER 6

# Working with Dynamic SQL

## In this chapter, you will learn:

- the two phases of processing an SQL statement;
- the difference between dynamic SQL and static SQL;
- when and how to use dynamic SQL using the EXECUTE IMMEDIATE statement;
- when and how to use dynamic SQL using the PREPARE and EXECUTE statements;
- restrictions and considerations of dynamic SQL.

Dynamic SQL is a method of SQL programming that allows you to write more robust and flexible code. So far, the distinction between dynamic SQL and static SQL has not been made, and up to this point, only the latter has been used for examples. At this stage, you may not even know that SQL programming can be classified as either static or dynamic, but don't worry, such details will be covered first. Then we will discuss the different ways of using dynamic SQL in SQL procedures.

## 6.1 PREPARE and EXECUTE: The Two Phases of Every SQL Statement

An SQL statement can be viewed as a request from the application to the database engine to do something, be it retrieve data, perform an insert, or update existing data. Whenever you submit an SQL statement to DB2, it passes through two general phases called PREPARE and EXECUTE. For the purpose of this discussion, PREPARE and EXCUTE will be explained in the context of SELECT (that is, retrieving data), but the concepts can be applied just as easily for other SQL statements.

In the PREPARE phase, the DB2 SQL optimizer examines your SQL statement and determines the optimal method to retrieve the requested data. There are many decisions that need to be made by the optimizer, including things such as:

- Are the syntax and semantics of the query correct?
- Can the query be rewritten so that it can be more easily optimized?
- What is the best combination of indexes to use?
- For queries that join tables, in what order should they be joined to optimize performance?

The method by which DB2 chooses to retrieve the data is called an access plan. Once the access plan has been determined, the query enters the EXECUTE phase. In the EXECUTE phase, the database uses the access plan to fetch the data. Figure 6.1 graphically illustrates the PREPARE and EXECUTE phases of SQL processing.

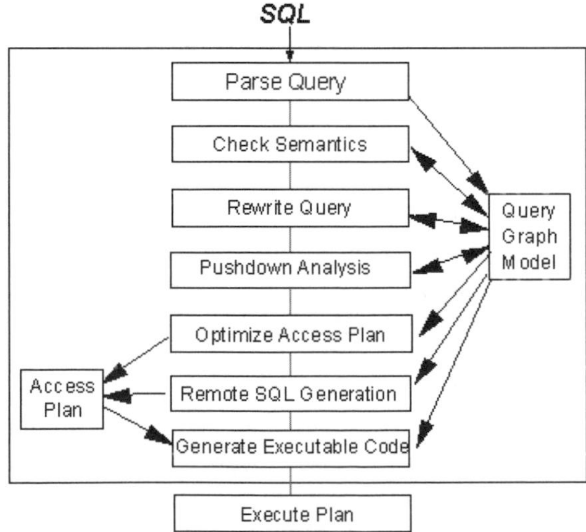


**Figure 6.1** The Flow of SQL from PREPARE to EXECUTE.

## 6.2 Dynamic SQL vs. Static SQL

SQL used within applications can be classified as either dynamic or static. In other words, applications are said to use dynamic SQL, static SQL, or both. Both dynamic and static SQL must go through the PREPARE and EXECUTE phases as just described. For static SQL, however, once the access plan for a query has been generated, it is stored and reusable in the database even if the database is restarted. Dynamic SQL means that the query is always prepared before execution, whether or not the same querys (and hence the same access plan) are used over and over again. To minimize this cost, DB2 does have a package cache (also known as the dynamic SQL cache), which keeps frequently used access plans in memory. The package cache significantly reduces the cost of actually performing repeated SQL prepare requests, but there is still the overhead of issuing and responding to them.

Writing queries using static SQL, as you can imagine, can yield performance benefits because DB2 no longer has to "think" about how to resolve queries at run-time. Dynamic SQL, however, offers flexibility that is not possible with static SQL. A comparison of dynamic SQL and static SQL is shown in Figure 6.2.

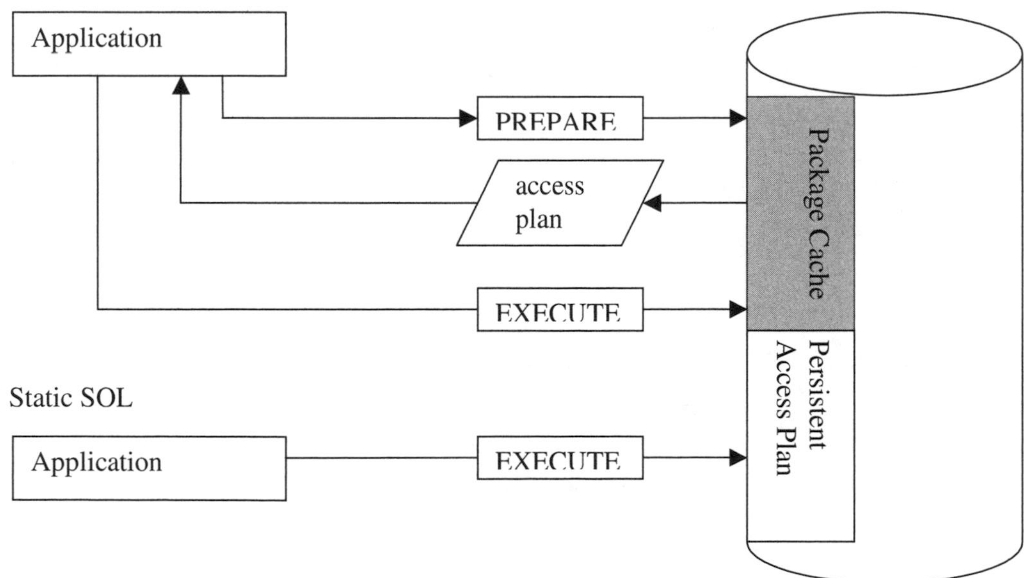


**Figure 6.2** Visual Comparison of the Difference Between Dynamic and Static SQL.

So far, the examples presented in this book have all used static SQL. The server-side nature of stored procedures makes writing static SQL relatively transparent.

Using dynamic SQL does not necessarily mean that you must take a performance hit relative to static SQL. For applications that use a set of queries very frequently, their access plans are kept and reused from DB2's package cache (also known as the dynamic SQL cache). The first execution of any given query, however, must incur the full cost of the PREPARE phase.

Static SQL is fast and easy to program in SQL procedures but there are circumstances where static SQL cannot be used. The most common need for dynamic SQL is when the final form of a query is not known until run-time, and therefore, the static access plans cannot be generated when the procedure is built.

There are different ways to use dynamic SQL in SQL procedures and the following sections will discuss each in turn.

## 6.3 Basic Dynamic SQL Usage with EXECUTE IMMEDIATE

The EXECUTE IMMEDIATE statement is the simplest way to use dynamic SQL. This method makes a single request to DB2 to perform both the PREPARE and EXECUTE phases for an SQL statement.

**Figure 6.3** The Syntax Diagram for EXECUTE IMMEDIATE

```
>>-EXECUTE--IMMEDIATE--sql-statement-------><
```

In Figure 6.3, the syntax diagram for EXECUTE IMMEDIATE is shown. The *sql-statement* is required and is a VARCHAR parameter that contains the actual SQL statement.

You should use EXECUTE IMMEDIATE if:

- the SQL statement only needs to be executed just once or infrequently.
- the SQL statement is not a SELECT statement.

Consider the example in Figure 6.4 of updating an employee table where the conditions of the update are generated at run-time.

**Figure 6.4** Example of Using EXECUTE IMMEDIATE for Dynamic SQL

```
CREATE PROCEDURE change_bonus(  IN p_new_bonus DECIMAL
                               ,IN p_where_cond VARCHAR(1000)
                               ,OUT p_num_changes INT )
    SPECIFIC change_bonus
    LANGUAGE SQL
cb: BEGIN
    DECLARE v_dynSQL VARCHAR(1000);                                     -- (1)

    SET v_dynSQL = 'UPDATE employee SET BONUS=' ||                      -- (2)
                   CHAR(p_new_bonus) || ' WHERE ' ||
                   p_where_cond;

    EXECUTE IMMEDIATE v_dynSQL;                                         -- (3)

    GET DIAGNOSTICS p_num_changes = row_count;                          -- (4)
END cb
```

In Figure 6.4, the procedure *change_bonus()* has three parameters. The IN parameters, *p_new_bonus* and *p_where_cond*, specify the new bonus value and the WHERE condition for the UPDATE SQL statement (which will change the bonuses), respectively.

The OUT parameter *p_num_changes* returns to the caller the number of records that were updated by the procedure.

To store the dynamic SQL statement, we declare a variable at (1) called *v_dynSQL* which is large enough to hold the entire statement. If the variable is not large enough, the SQL string is automatically truncated and probably will not execute as desired, so be careful! Next, we concatenate the UPDATE statement syntax with the two IN parameters to create the final SQL statement at (2).

Finally we issue EXECUTE IMMEDATE using the variable *v_dynSQL* to prepare and execute the UPDATE statement at (3). We then use GET DIAGNOSTICS at (4) to find out how many rows were updated.

Although we aren't required to issue GET DIAGNOSTICS to find out how many rows were updated, it is generally good practice to return a value to indicate how many rows were affected by an INSERT, UPDATE or DELETE.

Here is an example of how you could run this procedure code.

After you have created the procedure, execute the following from the DB2 command line processor (CLP):

```
CALL CHANGE_BONUS (1000, 'year(hiredate) < 1975', ?)
```

Here we are calling the procedure to give every employee that was hired before 1975 a bonus of $1000. Notice that we've used a question mark as a marker for the OUT parameter. Calling the procedure from the command line will result in output that is similar to the following:

```
Value of output parameters
--------------------------
Parameter Name  : P_NUM_CHANGES
Parameter Value : 20

Return Status = 0
```

The output above indicates that twenty rows were updated by the procedure.

## 6.4 Reusing Dynamic SQL Statements with PREPARE and EXECUTE

As mentioned in the previous section, EXECUTE IMMEDIATE is appropriate only for infrequently used SQL. If you have a dynamic SQL statement that needs to be executed many times within the same procedure, however, using EXECUTE IMMEDIATE incurs the unnecessary cost of implicit PREPARE requests. A better solution is to use PREPARE and EXECUTE separately, but the concept of parameter markers must first be introduced.

Parameter markers are useful if you have a set of very similar SQL statements to execute and differences between each statement exist only because certain variables change. Consider the following two UPDATE statements:

```
UPDATE EMPLOYEE SET BONUS=500 WHERE EMPNO='000300';
UPDATE EMPLOYEE SET BONUS=1000 WHERE EMPNO='000340';
```

From DB2's perspective, the access plan used to update the row for employee 000300 is the same as the one used to update the row for employee 000340. Hence, the value of the bonus and the employee number are irrelevant to the access plan chosen and the SQL statements can be reduced to the following general form:

```
UPDATE EMPLOYEE SET BONUS=? WHERE EMPNO=?;
```

In the above, the question marks are called parameter markers and act as placeholders for variables that can be replaced with values at a later time.

In SQL procedures, we can make use of parameter markers to avoid the overhead of preparing similar SQL statements that result in the same access plan. To do this, instead of using EXECUTE IMMEDIATE, we break up the process into two statements: PREPARE and EXECUTE.

The PREPARE statement has two parameters and its syntax diagram is presented in Figure 6.5.

**Figure 6.5** The Syntax Diagram for PREPARE

```
>>-PREPARE--statement-name--FROM--host-variable--------><
```

The *statement-name* is a STATEMENT object that you must have previously declared to hold the prepared form of an SQL statement. The *host-variable* is a VARCHAR variable that holds the text of the SQL statement to be prepared.

The EXECUTE statement takes one or more parameters and its syntax diagram is presented in Figure 6.6.

**Figure 6.6** The Syntax Diagram for EXECUTE

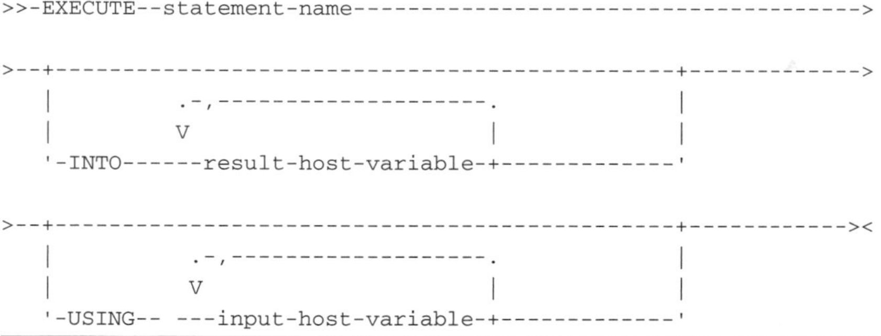

```
>>-EXECUTE--statement-name------------------------------------->

>--+---------------------------------------------+------------>
   |          .-,--------------------.           |
   |          V                      |           |
   '-INTO------result-host-variable-+-------------'

>--+---------------------------------------------+-----------><
   |           .-,-------------------.           |
   |           V                     |           |
   '-USING-- ---input-host-variable-+-------------'
```

In the least, *statement-name* must be specified and it must identify a STATEMENT object that has been previously prepared. Optionally, if the SQL statement has one or more parameter markers, a comma-delimited list of *host-variables* can be specified in the USING clause for parameter substitution. The optional INTO clause is used for dynamic CALL statements and will be discussed in a later section.

Consider the following example where a company increases bonuses for employees who are also department managers. To do this, a cursor is defined for all managers from which we fetch their current bonus. We then increase their current bonus by the amount specified by the *p_bonus_increase* parameter. This procedure is illustrated in Figure 6.7.

**Figure 6.7** Dynamic SQL Example Using PREPARE and EXECUTE USING

```
CREATE PROCEDURE change_mgr_bonus ( IN p_bonus_increase DECIMAL
                                   ,OUT p_num_changes INT )
    SPECIFIC change_mgr_bonus
    LANGUAGE SQL
cmb: BEGIN

    DECLARE v_dynSQL           VARCHAR(200);
    DECLARE v_new_bonus        DECIMAL;
    DECLARE v_no_data          SMALLINT DEFAULT 0;

    DECLARE v_mgrno            CHAR(6);
    DECLARE v_bonus            DECIMAL;

    DECLARE v_stmt1        STATEMENT;                                   -- (1)

-- cursor of all employees who are also managers
    DECLARE c_managers CURSOR FOR
        SELECT e.empno
             ,e.bonus
          FROM EMPLOYEE e
             ,DEPARTMENT d
         WHERE e.empno=d.mgrno;

    DECLARE CONTINUE HANDLER FOR NOT FOUND
        SET v_no_data=1;

    SET v_dynSQL = 'UPDATE EMPLOYEE SET BONUS=? WHERE EMPNO=?';
    SET p_num_changes=0;

    PREPARE v_stmt1 FROM v_dynSQL;                                      -- (2)

    OPEN c_managers;
    FETCH c_managers INTO v_mgrno, v_bonus;

    WHILE (v_no_data=0) DO
        SET p_num_changes = p_num_changes + 1;
        SET v_new_bonus = v_bonus + p_bonus_increase;

        EXECUTE v_stmt1 USING v_new_bonus, v_mgrno;                     -- (3)

        -- fetch the next row to be processed
        FETCH c_managers INTO v_mgrno, v_bonus;
    END WHILE;
    CLOSE c_managers;
END cmb
```

In procedure *change_mgr_bonus()* above, there are several things to note. First, we have declared a STATEMENT object called *v_stmt1* at (1) which is used to store the prepared form of the SQL text at (2). Once the prepared statement is ready, the cursor for all managers and their current bonus is opened and iterated with a WHILE loop. Within the WHILE loop, the EXECUTE statement at (3) uses the prepared statement for performing updates. To substitute real values for the parameter markers in the prepared statement, the USING clause of EXECUTE is used.

You can also issue EXECUTE without the USING clause if the dynamic SQL statement has no parameter markers.

Before running the procedure, take a look at the current bonus values for department managers and note the current bonus values.

```
SELECT e.empno, e.bonus FROM EMPLOYEE e, DEPARTMENT d
    WHERE e.empno=d.mgrno
```

Next, call the procedure from the CLP, passing in the value for the bonus increase. We can use a question mark for the second parameter (which is an OUT parameter) for passing out the number of rows that were updated.

```
CALL CHANGE_MGR_BONUS (100,?)
```

The output should look something like the following:

```
Value of output parameters
--------------------------
Parameter Name  : P_NUM_CHANGES
Parameter Value : 8

Return Status = 0"CHANGE_MGR_BONUS" RETURN_STATUS: "0"
```

In this example, eight rows were updated as indicated by *P_NUM_CHANGES*. To further verify that the result is correct, look at the data once again.

```
SELECT e.empno, e.bonus FROM EMPLOYEE e, DEPARTMENT d
    WHERE e.empno=d.mgrno
```

## 6.5 Using Dynamic SQL in Cursors

In previous examples, dynamic SQL has been used for single SQL statements. Sometimes, it may be necessary to iterate through a result set that was created using dynamic SQL. In this section, you'll see an example of how to do this.

Consider the example in Figure 6.8 where the previous example is repeated, only this time, the *c_managers* cursor is defined using dynamic SQL.

**Figure 6.8** Example of Using Dynamic SQL to Define Cursors

```
CREATE PROCEDURE change_mgr_bonus2 ( IN p_bonus_increase DECIMAL
                                    ,OUT p_num_changes INT)

    SPECIFIC change_mgr_bonus2
    LANGUAGE SQL
cmb2: BEGIN

    DECLARE v_dynMgrSQL      VARCHAR(200);                         -- (1)
    DECLARE v_dynSQL         VARCHAR(200);

    DECLARE v_new_bonus      DECIMAL;
    DECLARE v_no_data        SMALLINT DEFAULT 0;

    DECLARE v_mgrno          CHAR(6);
    DECLARE v_bonus          DECIMAL;

    DECLARE v_cur_stmt       STATEMENT;                            -- (2)
    DECLARE v_stmt1          STATEMENT;


    -- cursor of all employees who are also managers
    DECLARE c_managers CURSOR FOR v_cur_stmt;                      -- (3)

    DECLARE CONTINUE HANDLER FOR NOT FOUND
        SET v_no_data=1;

    -- SQL for c_managers cursor
    SET v_dynMgrSQL = 'SELECT e.empno,e.bonus FROM EMPLOYEE e, DEPARTMENT d ' ||
                      'WHERE e.empno=d.mgrno';


    SET v_dynSQL = 'UPDATE EMPLOYEE SET BONUS= ? WHERE EMPNO=?';
    SET p_num_changes=0;

    PREPARE v_stmt1 FROM v_dynSQL;

    PREPARE v_cur_stmt FROM v_dynMgrSQL;                           -- (4)
    OPEN c_managers;                                               -- (5)
    FETCH c_managers INTO v_mgrno, v_bonus;

    WHILE (v_no_data=0) DO

        SET p_num_changes = p_num_changes + 1;
        SET v_new_bonus = v_bonus + p_bonus_increase;
        EXECUTE v_stmt1 USING v_new_bonus, v_mgrno;
```

```
        -- fetch the next row to be processed
        FETCH c_managers INTO v_mgrno, v_bonus;
    END WHILE;

    CLOSE c_managers;
END cmb2
```

In Figure 6.8, the changes required to make the *c_managers* cursor use dynamic SQL have been highlighted.

First, a VARCHAR variable large enough to contain the SQL statement must be declared for the cursor at (1). Then, just as a STATEMENT object had been declared for the dynamic UPDATE statement in the previous example, another STATEMENT object is declared to hold the prepared form of *v_dynMgrSQL* at (2). In the cursor declaration at (3), notice how the cursor has been declared using the *v_cur_stmt* STATEMENT object. Before opening the *c_managers* cursor, the *v_cur_stmt* STATEMENT object is PREPAREd at (4) using the *v_dynMgrSQL* variable. When the *c_managers* cursor at (5) is opened, *v_cur_stmt* will define the cursor's contents.

Before running the procedure, take a look at the current bonus values for department managers.

```
SELECT e.empno, e.bonus FROM EMPLOYEE e, DEPARTMENT d WHERE
e.empno=d.mgrno
```

Then, call the procedure from the CLP, passing in the value for the bonus increase as the first parameter. We can use a question mark for the second parameter (which is an OUT parameter) for returning the number of rows that were updated.

```
CALL CHANGE_MGR_BONUS2 (100,?)
```

The output should look something like the following:

```
Value of output parameters
--------------------------
Parameter Name  : P_NUM_CHANGES
Parameter Value : 8

"CHANGE_MGR_BONUS2" RETURN_STATUS: "0"
```

In this case, eight rows were updated as indicated by *P_NUM_CHANGES*. To further verify that the code is correct, look at the data once again.

```
SELECT e.empno, e.bonus FROM EMPLOYEE e, DEPARTMENT d WHERE
e.empno=d.mgrno
```

## 6.6 Dynamic CALL Statements

A new feature in DB2 version 8 is the ability to dynamically prepare the CALL statement. In addition to EXECUTE USING, a dynamically prepared CALL can have an INTO clause to get the OUT or INOUT parameters.

**Figure 6.9** Example of Using EXECUTE ... USING ... INTO ... for Dynamically Prepared CALL Statements

```
CREATE PROCEDURE dynamicCall(IN procschema VARCHAR(50)
                            ,IN procname   VARCHAR(50) )
    SPECIFIC dynamicCall
    LANGUAGE SQL
dc: BEGIN

    DECLARE v_dynSQL        VARCHAR(200);

    DECLARE v_p1            INT;
    DECLARE v_p2            INT;
    DECLARE v_p3            INT;

    DECLARE v_stmt          STATEMENT;

    SET v_p1=100;
    SET v_p2=200;
    -- default to user schema if not supplied
    SET procschema = COALESCE (procschema, USER);                    -- (1)

    SET v_dynSQL = 'CALL ' || rtrim(procschema)
                       || '.'
                       || ltrim(procname)
                       || '(?,?,?)';                                 -- (2)

    PREPARE v_stmt FROM v_dynSQL;
    /* Assumption - Stored procedure being called
     * has 3 parameters :
     *      v_p1 - IN
     *      v_p2 - INOUT
     *      v_p3 - OUT
     */
    EXECUTE v_stmt INTO v_p2, v_p3 USING v_p1, v_p2;                 -- (3)
    RETURN v_p2 + v_p3;                                              -- (4)
END dc
```

In Figure 6.9 , the procedure *dynamicCall()* takes two parameters: a schema and a procedure name. The procedure checks if the schema has been supplied. If not, the procedure supplies the current connected user ID as the default schema at (1). The CALL statement is then dynamically formed by concatenating the procedure schema and procedure name together at (2). The *ltrim()* and *rtrim()* functions are used to eliminate the potential existence of blank spaces which may cause problems.

For best performance, use CALL with fully qualified procedure names.

For the purposes of this example, we assume that whatever procedure is called, it will have exactly three parameters in the following order: IN, INOUT, and OUT. The intention is to show you how to handle each of the three stored procedure parameter types using the least amount of code possible.

After the CALL statement has been prepared, it is executed at (3) USING variables *v_p1* and *v_p2* since only the first two parameters can contain input values. The INTO clause of the called procedure includes *v_p2* and *v_p3* since only parameters two and three of the called procedure can return an output value. Finally, the sum of *v_p2* and *v_p3* as passed out by the called procedure is RETURNed at (4).

To test *dynamicCall()*, connect to the database and create the procedure shown in Figure 6.10.

**Figure 6.10** A Simple Procedure to Be Called by dynamicCall()

```
CREATE PROCEDURE testCall (IN    v1 INT
                          ,INOUT v2 INT
                          ,OUT   v3 INT
                          )

SPECIFIC testCall
LANGUAGE SQL
tc: BEGIN
    SET v2 = v1+v2;
    SET v3 = v1;
END tc
```

The *testCall()* procedure is straightforward. The INOUT parameter *v2* is assigned a new value which is the sum of IN parameter *v1*, and its current value. In this case, the *dynamicCall()* will provide the initial value of *v2*. The value of OUT parameter *v3* will be set to the value of *v1*.

To test *dynamicCall()*, from the command line, execute the following:

```
CALL dynamicCall(null,'TESTCALL')
```

The expected output should be:

```
Return Status = 400
```

## 6.7 Restrictions and Considerations

There are several things to consider in deciding when to use dynamic SQL instead of static SQL.

Security for dynamic SQL is evaluated at run-time using the privileges of the user who calls the procedure, rather than the person who builds the procedure. For any dynamic SQL that you use, ensure that the user calling the procedure will have the proper privileges. For more information on how security is resolved, please see Appendix D, "Security Considerations for SQL Procedures."

The statement string to be prepared must be an executable statement that can be dynamically prepared. It must be one of the SQL statements shown in Figure 6.11.

**Figure 6.11** List of Statements that Can Be Dynamically Prepared

```
ALTER
CALL
COMMENT ON
COMMIT
CREATE
DECLARE GLOBAL TEMPORARY TABLE
DELETE
DROP
EXPLAIN
FLUSH EVENT MONITOR
GRANT
INSERT
LOCK TABLE
REFRESH TABLE
RELEASE SAVEPOINT
RENAME TABLE
RENAME TABLESPACE
REVOKE
ROLLBACK
SAVEPOINT
Select-statement
SET CURRENT DEFAULT TRANSFORM GROUP
SET CURRENT DEGREE
SET CURRENT EXPLAIN MODE
SET CURRENT EXPLAIN SNAPSHOT
SET CURRENT QUERY OPTIMIZATION
SET CURRENT REFRESH AGE
SET EVENT MONITOR STATE
SET INTEGRITY
SET PASSTHRU
SET PATH
SET SCHEMA
SET SERVER OPTION
UPDATE
```

Finally, note that parameter markers are un-typed. For various reasons, you may have a situation where a variable of the wrong type may be substituted for a parameter marker. You can protect yourself from errors by using CAST to guarantee the proper type. For example, in procedure *change_mgr_bonus()*, you could change the *v_dynSQL* variable to use the following SQL statement instead:

```
SET v_dynSQL = 'UPDATE EMPLOYEE SET BONUS= CAST(? AS DECIMAL)
    WHERE EMPNO=(CAST ? AS CHAR(6))';
```

Using CAST to guarantee the proper type, in most cases, will not be necessary and you should only use it if there is opportunity for type mismatch.

## 6.8 Chapter Summary

In this chapter, the PREPARE and EXECUTE phases of SQL processing was explained. This was required to make the distinction between static and dynamic SQL, describe how they differ, and the advantages of both. As you have seen in this chapter, dynamic SQL can be used for executing SQL statements or defining cursors that are not fully known until run-time. Such features of dynamic SQL enhance the flexibility and robustness of SQL procedures.

Different SQL PL keywords arc used to take advantage of dynamic SQL. A new variable type, STATEMENT, was introduced and through numerous examples, we described when and how to use the PREPARE, EXECUTE, and EXECUTE IMMEDIATE statements.

CHAPTER 7

# Working with Nested SQL Procedures

## In this chapter, you will learn:

- what nested SQL procedures are;
- how to pass parameters between nested SQL procedures;
- how to return values from nested SQL procedures;
- how to return and receive result sets from within nested SQL procedures;
- how to write recursive SQL procedures;
- security in nested SQL procedures.

DB2 supports the nesting of SQL procedures, that is, invoking an SQL procedure from another SQL procedure.

While all the information that has been described in this book so far is applicable to nested SQL procedures, you need a little more knowledge on how to pass data between SQL procedures to allow them to work effectively together. For example, there are some SQL statements unique to nested SQL procedures. These topics will be covered in this chapter.

In DB2, you can also implement stored procedures in a host programming language like C or Java. However, if you want to write nested stored procedures in mixed languages, you are only allowed to call stored procedures implemented in SQL or C from within another SQL procedure.

## 7.1 Basic Nested SQL Procedures

Figure 7.1 and Figure 7.2 are examples of basic nested SQL procedures:

**Figure 7.1** Example of a Called Procedure

```
CREATE PROCEDURE count_projects
    ( IN  p_empno CHAR(6)
     ,OUT p_total INT )
SPECIFIC count_projects
LANGUAGE SQL
cp: BEGIN
    -- Procedure logic
    SELECT COUNT(*)
    INTO   p_total
    FROM   emp_act
    WHERE  empno = p_empno;
END cp
```

**Figure 7.2** Example of a Caller Procedure

```
CREATE PROCEDURE bonus
    ( IN  p_empno CHAR(6)
     ,OUT p_bonus CHAR(1) )
SPECIFIC bonus
LANGUAGE SQL
bn: BEGIN
    -- Declare variables
    DECLARE v_min INT DEFAULT 5;
    DECLARE v_total INT DEFAULT 0;

    -- Procedure logic
    CALL count_projects(p_empno, v_total);

    IF ( v_total >= v_min )
    THEN
        SET p_bonus = 'Y';
    ELSE
        SET p_bonus = 'N';
    END IF;
END bn
```

The procedure *count_projects()* in Figure 7.1 returns the number of projects that one employee has completed. The employee is identified by an employee number. The procedure *bonus()* in Figure 7.2 is used to determine whether an employee should be awarded a bonus based on how many projects he or she has completed. It uses the output of the *count_projects()* procedure in its calculation.

In procedure *bonus()*, which is referred to as the caller, a CALL statement is issued to invoke procedure *count_projects()*, which is referred to as the called procedure.

By using nested SQL procedures, you can encapsulate business logic into smaller separate units. The code can become more readable, maintainable and reusable.

## 7.2 Passing Parameters between Nested SQL Procedures

As with procedures in any programming language, nested SQL procedures are not of much use unless you can pass values between the caller and the called procedures. As you can see from the examples in Figure 7.1 and Figure 7.2, you can pass values in and out by issuing the CALL statement in the caller procedure, with the number of parameters and their data types matching the called procedure signature. After the successful completion of a call statement, the OUT parameter values will be available to the caller procedure.

DB2 SQL PL uses strong data typing. This means that you will have to try to match the datatypes of the local variables with those of the parameters in the called procedure's signature if possible. You will have to use the explicit CAST functions if implicit conversion is not supported.

The local variables are matched to the called SQL procedure parameters by their positions in the CALL statement.

If you have overloaded the called SQL procedure, DB2 will determine which procedure to invoke by the number of parameters in the CALL statement. Overloading with the same number of parameters is not supported, even if the data types are different. For detailed information on overloaded SQL procedures, please refer to Chapter 2, "Basic SQL Procedure Structure."

## 7.3 Returning Values from Nested SQL Procedures

Besides using output parameters to pass values back from the called procedure, you can also return one integer as the return code (also known as the return value).

To return the value, use the SQL control statement RETURN. To access the return value, use the SQL control statement GET DIAGNOSTICS as illustrated in Figure 7.3.

**Figure 7.3** GET DIAGNOSTICS Syntax

```
>>-GET DIAGNOSTICS--SQL-variable-name--=----+-ROW_COUNT-----+--><
                                            '-RETURN_STATUS-'
```

The GET DIAGNOSTICS statement obtains the information about the previous SQL statement invoked.

If there is no previous statement, the value of return code can be any value.

The GET DIAGNOSTICS statement must be used immediately after a CALL statement if you want to catch its return code.

In Figure 7.4, procedure *get_emp_name()* uses a return code to indicate whether the record is found (code 99) or not (code 1000). The procedure itself returns the employee first name given an employee number.

**Figure 7.4** Example of Returning a Value from a Called Procedure

```
CREATE PROCEDURE get_emp_name
    ( IN  p_empno CHAR(6)
     ,OUT p_fname VARCHAR(10) )
SPECIFIC get_emp_name
LANGUAGE SQL
ge: BEGIN
    -- Declare variables
    DECLARE v_return_code INT DEFAULT 99;

    -- Declare condition handlers
```

```
    DECLARE CONTINUE HANDLER FOR NOT FOUND
    BEGIN
        SET v_return_code = 1000;
    END;

    -- Procedure logic
    SELECT firstnme
    INTO   p_fname
    FROM   employee
    WHERE  empno = p_empno;

    RETURN v_return_code;
END ge
```

The choice of return codes can be arbitrary. However, it is recommended that system defined SQLCODEs not be used as customized return codes. It may cause unnecessary confusion in interpreting error messages.

The caller *find_emp()* in Figure 7.5 shows how to use the GET DIAGNOSTICS statement to obtain the return code from the called procedure. Notice that the GET DIAGNOSTICS statement at (2) immediately follows the CALL statement at (1).

**Figure 7.5** Example of Receiving a Returned Value by a Caller Procedure

```
CREATE PROCEDURE find_emp
    ( IN  p_empno CHAR(6)
     ,OUT p_output VARCHAR(50) )
SPECIFIC find_emp
LANGUAGE SQL
fe: BEGIN
    -- Declare variables
    DECLARE v_rc INT;
    DECLARE v_fname VARCHAR(15);

    -- Procedure logic
    CALL get_emp_name( p_empno, v_fname );                          --(1)
    GET DIAGNOSTICS v_rc = RETURN_STATUS;                           --(2)

    IF ( v_rc = 99 )
    THEN
        SET p_output = 'The employee is: ' || v_fname || '.';
    ELSEIF ( v_rc = 1000 )
    THEN
        SET p_output = 'The employee does not exist!';
    ELSE
        SET p_output = 'Something else went wrong.';
    END IF;
END fe
```

In the example in Figure 7.5, the caller procedure assesses the execution of the called procedure by checking the return code. This value is then used to formulate more user-friendly messages.

Since an integer can be returned by both the return code and the output parameter, you might wonder which method should be used. As good SQL programming practice, you should reserve the use of return code for status indicators only. For all other situations, use an output parameter even if you only have one integer to return.

Use a return code for execution status only.

## 7.4 Returning Result Sets from Nested SQL Procedures

In previous chapters, you have learned how to use cursors to return result sets to calling applications. There is an additional consideration with returning result sets when nested SQL procedures are used. You can either:

- return your result set to the (direct) caller procedure;
- return your result set to the calling application (external client).

Where you return the result set can be defined by using the WITH RETURN clause of the DECLARE CURSOR statement.

**Figure 7.6** Partial DECLARE CURSOR Syntax

```
>>-DECLARE--cursor-name--CURSOR----+------------+-------------->
                                   '-WITH HOLD--'

>-----+----------------------------+------------------------->
      |               .-TO CALLER--.  |
      '-WITH RETURN--+------------+--'
                     '-TO CLIENT--'

>----FOR--+-select-statement-+-------------------------------><
          '-statement-name---'
```

As discussed in Chapter 4, "Cursors and Result Sets," the DECLARE CURSOR statement defines a cursor. When the WITH RETURN TO CALLER clause is used, the result sets will be returned to the direct caller, which can be either another SQL procedure, or an external application. When the WITH RETURN TO CLIENT clause is used, the result sets will be returned to the external application only. The result sets will be invisible to all intermediate SQL procedures.

### 7.4.1 Returning Result Sets to the Client

Figure 7.7 shows an example of an SQL procedure that uses a cursor to return result sets to the client. The procedure returns the first names, the last names and the salaries of all employees in one department for a given department number.

**Figure 7.7** Example of Returning Result Sets to Client

```
CREATE PROCEDURE emp_to_client
    ( IN  p_dept CHAR(3) )
SPECIFIC emp_to_client
DYNAMIC RESULT SETS 1
LANGUAGE SQL
ec: BEGIN
    -- Procedure logic
    DECLARE v_cur CURSOR WITH RETURN TO CLIENT
        FOR SELECT firstnme, lastname, salary
            FROM   employee
            WHERE  workdept = p_dept;
    OPEN v_cur;
END ec
```

The simple caller SQL procedure in Figure 7.8 demonstrates how it works.

**Figure 7.8** Example of Receiving Result Sets from Client

```
CREATE PROCEDURE call_client
    (  )
SPECIFIC call_client
LANGUAGE SQL
cc: BEGIN
    -- Declare variables
    DECLARE v_dept CHAR(3) DEFAULT 'A00';

    -- Procedure logic
    CALL emp_to_client(v_dept);
END cc
```

The procedure simply issues a CALL statement to *emp_to_client()* procedure. If you invoke the SQL procedure *call_client()* from the command window, you will see the output depicted in Figure 7.9.

**Figure 7.9** The Output of call_client()

```
FIRSTNME        LASTNAME         SALARY
CHRISTINE       HAAS             52750.00
VINCENZO        LUCCHESSI        46500.00
SEAN            O'CONNELL        29250.00
"CALL_CLIENT" RETURN_STATUS: "0"
```

Even though there is no cursor declared in the body of the SQL procedure *call_client()*, and there is no result set specified in its header, the calling application still received the result set. This is because the WITH RETURN TO CLIENT clause in the *emp_to_client()* SQL procedure told DB2 to bypass any intermediate SQL procedures and return the result sets directly to the application. The output you see is actually from the *emp_to_client()* procedure. You should see the same output if you invoke *emp_to_client()* directly without going through the *call_client()* caller procedure in the middle.

The cursor with the WITH RETURN TO CLIENT clause and its result sets are invisible to any intermediate SQL procedures.

Since the cursor and the result sets are invisible, you cannot use them in any intermediate SQL procedures. If you happen to need to use the result sets in both the caller SQL procedure and the client application, you will have to use WITH RETURN TO CALLER clause explained in the next section and re-return the rows in the caller SQL procedure.

## 7.4.2 Returning Result Sets to the Caller

To understand the difference between WITH RETURN TO CLIENT and WITH RETURN TO CALLER clauses, let's look at the two nested SQL procedures in Figures 7.10 and 7.11, which are very similar to the two in Figures 7.7 and 7.8.

Figure 7.10 shows the called SQL procedure using WITH RETURN TO CALLER clause.

**Figure 7.10** Example of Returning Result Sets to Caller

```
CREATE PROCEDURE emp_to_caller
    ( IN  p_dept CHAR(3) )
SPECIFIC emp_to_caller
DYNAMIC RESULT SETS 1
LANGUAGE SQL
ec: BEGIN
    -- Procedure logic
    DECLARE v_cur CURSOR WITH RETURN TO CALLER
        FOR SELECT firstnme, lastname, salary
            FROM   employee
            WHERE  workdept = p_dept;
    OPEN v_cur;
END ec
```

Figure 7.11 shows the caller SQL procedure that simply invokes the called SQL procedure.

**Figure 7.11** Example of Invoking a Procedure with RETURN TO CALLER Clause

```
CREATE PROCEDURE call_caller
    (  )
SPECIFIC call_caller
LANGUAGE SQL
cc: BEGIN
    -- Declare variables
    DECLARE v_dept CHAR(3) DEFAULT 'A00';

    -- Procedure logic
    CALL emp_to_caller(v_dept);
END cc
```

As you can see, the only differences between these two sets of nested SQL procedures are the WITH RETURN clauses in the called SQL procedures. In *emp_to_caller()*, the result sets are to be passed to its direct caller, be it an SQL procedure or client application.

If you invoke the *call_caller()* procedure, you will receive no result sets. This is because the result sets are for the *call_caller()* procedure, which did not re-return any result sets to its caller or its client application.

If you do not specify TO CLIENT or TO CALLER with WITH RETURN clause, by default, the result sets will be returned to the direct caller.

If you invoke the *emp_to_caller()* procedure directly, the output will be identical to that of the *emp_to_client()*. Obviously, it makes sense because you are working on two single procedures, instead of nested procedures, where the caller and the client application are always the same. There is no difference between WITH RETURN TO CALLER clause and WITH RETURN TO CLIENT clause outside the context of nested SQL procedures.

## 7.4.3 Receiving Result Sets as a Caller

To make use of the returned result sets from called procedures, you need to know how to access them in the calling procedure. In the previous chapters, you have learned how to receive result sets in client applications. For client applications, receiving result sets from nested SQL procedures is no different from receiving result sets from a single SQL procedure. The discussion of receiving result sets as a caller has been postponed until now.

In order to access and make use of the returned result sets, the ASSOCIATE LOCATORS statement and the ALLOCATE CURSOR statement must be used in the caller SQL procedure. The ASSOCIATE LOCATORS syntax is illustrated in Figure 7.12.

**Figure 7.12** ASSOCIATE LOCATORS Syntax

```
               .-RESULT SET--.
>>-ASSOCIATE--+-------------+---+-LOCATOR--+-------------------->
                                '-LOCATORS-'

        .-,---------------------.
        V                       |
>----(-----rs-locator-variable---+---)--WITH PROCEDURE--procedure-name->

>------------------------------------------------------------><
```

You can think of the RESULT SET LOCATORS as the pointers to the result sets in the caller procedure. ASSOCIATE LOCATORS, shown in Figure 7.13, obtain values for the result set locators.

**Figure 7.13** ALLOCATE CURSOR Syntax

```
>>-ALLOCATE--cursor-name--CURSOR FOR RESULT SET--rs-locator-variable-->

>--------------------------------------------------------------><
```

The ALLOCATE CURSOR statement allocates cursors for the result sets identified by the locator variables obtained by an ASSOCIATE LOCATORS statement.

The example in Figure 7.14 is a caller SQL procedure, which invokes the *emp_to_caller()* called procedure from Figure 7.10. The *emp_to_caller()* returns the first names, the last names and the salaries of all employees in one department. The caller SQL procedure, *total_salary()*, receives the result set and uses it to calculate the total salary of the department.

**Figure 7.14** Example of Receiving Result Sets from Caller Procedure

```
CREATE PROCEDURE total_salary
    ( in p_dept CHAR(3)
     ,OUT p_total DECIMAL(9,2) )
SPECIFIC total_salary
LANGUAGE SQL
ts: BEGIN
    -- Declare variables
    DECLARE v_fname VARCHAR(12);
    DECLARE v_lname VARCHAR(15);
    DECLARE v_salary DECIMAL(9,2) DEFAULT 0.0;
    DECLARE v_rs RESULT_SET_LOCATOR VARYING;                       --(1)
    -- Declare returncodes
    DECLARE SQLSTATE CHAR(5) DEFAULT '00000';

    -- Procedure logic
    CALL emp_to_caller(p_dept);                                    --(2)
    ASSOCIATE RESULT SET LOCATOR (v_rs)
        WITH PROCEDURE emp_to_caller;                              --(3)
    ALLOCATE v_rsCur CURSOR FOR RESULT SET v_rs;                   --(4)

    SET p_total = 0;

    WHILE ( SQLSTATE = '00000' ) DO
        SET p_total = p_total + v_salary;
        FETCH FROM v_rsCur INTO v_fname, v_lname, v_salary;
    END WHILE;
END ts
```

The result set locator variable is declared at (1).

After invoking the called SQL procedure at (2), the ASSOCIATE LOCATOR statement was used at (3) to obtain the result set locator variable. Then the ALLOCATE CURSOR statement was used at (4) to open the result set. The cursor name used in the ALLOCATE CURSOR statement must not be declared anywhere previous to the ALLOCATE CURSOR statement in the procedure. The locator variable in the ALLOCATE CURSOR statement must be associated beforehand.

Once declared with ALLOCATE CURSOR, the cursor can be used to fetch rows from the returned result set. In the example in Figure 7.14, a WHILE loop is used to fetch each row in order to calculate the department total salary. The SQLSTATE from the fetch statement is used as the exit condition for the loop, when the end of the result set is encountered.

## 7.4.4 Receiving Multiple Result Sets as a Caller

There are cases when a procedure will return more than one result set. To process multiple result sets in a caller procedure, the same statements as described in the previous section can be used. This is best illustrated using the example in Figure 7.15, which shows a called SQL procedure that returns multiple result sets.

**Figure 7.15** Example of Returning Multiple Result Sets to Caller Procedures

```
CREATE PROCEDURE emp_multi
    ( IN  p_dept CHAR(3) )
SPECIFIC emp_multi
DYNAMIC RESULT SETS 3
LANGUAGE SQL
em: BEGIN
    -- Procedure logic
    DECLARE v_cur1 CURSOR WITH RETURN TO CALLER
        FOR SELECT firstnme
            FROM   employee
            WHERE  workdept = p_dept;
    DECLARE v_cur2 CURSOR WITH RETURN TO CALLER
        FOR SELECT lastname
            FROM   employee
            WHERE  workdept = p_dept;
    DECLARE v_cur3 CURSOR WITH RETURN TO CALLER
        FOR SELECT salary
            FROM   employee
            WHERE  workdept = p_dept;
    OPEN v_cur1;
    OPEN v_cur2;
    OPEN v_cur3;
END em
```

The called SQL procedure *emp_multi()*, shown in Figure 7.15, is a simple rewrite of the previous called procedure *emp_to_caller()*, from Figure 7.10. Instead of returning three columns in one result set, each column is returned individually in a separate result set. Three cursors are declared and opened.

**Figure 7.16** Example of Receiving Multiple Result Sets from a Caller Procedure

```
CREATE PROCEDURE receive_multi
    ( in  p_dept  CHAR(3)
     ,OUT p_names VARCHAR(100)
     ,OUT p_total DECIMAL(9,2) )
SPECIFIC receive_multi
LANGUAGE SQL
rm: BEGIN
    -- Declare variables
    DECLARE v_fname VARCHAR(12) DEFAULT '';
    DECLARE v_lname VARCHAR(15) DEFAULT '';
    DECLARE v_salary DECIMAL(9,2) DEFAULT 0.0;
    DECLARE v_rs1, v_rs2, v_rs3 RESULT_SET_LOCATOR VARYING;
    -- Declare returncodes
    DECLARE SQLSTATE CHAR(5) DEFAULT '00000';

    -- Procedure logic
    CALL emp_multi(p_dept);
    ASSOCIATE RESULT SET LOCATOR (v_rs1, v_rs2, v_rs3)
        WITH PROCEDURE emp_multi;
    ALLOCATE v_rsCur1 CURSOR FOR RESULT SET v_rs1;
    ALLOCATE v_rsCur2 CURSOR FOR RESULT SET v_rs2;
    ALLOCATE v_rsCur3 CURSOR FOR RESULT SET v_rs3;

    SET p_names = 'The employees are:';
    WHILE (SQLSTATE = '00000') DO
        SET p_names = p_names || v_fname || ' ' ||  v_lname || ' ';
        FETCH FROM v_rsCur1 INTO v_fname;
        FETCH FROM v_rsCur2 INTO v_lname;
    END WHILE;

    SET p_total = 0;
    WHILE ( SQLSTATE = '00000' ) DO
        SET p_total = p_total + v_salary;
        FETCH FROM v_rsCur3 INTO v_salary;
    END WHILE;
END rm
```

The caller SQL procedure, *receive_multi()* in Figure 7.16, uses ASSOCIATE LOCATORS and ALLOCATE CURSOR statements, as in the *total_salary()* procedure from Figure 7.14, but multiple times to match the number of result sets returned. Three result set locator variables are declared and associated with the various result sets. Three cursors are allocated as well.

Another point this example demonstrates is that you can use the multiple result sets received both in parallel and sequentially. The first name and last name result sets are used in parallel to generate the string of employee names in the department. The salary result set is used after the first two result sets have been closed. Note that in this example, it is known that the two result sets used in parallel happen to have the same number of rows. In your project, if you choose to use two result sets with different numbers of rows in parallel, you must check the last row condition for each FETCH statement.

## 7.5 Levels of Nesting

If you implement an SQL procedure A() which calls SQL procedure B(), which in turn calls procedure C(), you have three levels of nested calls (A()->B()->C()). DB2 supports up to sixteen levels of SQL procedure nesting.

### 7.5.1 Recursion

SQL procedures can not only call other SQL procedures, but can also call themselves. This concept is called recursion. Recursive SQL procedures are a special case of nested SQL procedures.

Recursive procedures are sometimes the simplest solution to certain problems, even though they may be rewritten in a non-recursive way with the use of loops. Figure 7.17 is an example of a recursive procedure.

**Figure 7.17** Example of a Recursive Procedure

```
CREATE PROCEDURE managers
    ( IN  p_deptno CHAR(3)
     ,OUT p_report_chain VARCHAR(100) )
SPECIFIC managers
LANGUAGE SQL
mn: BEGIN
    -- Declare variables
    DECLARE v_manager_name VARCHAR(15);
    DECLARE v_admrdept CHAR(3);
    DECLARE v_report_chain VARCHAR(100);
    DECLARE v_stmt VARCHAR(100) DEFAULT 'CALL db2admin.managers(?,?)';      --(1)

    -- Procedure logic
    SELECT admrdept                                                          --(2)
      INTO v_admrdept
```

```
      FROM department
     WHERE deptno=p_deptno;

    SELECT lastname                                                          --(3)
      INTO v_manager_name
      FROM employee, department
     WHERE empno=mgrno
       AND deptno=p_deptno;

    IF (v_manager_name IS NULL) THEN
         SET v_manager_name = 'VACANT';
    END IF;

    IF ( v_admrdept = p_deptno ) THEN                                        --(4)
        SET p_report_chain = v_manager_name;
    ELSE
        PREPARE v_st from v_stmt;
        EXECUTE v_st INTO v_report_chain USING v_admrdept;                   --(5)
        SET p_report_chain = v_manager_name || ' -> ' || v_report_chain;
    END IF;
END mn
```

The procedure *managers()* finds the report chain of a department, which is indicated by a department number. For any department, there is an administrative department. The manager of a department is not considered a member of this department, but rather a member of the administrative department, except at the highest executive level.

The basic logic is to use a department number to find the administrative department number at (2). Then to use the new department number obtained as the input in turn to find the next level administrative department number at (5). The process will continue until the highest executive level is reached.

As with all recursive procedures, you need a terminating condition. In this case, the condition is the highest executive level where the department number is the same as the administrative department number. See lines (2) and (4).

The dynamic SQL at line (1) is required in order to compile the procedure. If static SQL is used instead, the procedure name will not be resolved at compile time and this will generate a compile error.

The limit on the number of recursions is the same as the limit for nesting levels which is sixteen. You need to know how much recursion your recursive SQL procedure will require. You might have to rewrite the code using an iterative solution if the limit is reached, or as a user-defined function.

The number of recursive calls for SQL procedures must be less than sixteen.

## 7.6 Security

Detailed information about security issues related to SQL procedures are discussed in Appendix D, "Security."

When you create an SQL procedure, you may specify CONTAINS SQL, READS SQL DATA or MODIFIES SQL DATA. The NO SQL clause is not valid for SQL procedures. Please refer to Chapter 2, "Basic SQL Procedure Structure for more information."

A nested SQL procedure will not be allowed to call a target procedure with a higher data access level. For example, an SQL procedure created with READS SQL DATA can call SQL procedures created with either CONTAINS SQL or READS SQL DATA, but cannot call SQL procedures created with MODIFIES SQL DATA.

With this restriction, a user without proper privileges will not be able to obtain access to confidential data, even if he knows the name and signature of the SQL procedure that reads the data or modifies the data.

## 7.7 Chapter Summary

In this chapter, nested SQL procedures were covered. Data is passed between the procedures and external applications via parameters or result sets. Output parameters are used to return single values, while result sets are used to return rows of data. The return status, which is of integer type, should be reserved as an execution status indicator only.

You have two options in returning result sets. By using the TO CALLER or TO CLIENT clauses, you can control the destination and the visibility of the result sets. Use TO CLIENT if the result set is meant for an external application only. Use TO CALLER if the result set is meant for direct callers.

Recursive SQL procedures are special cases of nested SQL procedures. Dynamic SQL is required to implement recursive procedures.

CHAPTER 8

# Leveraging DB2 Advanced Features

## In this chapter, you will learn:

- the differences between identity columns and sequence objects and how to use them;
- how to use declared user-temporary tables;
- how to use savepoints for finer transaction control;
- the characteristics of large objects;
- how to wrap these DB2 features in SQL procedures.

At this point you should know almost everything about coding DB2 SQL procedures. You learned about SQL PL structure, logic flow control, cursor usage, condition handling, dynamic SQL and nested procedure calls. In this chapter, DB2 advanced features and common programming techniques will be introduced. They can be used to simplify existing code and improve performance. Examples of some DB2 advanced features are presented with techniques you learned from the previous chapters. If you are already familiar with the features, you may jump directly into sections on how they can be used in SQL procedures.

# 8.1 Working with Identity Columns and Sequence Objects

## 8.1.1 Automatic Numbering

Numeric generation is a very common requirement for many types of applications, such as generation of new employee numbers, order purchase numbers, ticket numbers and so on. In a heavy online transaction processing (OLTP) environment with a high number of concurrent users, use of database tables and user-defined programmatic increment methods usually degrades performance. The reason is that the database system has to lock a table row when a value is requested to guarantee no duplicated values are used. Instead of relying on your own methods for generating unique IDs, you can make use of facilities provided by DB2 UDB.

DB2 UDB provides two mechanisms to implement such sets of numbers: identity columns and sequence objects.

As you explore the usage of identity columns and sequence objects, you will see that both of them achieve basically the same goal: automatically generating numeric values. Their behaviors can be tailored by using different options to meet specific application needs. Although they are created and used differently, DB2 treats both of them as sequences. An identity column is a system-defined sequence and a sequence object is a user-defined sequence. Their definitions are stored in the SYSCAT.SEQUENCES catalog table. Under the column ORIGIN, "S" means system-defined and "U" means user-defined.

Because DB2 supports both sequence objects and identity columns, you have one less worry when migrating your application from other database products to DB2.

## 8.1.2 Identity Column

An identity column is a numeric column defined in a table for which the column values can be generated automatically by DB2. Definition of an identity column is specified at table creation time. Existing tables cannot be altered to add or drop an identity column. Figure 8.1 shows the syntax of an identity column clause used in a CREATE TABLE statement. Only one column in a table can be defined to be an identity column.

**Figure 8.1** Syntax of the Identity Column Clause

```
|---column-name----+--------------------+-------------------->
                   |                    |
                   '-| data-type |-------'

>----GENERATED--+-ALWAYS--+---AS--+-| identity-clause |-----+->
                '-BY DEFAULT-'

 identity-clause
|---IDENTITY--+------------------------------------------------------+->
              |     .-,---------------------------------------.      |
              |     V              |---1--------------------|      |
              '-(------+-START WITH--+-numeric-constant-+---+--+---)--'
                       |               |---1---------------|
                       +-INCREMENT BY--+-numeric-constant-+-+
                       +-NO MINVALUE----------------------+-+
                       |'-MINVALUE--numeric-constant-'      |
                       +-NO MAXVALUE----------------------+-+
                       |'-MAXVALUE--numeric-constant-'      |
                       +-NO CYCLE-------------------------+-+
                       |'-CYCLE----'                        |
                       +-CACHE--20--------------------------|
                       |'-+-NO CACHE-'                      |
                       |'-+-CACHE--integer-constant-'       |
                       +-NO ORDER-------------------------+-+
                       |'-ORDER----'                        |
>-----------------------------------------------------------|
```

*Data types* for identity columns can be any exact numeric data type with a scale of zero such as SMALLINT, INTEGER, BIGINT, or DECIMAL. Single and double precision floating point are considered to be approximate numeric data types and they cannot be used as identity columns. Refer to the SQL Reference for details about data types.

Values will be generated for the column when a row is inserted to the table. An identity column is a generated column and two options are supported, namely GENERATED ALWAYS and GENERATED BY DEFAULT. For a GENERATED ALWAYS identity column, DB2 has full control over the values generated and uniqueness is guaranteed. An error will be raised if an explicit value is specified. On the other hand, the GENERATED BY DEFAULT option does not guarantee uniqueness. DB2 will only generate a value for the column when no value is specified at the time of insert.

Within the IDENTITY clause, there are number of options you can set to customize the behavior of an identity column. Before going into discussion of these options, let's look at Figure 8.2 to see how a table can be created with an identity column.

**Figure 8.2** Example of a Table Definition with an Identity Column

```
CREATE TABLE service_rq
    ( rqid SMALLINT NOT NULL
        CONSTRAINT rqid_pk
        PRIMARY KEY                                                         -- (1)
    , status VARCHAR(10) NOT NULL
        WITH DEFAULT 'NEW'
        CHECK ( status IN ( 'NEW', 'ASSIGNED', 'PENDING', 'CANCELLED' ) ) -- (2)
    , rq_desktop CHAR(1) NOT NULL
        WITH DEFAULT 'N'
        CHECK ( rq_desktop IN ( 'Y', 'N' ) )                                -- (3)
    , rq_ipaddress CHAR(1) NOT NULL
        WITH DEFAULT 'N'
        CHECK ( rq_ipaddress IN ( 'Y', 'N' ) )                              -- (4)
    , rq_unixid CHAR(1) NOT NULL
        WITH DEFAULT 'N'
        CHECK ( rq_unixid IN ( 'Y', 'N' ) )                                 -- (5)
    , staffid INTEGER NOT NULL
    , techid INTEGER
    , accum_rqnum INTEGER NOT NULL                                          -- (6)
        GENERATED ALWAYS AS IDENTITY
        ( START WITH 1
      , INCREMENT BY 1
      , CACHE 10 )
    , comment VARCHAR(100))
```

Figure 8.2 is the data definition language (DDL) of a table called *service_rq*, which will be used in a later sample. The *service_rq* table contains an identity column called *accum_rqnum* (6). Note that the GENERATED ALWAYS option is specified and therefore DB2 will always generate a unique integer. The value of *accum_rqnum* will start at 1 and increment by 1.

From examining the other column definitions (2,3,4 and 5), you will see that some are defined with a CHECK constraint so that only the specified values are allowed as column values. A primary key is also defined for this table (1). Figures 8.3 and 8.4 show two different ways to insert a record into the *service_rq* table.

**Figure 8.3** First Method of Inserting into Table with Identity Column

```
INSERT INTO service_rq
    ( rqid
    , rq_desktop
    , rq_ipaddress
    , rq_unixid
    , staffid
    , comment )
```

```
VALUES
     ( 1
     , 'Y'
     , 'Y'
     , 'Y'
     , 10
     , 'First request for staff id 10' )
```

**Figure 8.4** Second Method of Inserting into Table with Identity Column

```
INSERT INTO service_rq
     ( rqid
     , status
     , rq_desktop
     , rq_ipaddress
     , rq_unixid
     , staffid
     , techid
     , accum_rqnum
     , comment )
VALUES
     ( 2
     , DEFAULT                                                        -- (1)
     , 'Y'
     , 'Y'
     , 'Y'
     , 10
     , NULL
     , DEFAULT                                                        -- (2)
     , 'Second request for staff id 10' )
```

Notice that in Figure 8.3, not every column is specified in the INSERT statement. If they are omitted, DB2 will automatically substitute default values according to the column definitions. On the other hand, the example shown in Figure 8.4 specifies all the columns defined in the table and the associated values. This option allows you to easily identify a mismatch or missing column names and values. Notice how the reserved word DEFAULT is used at (2) in Figure 8.4. It is mandatory for the identity column value because only DB2 generated values are allowed in a GENERATED ALWAYS identity column. DEFAULT is also used at (1) so that DB2 will supply the default value for the *status* column in Figure 8.2.

DEFAULT is a DB2 reserved word. It is mandatory if a GENERATED ALWAYS identity column name is specified in an INSERT statement. Specifying all values for the columns in the VALUES clause of an INSERT statement is a good practice because it gives a clear view of what values are being inserted.

As shown in Figure 8.1, few other options are available when defining the identity attribute. The START WITH option indicates the first value of the identity column and can be a positive or negative value. Identity values can be generated in ascending or descending order and this can be controlled by the INCREMENT BY clause. The default behavior is to auto increment by 1 (and therefore, is ascending). Options MINVALUE and MAXVALUE allow you to specify the lower and upper limit of the generated values. These values must be within the limit of the data type. For example, the smallest and largest SMALLINT values are -32768 and +32767 respectively. You can find a complete list of SQL limits in Appendix A of the *DB2 SQL Reference Guide.* If the minimum or maximum limit has been reached, you can use CYCLE to recycle the generated values from the minimum or maximum value governed by the MINVALUE and MAXVALUE option.

The CACHE option can be used to provide better performance. Without caching, option NO CACHE, DB2 will check the catalog table every time the next value is requested. Performance can be degraded if the insert rate of a table with an identity column is heavy. To minimize this synchronous effect, specify the CACHE option so that a block of values is obtained and stored in memory to serve subsequent identity value generation requests. When all the cached values are used, the next block of values will be obtained. In the example shown in Figure 8.2, ten values are generated and stored in memory cache. When applications request a value, it will be obtained from the cache rather than from the system tables that are stored on disk. If DB2 is stopped before all cached values are used, any unused cached values will be discarded. After DB2 is restarted, the next block of values is generated and cached, introducing gaps between values. If your application does not allow value gaps, specify the default value of NOCACHE.

## 8.1.3 Generate Value Retrieval

It is often useful to be able to use the identity value previously generated by DB2 in subsequent application logic. The generated value can be obtained by executing the function, IDENTITY_VAL_LOCAL(), within the same session of the INSERT statement; otherwise NULL is returned. The function does not take any parameters. Figure 8.5 demonstrates two different ways to use the IDENTITY_VAL_LOCAL() function.

**Figure 8.5** Example of Using IDENTITY_VAL_LOCAL

```
CREATE PROCEDURE addnewrq
    ( IN p_rqid SMALLINT
    , IN p_staffid INTEGER
    , IN p_comment VARCHAR(100)
    , OUT p_accum_rqnum INTEGER )
    SPECIFIC addnewrq
    LANGUAGE SQL

anr:  BEGIN
    INSERT INTO service_rq
        ( rqid, status, rq_desktop
        , rq_ipaddress, rq_unixid, staffid
        , techid, accum_rqnum, comment )
    VALUES
        ( p_rqid, DEFAULT, 'Y'
        , 'Y', 'Y', p_staffid
        , NULL, DEFAULT, p_comment ) ;

    SELECT                                                        -- (1)
        identity_val_local()
    INTO
        p_accum_rqnum
    FROM
        sysibm.sysdummy1;

    VALUES                                                        -- (2)
        identity_val_local()
    INTO
        p_accum_rqnum;

END anr
```

In Figure 8.5, procedure *addnewrq* uses two ways to obtain the value just inserted into *service_rq*. At (1), it uses the SYSIBM.SYSDUMMY1 table. As the name indicates, it is a *dummy* table. Another method is to use the VALUES clause instead shown at (2). If you call the procedure multiple times with the same *rqid* value, for example:

```
CALL addnewrq(3, 1050, 'New Request', ?)
```

You will get an error with SQLSTATE 23505 indicating a unique constraint was violated because the *rqid* column is defined as a primary key in Figure 8.2. Note that the result of IDENTITY_VAL_LOCAL() keeps increasing even though the INSERT statement fails. This indicates that once an identity value is assigned by DB2, it will not be reused regardless of the success or failure of the previous INSERT statement.

Notice that the example in Figure 8.5 only involves a single row insert. If the statement inserts multiple rows prior to execution of IDENTITY_VAL_LOCAL(), it will not return the last value generated, it will return NULL. Consider the example in Figure 8.6.

**Figure 8.6** Example of Multi-Row Insert Before IDENTITY_VAL_LOCAL

```
CREATE PROCEDURE insert_multirow
    ( OUT p_id_generated INTEGER )
    SPECIFIC insert_multirow
    LANGUAGE SQL

imr:  BEGIN
    INSERT INTO service_rq                                              -- (1)
        ( rqid
        , staffid
        , accum_rqnum
        , comment )
    VALUES
        ( 30000                                                         -- (2)
        , 1050
        , DEFAULT
        , 'INSERT1')
        ,                                                               -- (3)
        ( 30001                                                         -- (4)
        , 1050
        , DEFAULT
        , 'INSERT2')
    ;
    VALUES                                                              -- (5)
        identity_val_local()
    INTO
        p_id_generated;

    -- For clean up purpose
    DELETE FROM svcrq
        WHERE rqid = 30000 or rqid = 30001;

END imr
```

Two sets of values at (2) and (4) are being inserted with a single INSERT statement. They are separated by a comma at (3). The output parameter *p_id_generated* is assigned to the result of IDENTITY_VAL_LOCAL() function at (5). Successfully completion of *insert_multirow* will give you the following:

```
P_ID_GENERATED: NULL
"INSERT_MULTIROW" RETURN_STATUS: "0"
```

## 8.1.4 Change of Identity Column Characteristics

Since an identity column is part of a table definition, to reset or change a characteristic of an identity column you need to issue an ALTER TABLE statement as shown in Figure 8.7.

**Figure 8.7** Syntax and Example of Altering Identity Column Characteristics

```
>>-ALTER TABLE--table-name---column-name----------------------->
|--column-name--+-----------------+----------------------->
|-----------+-SET INCREMENT BY--numeric-constant--+-+----------|
            +-SET--+-NO MINVALUE---------------+-+
            |      '-MINVALUE--numeric-constant-' |
            +-SET--+-NO MAXVALUE---------------+-+
            |      '-MAXVALUE--numeric-constant-' |
            +-SET--+-NO CYCLE-+------------------+
            |      '-CYCLE----'                  |
            +-SET--+-NO CACHE---------------+----+
            |      '-CACHE--integer-constant-'    |
            +-SET--+-NO ORDER-+------------------+
            |      '-ORDER----'                  |
            '-RESTART--+-----------------------+-'
                       '-WITH--numeric-constant-'
```

Except for the RESTART option (which has not been introduced), the options listed in Figure 8.7 behave exactly the same as they were described above. If you want the identity column to be restarted at a specific value at any time, you will find the RESTART option very useful. Simply alter the table, provide the RESTART WITH clause, and explicitly specify a numeric constant.

## 8.1.5 Sequence Objects

A sequence is a database object that allows automatic generation of values. Unlike an identity column, which is bound to a specific table, a sequence is a global and standalone object that can be used by any table in the same database. The same sequence object can be used for one or more tables. Figure 8.8 lists the syntax for creating a sequence object.

**Figure 8.8** Syntax of CREATE SEQUENCE Statement

```
                                              .-AS INTEGER-----.
>>-CREATE SEQUENCE--sequence-name---*----+----------------+--*-->
                                              '-AS--data-type--'
>-----+-------------------------------+--*---------------------->
      '-START WITH--numeric-constant--'
      .-INCREMENT BY 1-----------------.
>-----+--------------------------------+--*-------------------->
      '-INCREMENT BY--numeric-constant--'
      .-NO MINVALUE-----------------.
>-----+-----------------------------+--*----------------------->
      '-MINVALUE--numeric-constant--'
      .-NO MAXVALUE-----------------.        .-NO CYCLE--.
>-----+-----------------------------+--*----+-----------+--*---->
      '-MAXVALUE--numeric-constant--'        '-CYCLE-----'
      .-CACHE 20-----------------.        .-NO ORDER--.
>-----+--------------------------+--*----+-----------+--*------><
      +-CACHE--integer-constant--+        '-ORDER-----'
      '-NO CACHE-----------------'
```

As with identity columns, any exact numeric data type with a scale of zero can be used for the sequence value. These include SMALLINT, INTEGER, BIGINT, or DECIMAL. In addition, any user-defined distinct type based on these data types can hold sequence values. This extends the usage of user-defined distinct types in an application. You may already notice that options supported for sequence objects are the same as the ones for identity columns. Please refer to the previous subsection for their descriptions.

**Figure 8.9** Example of Sequence staff_seq

```
CREATE SEQUENCE staff_seq AS INTEGER
    START WITH 360
    INCREMENT BY 10
    NO MAXVALUE
    NO CYCLE
    NO CACHE
```

**Figure 8.10** Example of Sequence service_rq_seq

```
CREATE SEQUENCE service_rq_seq AS SMALLINT
   START WITH 1
   INCREMENT BY 1
   MAXVALUE 5000
   NO CYCLE
   CACHE 50
```

Figure 8.9 and Figure 8.10 show creation of two sequence objects. For example, sequence *staff_seq* is used to provide a numeric ID to each staff member. It is declared as an INTEGER, starts at 360, is incremented by 10, and no maximum value is explicitly specified. It is implicitly bound by the limit of the data type. In this example, values generated are within the limit of an INTEGER data type. The NO CYCLE option indicates that if the maximum value is reached, SQLSTATE 23522 will be raised. The second sequence object, in Figure 8.10, is defined as SMALLINT and used to generate ticket numbers for service requests. This sequence object will start at 1 and increment by 1. Since NO CYCLE is specified, the maximum value generated will be 5000. The CACHE 50 option indicates that DB2 will acquire and cache 50 values at a time for application use. Like identity columns, if DB2 is stopped and sequence values were cached, gaps in sequence values may result.

## 8.1.6 Change of Sequence Object Characteristics

At any time, you can either drop and recreate the sequence object or alter the sequence to change its behavior. Figure 8.11 and Figure 8.12 show the syntax of the ALTER SEQUENCE and DROP SEQUENCE statements respectively.

**Figure 8.11** Syntax of ALTER SEQUENCE Statement

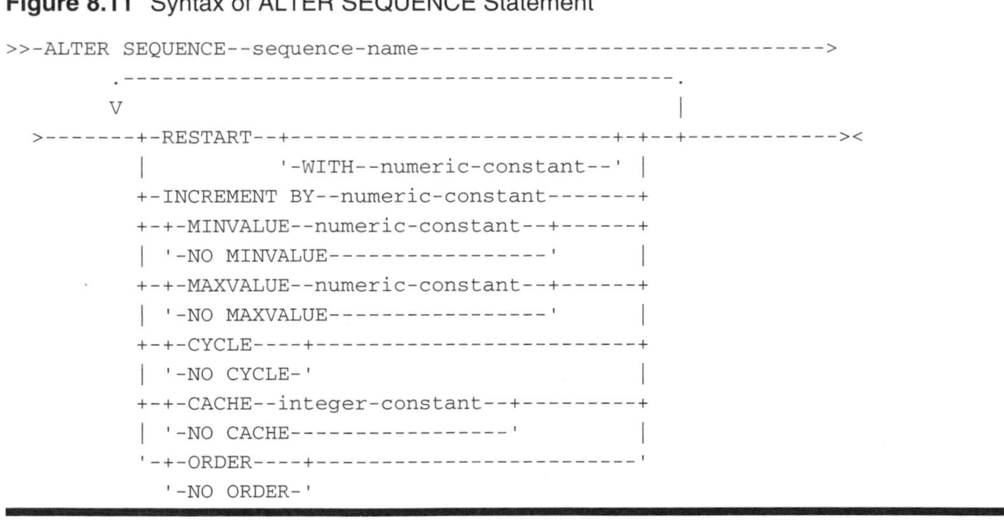

```
>>-ALTER SEQUENCE--sequence-name-------------------------------->

        .-----------------------------------------.
        V                                         |
  >-------+-RESTART--+-----------------------+-+--+------------><
          |          '-WITH--numeric-constant--' |
          +-INCREMENT BY--numeric-constant-------+
          +-+-MINVALUE--numeric-constant--+------+
          | '-NO MINVALUE-----------------'      |
          +-+-MAXVALUE--numeric-constant--+------+
          | '-NO MAXVALUE-----------------'      |
          +-+-CYCLE----+-----------------------+
          | '-NO CYCLE-'                         |
          +-+-CACHE--integer-constant--+---------+
          | '-NO CACHE-----------------'         |
          '-+-ORDER----+-----------------------'
            '-NO ORDER-'
```

**Figure 8.12** Syntax of DROP SEQUENCE Statement

```
>>- DROP SEQUENCE--sequence-name--RESTRICT--------------------------><
```

## 8.1.7 Privilege Required for Using Sequence Object

Just like other database objects in DB2, use of sequence objects is controlled by privileges. By default, only the sequence creator, SYSADM, and DBADM hold the USAGE privilege of the object. If you want other users be able to use the sequence, you need to issue:

```
GRANT USAGE ON <sequence_object_name> TO PUBLIC
```

which cannot be revoked once granted.

## 8.1.8 Generated Value Retrieval of Sequence Objects

Two expressions, NEXTVAL and PREVVAL, are provided to generate and retrieve a sequence value. Figure 8.13 is an example of their usage.

**Figure 8.13** Usage of the NEXTVAL and PREVVAL Expressions

```
CREATE PROCEDURE seqexp
    ( out p_prevval1 int
    , out p_nextval1 int
    , out p_nextval2 int
    , out p_prevval2 int )
    SPECIFIC seqexp
    LANGUAGE SQL

se:  BEGIN

    -- DECLARE host variables
    DECLARE v_prevstaffno INT;

    -- Procedure logic
    INSERT INTO staff
        ( id, name, dept
        , job, years, salary
        , comm )
    VALUES
        ( NEXTVAL FOR staff_seq, 'Bush', 55
        , 'Mgr', 30, NULL
        , NULL);

    UPDATE staff
       SET id = ( NEXTVAL FOR staff_seq )
     WHERE name='Bush';

    VALUES PREVVAL FOR staff_seq INTO v_prevstaffno;                      -- (1)

    DELETE FROM staff WHERE id = v_prevstaffno;                           -- (2)
```

```
    VALUES                                                        -- (3)
        ( PREVVAL FOR staff_seq
        , NEXTVAL FOR staff_seq
        , NEXTVAL FOR staff_seq
        , PREVVAL FOR staff_seq )
    INTO p_prevval1, p_nextval1, p_nextval2, p_prevval2;

END se
```

You can use the NEXTVAL and PREVVAL expressions in SELECT, VALUES, INSERT, and UPDATE statements. In Figure 8.13 at (2), the DELETE statement needs to reference the value just generated in the WHERE clause. Since NEXTVAL and PREVVAL cannot be used in a WHERE clause, you need to use two separate SQL statements. Use a VALUES INTO statement to obtain and store the generated value in a variable, *v_prevstaffno*. The DELETE statement can then specify the variable in the WHERE clause.

The last VALUES statement at (3) in the example shows that if more than one sequence expression for a single sequence object is used in a statement, DB2 will execute NEXTVAL and PREVVAL only once. In the example, assuming the value last generated is 500, statement (3) will have the result 500, 501, 501, 500.

There are other places where NEXTVAL and PREVVAL cannot be used:

- CASE expression
- Parameter list of an aggregate function
- Subquery in a context other than those explicitly allowed above
- SELECT statement for which the outer SELECT contains a DISTINCT operator
- Join condition of a join
- SELECT statement for which the outer SELECT contains a GROUP BY clause
- SELECT statement for which the outer SELECT is combined with another SELECT statement using the UNION, INTERSECT, or EXCEPT
- Set operator
- Nested table expression
- Parameter list of a table function
- WHERE clause of the outermost SELECT statement, or a DELETE or UPDATE statement
- ORDER BY clause of the outermost SELECT statement

- Select-clause of the fullselect of an expression, in the SET clause of an UPDATE statement
- IF, WHILE, DO ... UNTIL, or CASE statement in an SQL routine

### 8.1.9 Using Identity Columns and Sequence Objects in SQL Procedures

To use identity columns in SQL procedures, simply use INSERT to generate numeric values and the IDENTITY_VAL_LOCAL() function to retrieve generated values. Examples of using sequence objects inside SQL procedures are shown below.

It is common for applications to support different back-end database systems. You may notice that the syntax for referencing a sequence in disparate databases is not the same. In order to minimize the cost of maintaining different application code base for different database systems, SQL procedure can be used to provide a consistent syntax for getting the next value of a given sequence object. The stored procedures can be maintained along with other database objects. An example is shown in Figure 8.14.

While pointing out the advantage of wrapping NEXTVAL in SQL procedures, you should also understand that there is overhead to load and run stored procedures.

**Figure 8.14** Sequence Value Generation Wrapped in an SQL Procedure

```
CREATE PROCEDURE seqnextval
    ( IN p_seqname VARCHAR(50)
    , OUT p_nextval INT )
    SPECIFIC seqnextval
    LANGUAGE SQL

snv: BEGIN
    -- DECLARE VARIABLES
    DECLARE v_dynstmt VARCHAR(100);

    -- DECLARE CONDITIONS                                                -- (1)
    -- SQLSTATE 42704, object not found
    DECLARE seq_notfound CONDITION FOR SQLSTATE '42704';
    -- SQLSTATE 42501, object privilege error
    DECLARE obj_access_error CONDITION FOR SQLSTATE '42501';

    -- DECLARE STATEMENT
    DECLARE v_prepstmt STATEMENT;

    -- DECLARE CURSORS
    DECLARE c_nextval CURSOR FOR v_prepstmt;

    -- DECLARE HANDLERS                                                  -- (2)
```

```
    DECLARE EXIT HANDLER FOR seq_notfound
        RESIGNAL SQLSTATE '70000'
          SET MESSAGE_TEXT = 'Sequence Object NOT FOUND';
    DECLARE EXIT HANDLER FOR obj_access_error
        RESIGNAL SQLSTATE '70001'
          SET MESSAGE_TEXT = 'User encounters privilege problems';

    -- Procedure body
    SET v_dynstmt = 'VALUES NEXTVAL for ' || p_seqname ;                -- (3)
    PREPARE v_prepstmt FROM v_dynstmt;                                  -- (4)
    OPEN c_nextval;
    FETCH c_nextval INTO p_nextval;                                     -- (5)
    CLOSE c_nextval;

END snv
```

This SQL procedure takes a sequence object name as input and returns the next sequence value. The statement at (3) is used to generate the value and must be prepared dynamically at (4) since the sequence object name is not known until the time of execution. The generated value is then fetched at (5) and stored in the OUT parameter. Conditions and error handlers are defined at (1) and (2) to catch object-not-found and privilege errors. If the given sequence is not defined or the sequence schema name is not correctly provided, the SQL procedure will result in an object not found error. A privilege error may result if the user does not have USAGE on the sequence or the user does not have EXECUTE on the stored procedure package itself. For more information about privileges required for creating or executing an SQL procedure, refer to Appendix D, "Security Considerations in SQL Procedures."

The behavior of a sequence object can be changed with the ALTER SEQUENCE statement as mentioned in the section above. Another SQL procedure can be defined to alter a sequence object with specific options. Figure 8.15 shows such an example.

**Figure 8.15** Sequence Object Alteration Wrapped in an SQL Procedure

```
CREATE PROCEDURE alterseq
    ( IN p_seqname VARCHAR(50)
    , IN p_options VARCHAR(100) )
    SPECIFIC alterseq
    LANGUAGE SQL

aseq: BEGIN
    -- DECLARE VARIABLES
    DECLARE v_dynstmt VARCHAR(100);
    DECLARE v_retcode INTEGER DEFAULT 0;

    -- DECLARE CONDITIONS
```

```
    -- SQLSTATE 42704, object not found
    DECLARE seq_notfound CONDITION FOR SQLSTATE '42704';
    -- SQLSTATE 42501, object privilege error
    DECLARE obj_access_error CONDITION FOR SQLSTATE '42501';

    -- DECLARE STATEMENT
    DECLARE v_prepstmt STATEMENT;

    -- DECLARE HANDLERS
    DECLARE EXIT HANDLER FOR seq_notfound
        RESIGNAL SQLSTATE '70000'
          SET MESSAGE_TEXT = 'Sequence Object NOT FOUND';
    DECLARE EXIT HANDLER FOR obj_access_error
        RESIGNAL SQLSTATE '70001'
          SET MESSAGE_TEXT = 'User encounters privilege problems';
    DECLARE EXIT HANDLER FOR SQLEXCEPTION
        RESIGNAL SQLSTATE '70002'
          SET MESSAGE_TEXT = 'SQL Exception raised';

    -- Procedure body
    SET v_dynstmt = 'ALTER SEQUENCE ' || p_seqname || ' ' || p_options;
    PREPARE v_prepstmt FROM v_dynstmt;
    EXECUTE v_prepstmt;

END aseq
```

To test the ALTERSEQ SQL procedure, you can issue:

```
call alterseq('staff_seq', 'restart with 500')
```

This will RESTART the sequence number at 500.

## 8.1.10 Bringing It All Together

In this section, all the scripts presented so far will be put together. The SAMPLE database provided with the DB2 installation is required. Setup instructions can be found in Appendix A, "Getting Started With DB2" .

The following describes the scenario for the example:

- The STAFF table in the sample database contains information about each staff member in the company. Each staff member has an ID assigned that is generated by the *staff_seq* sequence object (object definition shown in Figure 8.9).
- When a new person joins the company, their information will be added to the *staff* table.

- The IT department needs to perform some setup tasks for every new staff member, such as setting up a desktop computer, creating a user account, assigning IP addresses, and so on.
- To track all IT service requests and processes, two new tables are required to store assigned technician, new staff ID, requirements, and status of the service requests (see Figure 8.2 for table definitions).
- Each request is uniquely identified by a ticket number. The service_rq_seq sequence object acts as the ticket number generator (see Figure 8.10).

The flow of the *addnewstaff* SQL procedure is illustrated in Figure 8.16.

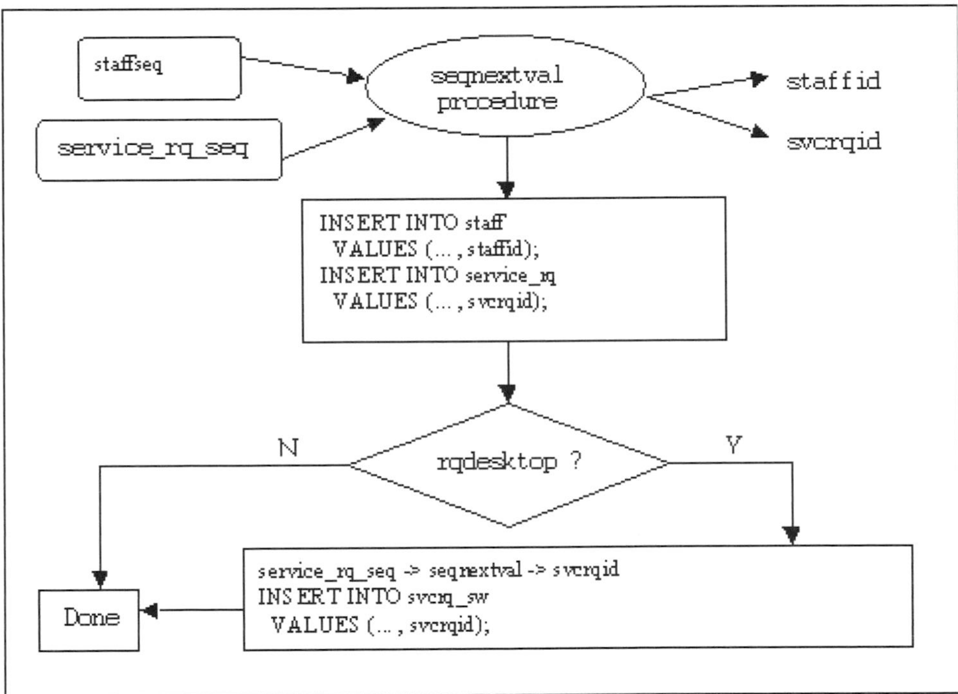


**Figure 8.16** Flow Diagram of Adding New Staff

Figure 8.17 is an SQL procedure that inserts new staff into the *staff* table, and creates a service request for the staff. This example requires the *service_rq* and *svcrq_sq* tables, *staff_seq* and *service_rq* sequence objects, and *seqnextval* SQL procedure.

**Figure 8.17** Add New Staff Members and Service Requests Using an SQL Procedure

```
CREATE PROCEDURE addnewstaff
    ( IN p_staffname VARCHAR(9)
    , IN p_dept SMALLINT
    , IN p_job CHAR(5)
    , IN p_rqdesktop CHAR(1)
    , IN p_rqipadd CHAR(1)
    , IN p_rqunixid CHAR(1) )
    SPECIFIC addnewstaff
    LANGUAGE SQL

ans:  BEGIN
    -- DECLARE host variables
    DECLARE v_staffid INT;
    DECLARE v_svcrqid INT;
    DECLARE v_staff_seq VARCHAR(50) DEFAULT 'staff_seq';
    DECLARE v_svcrq_seq VARCHAR(50) DEFAULT 'service_rq_seq';
    DECLARE v_alterseq_opt VARCHAR(50) DEFAULT 'RESTART';

    -- Procedure body
    CALL seqnextval( v_staff_seq, v_staffid );                       -- (1)
    CALL seqnextval( v_svcrq_seq, v_svcrqid );                       -- (1)

    INSERT INTO staff                                                -- (2)
        ( id, name, dept
        , job, years, salary
        , comm)
     VALUES
        ( v_staffid, p_staffname, p_dept
        , p_job, 0, NULL
        , NULL );

    INSERT INTO service_rq                                           -- (3)
        ( rqid, status, rq_desktop
        , rq_ipaddress, rq_unixid, staffid
        , techid, accum_rqnum, comment )
    VALUES
        ( SMALLINT( v_svcrqid ), DEFAULT, p_rqdesktop
        , p_rqipadd, p_rqunixid, v_staffid
        , NULL, DEFAULT, NULL );

    IF p_rqdesktop = 'Y' THEN                                        -- (4)
        CALL seqnextval( v_svcrq_seq, v_svcrqid );
        INSERT INTO svcrq_sw
            ( rqid, status, ostype
            , staffid, techid, comment )
        VALUES
            ( v_svcrqid, DEFAULT, DEFAULT
            , v_staffid, NULL, NULL );
    END IF;

END ans
```

In order to add a new staff member and the associated service request, SQL procedure *seqnextval* is called to obtain the next value for sequences *staff_seq* and *service_rq_seq* at (1). The statement at (2) inserts the appropriate values into the *staff* table where *v_staff* is a sequence value generated by *staff_seq*. Similarly, the statement at (3) inserts a record into the *service_rq* table. The generic SQL procedure *seqnextval* produces a value of INTEGER type but the *rqid* column is defined as SMALLINT. You therefore need to cast *v_svcrqid* to SMALLINT for the INSERT.

There is also an identity column, *accum_rqnum*, defined in the *service_rq* table. Assume that the IT department also wants to keep track of the total number of hardware services requested so far. Since all hardware requests are stored only in the *service_rq* table, an identity column is sufficient to serve this purpose. The IF block shows that if desktop is requested, a separate request will be inserted to the *svcrq_sw* table. Notice that the *seqnextval* procedure is used to get the next value of the *service_rq_seq* sequence object. This demonstrates that a sequence object can be used by multiple tables in the same database. Another reason for you to choose a sequence object over an identity column is that with sequence objects, a value can be generated without having to insert a row.

# 8.2 Working with Temporary Tables

## 8.2.1 Introduction to Temporary Tables

As the name implies, temporary tables are not permanent database objects. A temporary table behaves like a normal table except that not all features and options are supported and/or required. They persist only for the duration of a connection. When the connection is closed, all temporary tables declared in it will be dropped automatically. To declare temporary tables, a USER temporary table space (which is different from, and often confused with, a SYSTEM temporary table space) must exist to store the definition and content of the temporary table.

Only the session or application that declares a temporary table will have access to it. If two applications create a temporary table with the same name, each instance of the temporary table is unique. Regardless of name used, a temporary table is always qualified with the schema SESSION (i.e. SESSION.temptable1). Thus, you do not need to be concerned about any temporary data collision scenarios. Since a temporary table only allows single connection access, locking is not required. This is one of the main performance benefits of using temporary tables. Let's now look at how to declare and use a temporary table. The temporary table syntax diagram and a declaration example are shown in Figures 8.18 and 8.19, respectively.

**Figure 8.18** Syntax of Declaring a Global Temporary Table

```
>>-DECLARE GLOBAL TEMPORARY TABLE--table-name------------------->
           .-,------------------------.
           V                          |
>-----+-(-----| column-definition |---+---)-------------------------+>
      +-LIKE--+-table-name2-+---+------------------+----------------+
      |       '-view-name---'   '-| copy-options |--'               |
      '-AS--(--fullselect--)--DEFINITION ONLY--+-------------------+-'
                                               '-| copy-options |--'
                             .-ON COMMIT DELETE ROWS---.
>----*--+--------------+--*--+------------------------+---*--NOT LOGGED--*->
        '-WITH REPLACE-'     '-ON COMMIT PRESERVE ROWS-'
>----+---------------------+---*------------------------------>
     '-IN--tablespace-name--'
```

You can also define an identity column in a temporary table

**Figure 8.19** Example of Creating a USER Temporary Table Space

```
CREATE USER TEMPORARY TABLESPACE usertempspace
    MANAGED BY SYSTEM USING ('d:\sqlsp\usertempspace') ;
```

At database creation time, a default temporary table space TEMPSPACE1 is created. It is a system temporary table space and cannot be used for temporary tables. Therefore you need to explicitly create a USER temporary table space. Figure 8.19 creates one called USERTEMPSPACE defined as System Managed Space (SMS). Refer to the DB2 SQL Reference for different table space options.

**Figure 8.20** Example of Declaring a Temporary Table

```
DECLARE GLOBAL TEMPORARY TABLE tempnewproj
      ( projno CHAR(6)
      , projname VARCHAR(24)
      , projsdate DATE
      , projedate DATE
      , category VARCHAR(10)
      , desc VARCHAR(100) )
      WITH REPLACE
      ON COMMIT PRESERVE ROWS
      NOT LOGGED
      IN usertempspace ;
```

Figure 8.20 declares the *tempnewproj* temporary table. The column definition clause is just like the one used for normal table creation except that BLOB, CLOB, DBCLOB,

LONG VARCHAR, LONG VARGRAPHIC, DATALINK, reference, and structured types cannot be used. NOT LOGGED is a mandatory clause that indicates logging is not performed. Due to the nature of a temporary table, there is no point of logging any changes or being able to restore such a table. This also means better performance. The IN clause specifies which USER temporary table space is to be used to store the temporary table. The ON COMMIT option allows you to specify whether you want to preserve or delete data in the temporary table on commit.

Before you can declare another temporary table with the same name in the same session, the temporary table has to be explicitly dropped. Alternatively, you can specify the WITH REPLACE option as shown in the example above so that DB2 will implicitly delete all data, drop the temporary table, and recreate it with the new definition. As a good practice, you should explicitly drop temporary tables after use and specify the WITH REPLACE option during temporary table declaration.

The WITH REPLACE option is very important when connection pooling is used. Connection pooling is a mechanism to reuse database connections so that resources are not allocated and deallocated on demand. These operations are quite costly especially when there are large numbers of connections that perform relatively short transactions. Since connections are not released, it is possible that previously used temporary tables are not cleaned up. The next application using that connection may pick up data left from the previous execution.

In some cases, you may want to store a large amount of data in temporary tables. Just like accessing data from a normal table, you still want to avoid table scans as much as possible. Therefore, DB2 allows you to create indexes on temporary tables. Creation of indexes is the same as for persistent tables but remember that temporary tables have to be referenced with the SESSION schema.

## 8.2.2 Using Temporary Tables in SQL Procedures

You can declare, manipulate, and drop temporary tables in an SQL procedure. To better explain the characteristics and usage of temporary tables, the following example is used:

A project deployment manager is responsible for assigning projects to employees according to their skills and availability. When a project is approved, the project manager will assess it and assign it to appropriate staff. Three SQL procedures are used to automate the assignment process. The first SQL procedure crtnewproj accepts information about the project as input parameters. A temporary table is declared in the SQL procedure and all the information is inserted into it. crtnewproj then calls two other SQL procedures, deptsearch and staffsearch, to evaluate the project requirements and assign it to staff accordingly. A flow diagram is shown in Figure 8.21.

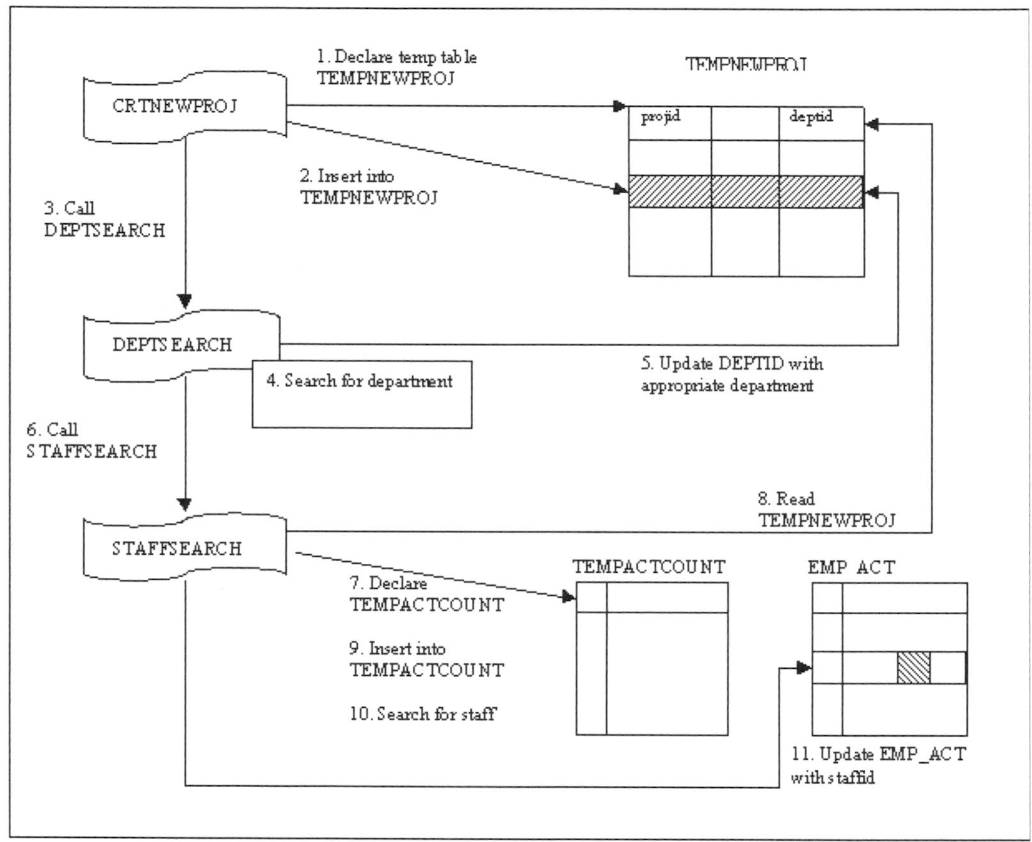


**Figure 8.21** Flow Diagram of Assigning Project to a Staff Member

**Figure 8.22** SQL Procedure CRTNEWPROJ

```
CREATE PROCEDURE crtnewproj
    ( IN p_projno CHAR(6)
    , IN p_projname VARCHAR(24)
    , IN p_actno SMALLINT
    , IN p_projsdate CHAR(10)
    , IN p_projedate CHAR(10)
    , IN p_category VARCHAR(20)
    , IN p_desc VARCHAR(100) )
    SPECIFIC crtnewproj
    LANGUAGE SQL
```

```
cnp: BEGIN
    -- DECLARE VARIABLES                                              -- (1)
    DECLARE v_dynStmt VARCHAR(100);
    DECLARE at_end int default 0;
    DECLARE SQLSTATE CHAR(5) DEFAULT '00000';

    -- DECLARE CONDITIONS                                             -- (2)
    DECLARE TTABLE_EXIST CONDITION FOR SQLSTATE '42710';
    DECLARE TTBSP_NOTFOUND CONDITION FOR SQLSTATE '42704';

    -- DECLARE STATEMENTS                                             -- (3)
    DECLARE s1 STATEMENT;

    -- DECLARE CURSORS                                                -- (4)
    DECLARE cursor1 CURSOR WITH RETURN FOR s1;

    -- DECLARE HANDLERS                                               -- (5)
    DECLARE EXIT HANDLER FOR TTBSP_NOTFOUND
       RESIGNAL SQLSTATE '70001'
         SET MESSAGE_TEXT = 'User temporary table space does not exists';
    DECLARE CONTINUE HANDLER FOR NOT FOUND
       SET at_end=1;

    -- DECLARE TEMPORARY TABLES                                       -- (6)
    DECLARE GLOBAL TEMPORARY TABLE tempnewproj
        ( projno CHAR(6)
        , projname VARCHAR(24)
        , actno SMALLINT
        , projsdate DATE
        , projedate DATE
        , category VARCHAR(20)
        , deptno CHAR(3) )
        WITH REPLACE
        ON COMMIT PRESERVE ROWS
        NOT LOGGED
        IN USERTEMPSPACE;

    -- Procedure body
    INSERT INTO session.tempnewproj
      VALUES
         ( p_projno
         , p_projname
         , p_actno
         , DATE( p_projsdate )
         , DATE( p_projedate )
         , p_category
         , NULL );
    COMMIT;                                                           -- (7)
    CALL deptsearch();
    CALL staffsearch();
    DROP TABLE session.tempnewproj;                                   -- (8)

END cnp
```

Let's go through the *crtnewproj* procedure in Figure 8.22. The temporary table tempnewproj is declared at (6) with seven columns and the WITH REPLACE and ON COMMIT PRESERVE ROWS options. Information stored in *tempnewproj* is intended for use in other SQL procedure calls of the same session, therefore you want to preserve all rows in the temporary table on COMMIT. Note that if ROLLBACK is specified at (7) instead of a COMMIT, tempnewproj declared at (6) will be dropped. In addition, if a nonempty tempnewproj temporary table already exists before this SQL procedure is called, a ROLLBACK will only restore the previous table definition and all its data is lost. As discussed above, you should explicitly drop the temporary table after use as shown at (8).

Notice that in the script, the temporary table is referenced through schema SESSION. Temporary tables are not owned by SYSADM, or DBADM, or a particular user. They belong to the session in which they are created. All temporary tables belong to schema SESSION. You have to fully qualify the temporary tables with SESSION for all temporary table references otherwise DB2 will look for a persistent table in the current schema instead.

*A table space not exist* handler, *ttbsp_notfound*, is defined in (5). Checking for existence of a user-temporary table space is recommended in case, for some reason, the temporary table space is not available. This type of error should be handled.

**Figure 8.23** SQL Procedure DEPTSEARCH

```
CREATE PROCEDURE deptsearch ()
    SPECIFIC deptsearch
    LANGUAGE SQL

ds: BEGIN
    -- DECLARE VARIABLES
    DECLARE v_dynStmt VARCHAR(100);
    DECLARE v_category VARCHAR(20);
    DECLARE v_deptno CHAR(3);
    DECLARE SQLSTATE CHAR(5) DEFAULT '00000';

    -- DECLARE CONDITIONS
    DECLARE TAB_NOTFOUND CONDITION FOR SQLSTATE '42704';

    -- DECLARE STATEMENTS
    DECLARE selectstmt STATEMENT;
    DECLARE updatestmt STATEMENT;

    -- DECLARE CURSORS
    DECLARE c_temptab CURSOR FOR selectstmt;

    -- DECLARE HANDLERS
```

```
    DECLARE EXIT HANDLER FOR TAB_NOTFOUND
       RESIGNAL SQLSTATE '70000'
         SET MESSAGE_TEXT = 'Table not found';

    -- Procedure body
    SET v_dynStmt = 'SELECT category FROM session.tempnewproj';          -- (1)
    PREPARE selectstmt FROM v_dynStmt;
    OPEN c_temptab;
    FETCH c_temptab INTO v_category;
    CLOSE c_temptab;

    VALUES                                                               -- (2)
        CASE UPPER( v_category )
        WHEN 'SPIFFY' THEN 'A00'
        WHEN 'PLANNING' THEN 'B01'
        WHEN 'DATAMANAGEMENT' THEN 'C01'
        WHEN 'DEVELOPMENT' THEN 'D01'
        WHEN 'MANUFACTURING' THEN 'D11'
        WHEN 'ADMINISTRATION' THEN 'D21'
        WHEN 'HARDWARE' THEN 'E01'
        WHEN 'OPERATIONS' THEN 'E11'
        WHEN 'SOFTWARE' THEN 'E21'
        ELSE 'NA'
        END
    INTO v_deptno;

    SET v_dynStmt = 'UPDATE session.tempnewproj SET deptno = ?'          -- (3)
    PREPARE updatestmt FROM v_dynStmt;
    EXECUTE updatestmt USING v_deptno;

END ds
```

The procedure in Figure 8.23 performs a search to find a department that can handle the new project with the category provided. The project keyword stored in category in the temporary table is extracted at (1). Dynamic SQL is required here because *session.tempnewproj* is unknown at compile time, and is not known until it is declared in SQL procedure *crtnewproj*. CASE statements used at (2) assign the new project to the appropriate department number. Of course in a real scenario, more sophisticated logic might be used. Once a department number is found, it is then inserted into the tempnewproj temporary table and will be used by the next SQL procedure STAFF-SEARCH.

**Figure 8.24** SQL Procedure STAFFSEARCH

```
CREATE PROCEDURE staffsearch ()
    SPECIFIC staffsearch
    LANGUAGE SQL

ss: BEGIN
    -- DECLARE VARIABLES
    DECLARE v_dynStmt VARCHAR(100);
    DECLARE v_category VARCHAR(20);
    DECLARE v_deptno CHAR(3);
    DECLARE v_empno CHAR(6) DEFAULT NULL;
    DECLARE v_projno CHAR(6);
    DECLARE v_actno SMALLINT;
    DECLARE v_emsdate DATE;
    DECLARE v_emedate DATE;
    DECLARE v_numjob INT;
    DECLARE v_foundstaff INT DEFAULT 0;
    DECLARE SQLSTATE CHAR(5) DEFAULT '00000';

    -- DECLARE CONDITIONS
    DECLARE tab_notfound CONDITION FOR SQLSTATE '42704';

    -- DECLARE STATEMENTS
    DECLARE selectstmt STATEMENT;
    DECLARE selectstmt2 STATEMENT;
    DECLARE insertstmt STATEMENT;

    -- DECLARE CURSORS
    DECLARE c_temptab CURSOR FOR selectstmt;
    DECLARE c_emptab CURSOR FOR selectstmt2;

    -- DECLARE HANDLERS
    DECLARE CONTINUE HANDLER FOR NOT FOUND
    SET v_foundstaff=1;

    DECLARE EXIT HANDLER FOR tab_notfound
       RESIGNAL SQLSTATE '70000'
         SET MESSAGE_TEXT = 'Table not found';

    -- DECLARE TEMPORARY TABLE
    DECLARE GLOBAL TEMPORARY TABLE tempactcount                          -- (1)
      (empno CHAR(6), numjob INT)
      WITH REPLACE
      ON COMMIT PRESERVE ROWS
      NOT LOGGED
      IN USERTEMPSPACE;

    -- Procedure body
    SET v_dynStmt = 'SELECT projno, actno, projsdate, projedate, deptno '
                 || 'FROM session.tempnewproj';
    PREPARE selectstmt FROM v_dynStmt;
```

```
    OPEN c_temptab;
    FETCH c_temptab INTO v_projno, v_actno, v_emsdate, v_emedate, v_deptno;
    CLOSE c_temptab;

    -- search the employee table to find all staffs under the department
    -- order those employees in job order
    INSERT INTO session.tempactcount                                    -- (2)
        ( SELECT empno, count(*) AS numact FROM emp_act GROUP BY (empno) )
        UNION
        ( SELECT empno, 0 FROM employee EXCEPT SELECT empno, 0 FROM emp_act );

    -- search those employee against emp_act,
    -- if employee has more than 2 jobs, choose the next one
    SET v_dynStmt = 'SELECT empno FROM employee WHERE workdept=? ORDER BY
edlevel DESC';
    PREPARE selectstmt2 FROM v_dynStmt;
    OPEN c_emptab USING v_deptno;                                       -- (3)
    WHILE v_foundstaff=0 DO
        FETCH c_emptab INTO v_empno;
        SELECT numjob
        INTO v_numjob
        FROM session.tempactcount
        WHERE empno=v_empno;
        IF v_numjob < 2 THEN
            SET v_foundstaff=1;
        END IF;
    END WHILE;
    CLOSE c_emptab;

    IF v_empno IS NULL THEN
        SET v_empno='NOTASN';
    END IF;

    SET v_dynStmt = 'INSERT INTO emp_act
                     (empno, projno, actno, emptime, emstdate, emendate)
                     VALUES (?, ?, ?, NULL, ?, ?)';
    PREPARE insertstmt FROM v_dynStmt;
    EXECUTE insertstmt
        USING v_empno, v_projno, v_actno, v_emsdate, v_emedate;
    DROP TABLE session.tempactcount;

END ss
```

The example in Figure 8.24 uses the department number found in the *deptsearch* stored procedure and searches for a staff member for project assignment. The search logic here is to choose an employee with the highest education level from the department. It is assumed that higher education level correlates to an employee's capacity to handle a project. However if the employee is already working on more than two projects, the next eligible employee will be considered.

Cursor c_emptab shown at (3) contains only employee numbers that belong to the department. Each employee number is then checked against the emp_act table for eligibility. Table emp_act stores information such as owner and start and end time of the project. To search through this table and perform a count on the number of projects assigned for each employee, one option is to perform 'SELECT COUNT(*) FROM emp_act WHERE EMPNO=v_empno' for each row of the cursor. If the count is greater than two, move on to the next row because the employee is already working on two or more projects. COUNT(*) is usually costly and you want to minimize its usage as much as possible. In this example, the GROUP BY function, UNION, and EXCEPT operators are used instead. Let's break down the statement at (2) and discuss each part separately. Figure 8.25 shows the output of the first half of the UNION operator. It groups the result with empno and provides a total of each occurrence of the employee number in the numact column.

**Figure 8.25** Results of Statement with GROUP BY

```
SELECT empno, count(*) AS numact FROM emp_act GROUP BY (empno);

EMPNO  NUMACT
------ -----------
000010           3
000020           2
000030           2
000050           2
000070           1
000090           1
000100           1
000110           1
000130           2
000140           5
000150           2
000160           1
000170           3
000180           1
000190           2
000200           2
000210           2
000220           1
000230           5
000240           2
000250          10
000260           7
000270           7
000280           1
000290           1
000300           1
000310           1
```

```
000320          2
000330          2
000340          2
```

Notice that the statement does not contain every employee in the company, so employees that are currently not working on any project should be included with number of activity *numact* sets to zero. The second half of the UNION operator uses EXCEPT to get the employee numbers from the employee table that are not in the *emp_act* table. Examine Figure 8.26 for the result of the EXCEPT operator.

**Figure 8.26** Results of Statement with EXCEPT Operator

```
(SELECT empno, 0 FROM employee) EXCEPT (SELECT empno, 0 FROM emp_act);
EMPNO  2
------ -----------
000060          0
000120          0
```

The UNION operator then combines the two result sets and inserts it into a temporary table called *tempactcount*. Declaration of the temporary table at (1) of Figure 8.24 is very similar to the one illustrated in SQL procedure *crtnewproj*. Temporary table *tempactcount* now contains the number of projects assigned for every single employee in the company. The next step is to simply use the *numact* column and verify that the eligible employee does not have more than two projects. If no employee is found to meet all the requirements, the employee number is set to 'NOTASN' indicating that the project is not assigned and requires special handling.

# 8.3 Working with Savepoints

## 8.3.1 Introduction to Application Savepoints

An application savepoint is a mechanism to control transactions within an application program such as an SQL procedure. There are three kinds of savepoints:

- Statement savepoint
- Compound SQL savepoint
- External savepoint

By default, a savepoint is internally created before the execution of each SQL statement. If an SQL statement fails with an error, DB2 will rollback to the internal savepoint. Statement savepoints are only used by DB2.

With a compound SQL savepoint, DB2 performs a block of SQL statements as one transaction. If any of the substatements fail, all actions within the compound SQL block are rolled back. What does this behavior sound like? Yes, it's atomic compound SQL.

Atomic compound SQL is actually a kind of savepoint named compound SQL savepoint. See Chapter 3, "Flow Control" for a discussion of atomic compound SQL. The third kind of savepoint is one that will be focused in this chapter. From this point on, any reference to the term savepoint implies external savepoint. An external savepoint is like an atomic compound block but with more granular transaction control. After establishing a savepoint, only the failed substatement will be rolled back, others can still be committed to the database.

Compared to the simple BEGIN ATOMIC... END keywords for atomic compound statements, external savepoints offer a few more options as shown below. Syntax diagrams for creating, releasing, and rolling back to a savepoint are shown in Figures 8.27, 8.28, and 8.29 respectively.

**Figure 8.27** Syntax Diagram of Creating a Savepoint

```
>>-SAVEPOINT--savepoint-name----+---------+-------------------->
                                '-UNIQUE--'
                                 .-ON ROLLBACK RETAIN LOCKS--.
>----ON ROLLBACK RETAIN CURSORS--+--------------------------+--><
```

**Figure 8.28** Syntax Diagram of Releasing a Savepoint

```
            .-TO-.
>>-RELEASE--+----+--SAVEPOINT--savepoint-name-----------------><
```

**Figure 8.29** Syntax Diagram of Rolling Back to a Savepoint

```
>>-ROLLBACK----+-------+-------------------------------------->
 >-----+-------------------------------------+------------------><
       '-TO SAVEPOINT--+-----------------+--'
                       '-savepoint-name--'
```

Before issuing the first substatement of the block, you need to create a savepoint and specify its characteristics. The keyword UNIQUE indicates that this savepoint name will not be reused in the transaction. The ON ROLLBACK RETAIN CURSORS is a mandatory clause that describes cursor behavior within the savepoint. If a cursor is opened or referenced in a savepoint, rolling back to the savepoint will keep the cursor open and positioned at the next logical row of the result set. At the completion of a transaction, DB2 by default releases all database locks acquired in it. This is also the default behavior when you rollback to a savepoint. With the ON ROLLBACK RETAIN LOCKS option, DB2 will not release locks obtained within the savepoint.

After the last substatement of the block, you may choose to rollback to the savepoint or release the savepoint. Once the savepoint is released, rollback to the savepoint is no longer possible. A savepoint is implicitly released when the transaction is completed. Rolling back to a savepoint is not considered the end of a transaction, therefore the savepoint is not released.

Nested savepoints are not supported. If you want to establish another savepoint with the same name within the same transaction, you need to explicitly release the savepoint or end the whole transaction with COMMIT or ROLLBACK statements.

Atomic Compound SQL is a type of savepoint and nested savepoints are not supported. Therefore an external savepoint cannot be created in an atomic compound block. You can only create external savepoints in non-atomic compound blocks.

## 8.3.2 Considerations When Using Savepoints

Cursor blocking, as discussed in Chapter 4,"Cursors and Result Sets," enables DB2 to retrieve a block of data for cursors rather than getting one row of data per request. With this option enabled, using a cursor within the scope of a savepoint may retrieve incorrect data. The example in Figure 8.30, extracted from the DB2 Application Development Guide, demonstrates this problem.

**Figure 8.30** Example of Savepoint Usage with Cursor Blocking

```
CREATE TABLE t1( c1 INTEGER );
          DECLARE CURSOR c1 AS 'SELECT c1 FROM t1 ORDER BY c1';
          INSERT INTO t1 VALUES ( 1 );                                     -- (1)
          SAVEPOINT showFetchDelete ON ROLLBACK RETAINS CURSORS            -- (2)
             INSERT INTO t1 VALUES ( 2 );                                  -- (3)
             INSERT INTO t1 VALUES ( 3 );
             OPEN CURSOR c1;
             FETCH c1; -- get first value and cursor block                 -- (4)
          ROLLBACK TO SAVEPOINT;                                           -- (5)
FETCH c1; -- retrieves second value from cursor block                      -- (6)
```

A single row is inserted into table *t1* at (1). A savepoint is created at (2) and two more rows are inserted into *t1* at (3). After the first row of the cursor is fetched at (4), there is a request to rollback to the savepoint at (5). At this point, the new rows inserted at (3) are rolled back. According to the behavior of ROLLBACK TO SAVEPOINT, the cursor will remain open and positioned on the next logical row. Since a block of rows for the cursor is already retrieved and stored in the memory, the phantom rows are still visible to the application. When the next row is fetched at (6), a phantom row is returned. To prevent this from happening, you may consider not enabling cursor blocking if a savepoint is used in the application. Set the DB2 registry variable DB2_SQLROUTINE_PREPOPT="BLOCKING OFF" to disable cursor blocking.

Data definition language (DDL) is supported within a savepoint. ROLLBACK TO SAVEPOINT will drop or undo changes made to database objects. If a cursor references any of these objects, ROLLBACK TO SAVEPOINT will cause the cursor to be marked invalid because the database object may no longer exist.

During creation of a table, the NOT LOGGED INITIALLY option can be specified to change the default logging behavior for the table. If it is specified and enabled, DB2 will not log any changes made to the table in the same unit of work. Performance of such operations is enhanced since database logging does not take place. When the NOT LOGGED INITIALLY option is used in a savepoint either through a CREATE TABLE or ALTER TABLE statement, rollback to savepoint will be upgraded to unit of work rollback. In other words, the whole transaction is rolled back.

## 8.3.3 Using Application Savepoints in SQL Procedures

It is now a good time to show how savepoints can be used in an SQL procedure. In Figure 8.31, an SQL procedure *bonus_incr* is illustrated. It is used to automate bonus increases for employees in a company. Company ABC is doing so well that every employee is getting a ten percent increase in bonus. Given that the total amount of bonuses for some department is already quite high, management has decided that if the total bonus of a department is greater than $3000, its employees will not receive the increase immediately and will be evaluated individually.

**Figure 8.31** SQL Procedure BONUS_INCR

```
CREATE PROCEDURE bonus_incr ()
    SPECIFIC bonus_incr
    LANGUAGE SQL

bi: BEGIN
    -- DECLARE VARIABLES
    DECLARE v_dept, v_actdept CHAR(3);
    DECLARE v_bonus, v_deptbonus, v_newbonus DECIMAL(9,2);
    DECLARE v_empno CHAR(6);
    DECLARE v_atend SMALLINT DEFAULT 0;

     -- DECLARE CURSORS
    DECLARE c_sales CURSOR WITH HOLD FOR                                  -- (1)
        SELECT workdept, bonus, empno FROM employee
        ORDER BY workdept;

    -- DECLARE HANDLERS
    DECLARE CONTINUE HANDLER FOR NOT FOUND
        SET v_atend=1;
    DECLARE EXIT HANDLER FOR SQLEXCEPTION                                 -- (2)
        SET v_atend=1;

    -- Procedure body
    OPEN c_sales;
    FETCH c_sales INTO v_dept, v_bonus, v_empno;

    nextdept:                                                             -- (3)
        IF v_atend = 0 THEN
            SAVEPOINT svpt_bonus_incr ON ROLLBACK RETAIN CURSORS;         -- (4)
            SET v_actdept = v_dept;
            SET v_deptbonus = 0;
            WHILE ( v_actdept = v_dept ) AND ( v_atend = 0 ) DO           -- (5)
                SET v_newbonus = v_bonus * 1.1;
                UPDATE employee                                           -- (6)
                    SET bonus = v_newbonus
                    WHERE empno = v_empno;
                SET v_deptbonus = v_deptbonus + v_newbonus;
                FETCH c_sales INTO v_dept, v_bonus, v_empno;
            END WHILE;

            IF v_deptbonus <= 3000.00 THEN
                COMMIT;                                                   -- (7)
            ELSE
                ROLLBACK TO SAVEPOINT svpt_bonus_incr;                    -- (8)
                RELEASE SAVEPOINT svpt_bonus_incr;                        -- (9)
            END IF;
            GOTO nextdept;                                               -- (10)
        END IF;

END bi
```

At statement (1), a cursor is declared to retrieve a result set of every employee sorted by department number. The statement at (3) defines a savepoint *svpt_bonus_incr*. This is the point to which the application can roll back. The WHILE loop iterates through every employee in a single department and performs the bonus increase. If the total amount of bonus for a department is 3000 or less, changes made since the savepoint are committed at (7). In order to keep the cursor open so that other departments can be processed, the cursor is declared at (1) with the WITH HOLD option. On the other hand, if the total bonus for a department is greater than 3000, updates to the database since the last savepoint will be rollback at (8). The savepoint is also released at (9) so that it can be created again at (3). The GOTO statement at (10) routes the execution pointer back to the *nextdept* label, allowing continuous processing of the next department.

What happens if a statement used in the savepoint fails? Does DB2 roll back only the statement, to the savepoint block, or the whole SQL procedure? The answer depends on whether a HANDLER is defined to catch the error. Without a HANDLER declared for the error, any statement failure raised in a savepoint will cause all changes made in the SQL procedure to be rolled back regardless if they are defined inside or outside of the savepoint. Conversely, if a HANDLER is defined for the error, only the failed statement is rolled back. This is the expected behavior when a savepoint is used. To make the example in Figure 8.31 more complete, an EXIT HANDLER is defined at (2). This makes sure that only the statement in error is rolled back and exits the stored procedure call.

# 8.4 Working with Large Objects

## 8.4.1 Introduction to Large Objects

Large objects are objects that can store data greater than 32k bytes. Starting with DB2 UDB v7.1, the maximum length of a VARCHAR data type is 32,672 bytes. However, that is often still not large enough to hold data such as a long XML document, an audio file, or a picture. You can store such data in large objects (LOBs) as strings of up to two gigabytes in size. Three kinds of LOB data types are provided by DB2 namely Binary Large Objects (BLOBs), single-byte Character Large Objects (CLOBs), and Double-Byte Character Large Objects (DBCLOBs).

With regular data types, DB2 uses buffer pool(s) to cache data and index pages for faster in-memory reads and writes. However, LOBs can be as large as two gigabytes and the system may not have that much memory. Even if there is, it does not make sense to page all existing data out of the buffer pool just to serve one LOB data object. Therefore, LOBs are accessed directly from disk without going through the buffer pool. This is called a direct I/O operation. As you may imagine, such access is slower than in-memory buffer pool access.

For storage and performance reasons, do not use LOBs for small data values. Use VARCHAR or VARCHAR FOR BIT DATA if possible which can hold a maximum of 32,672 bytes of data.

## 8.4.2 Using Large Objects in SQL Procedures

You can use large objects as IN, OUT, or INOUT parameters of an SQL procedure. Figure 8.32 demonstrates very simple manipulations of large objects and returns a CLOB to the stored procedure caller.

**Figure 8.32** SQL Procedure STAFFRESUME

```
CREATE PROCEDURE staffresume
    ( IN p_empno CHAR(6)
    , OUT p_resume CLOB(1M) )
    SPECIFIC staffresume
    LANGUAGE SQL

sr: BEGIN
    SELECT resume INTO p_resume
        FROM emp_resume
        WHERE empno=p_empno AND resume_format = 'ascii';
    INSERT INTO emp_resume
        VALUES
        ( p_empno
        , 'backupcopy'
        , p_resume );

END sr
```

## 8.5 Chapter Summary

With the SQL Procedural Language and DB2 advanced features, you can write more complex code segments and wrap them into SQL procedures. As you have seen in this chapter, DB2's advanced features enable you to code application logic more easily and effectively. Utilizing these features in SQL procedures can result in performance gains and increased code manageability. As you learn more and more about DB2, you will find that you can write very powerful code with the combination of DB2 advanced features and SQL procedures.

CHAPTER 9

# Deploying SQL Procedures

### In this chapter, you will learn:

- several methods for deploying SQL procedures;
- the pros and cons associated with each of the various deployment methods;
- considerations for deploying and working with SQL procedures.

*Deployment* of SQL procedures is the task of moving SQL procedures from one environment to another, for example, moving SQL procedures from a development environment to a test or production environment. This chapter discusses several ways in which this can be done. The method chosen to deploy will depend on your requirements.

## 9.1 How to Deploy SQL Procedures

### 9.1.1 Deploying SQL Procedures Using DDL

The most straightforward way to deploy SQL procedures is to export them in DDL form, from the source environment and apply them against the target environment. The *export* command in the DB2 Development Center can be used to generate the DDL file. To do this, after launching the DB2 Development Center, right-click on the Stored Procedures folder within a project and select Export (Figure 9.1) to launch the Export Wizard.

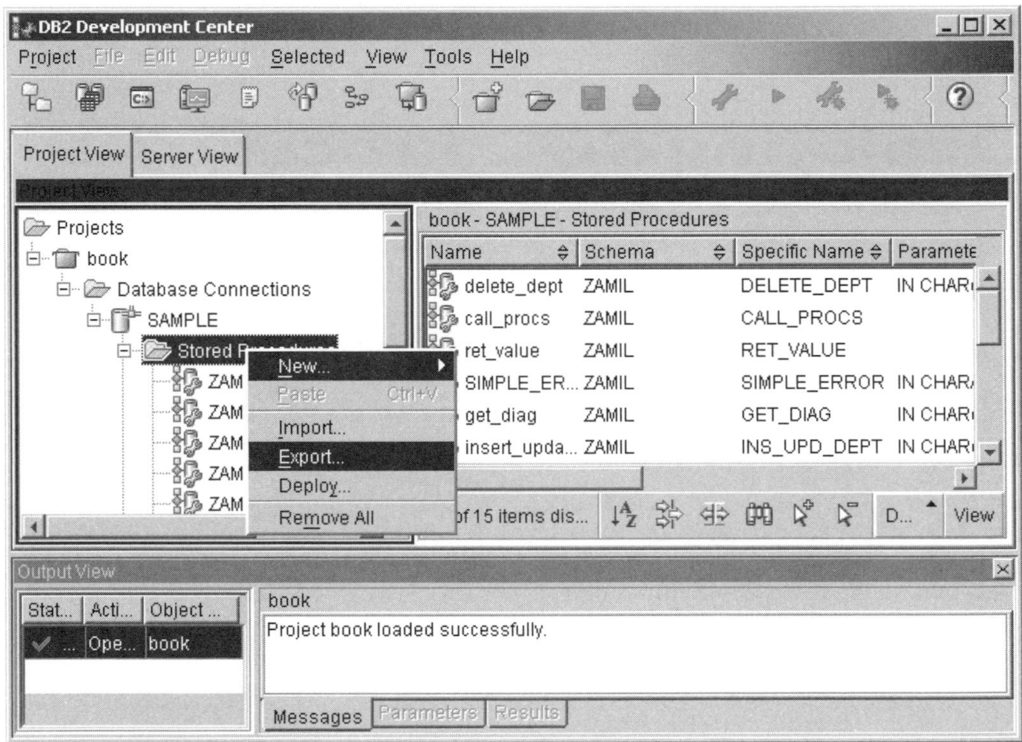


**Figure 9.1** Initiating Export

The first screen of the wizard gives you the option of choosing which SQL Stored Procedures you want to export (Figure 9.2).

Select the procedures you want to export in the order that you want to create them. For example if there are any inter-dependencies between the stored procedures, ensure that the called procedures are selected before the calling procedure.

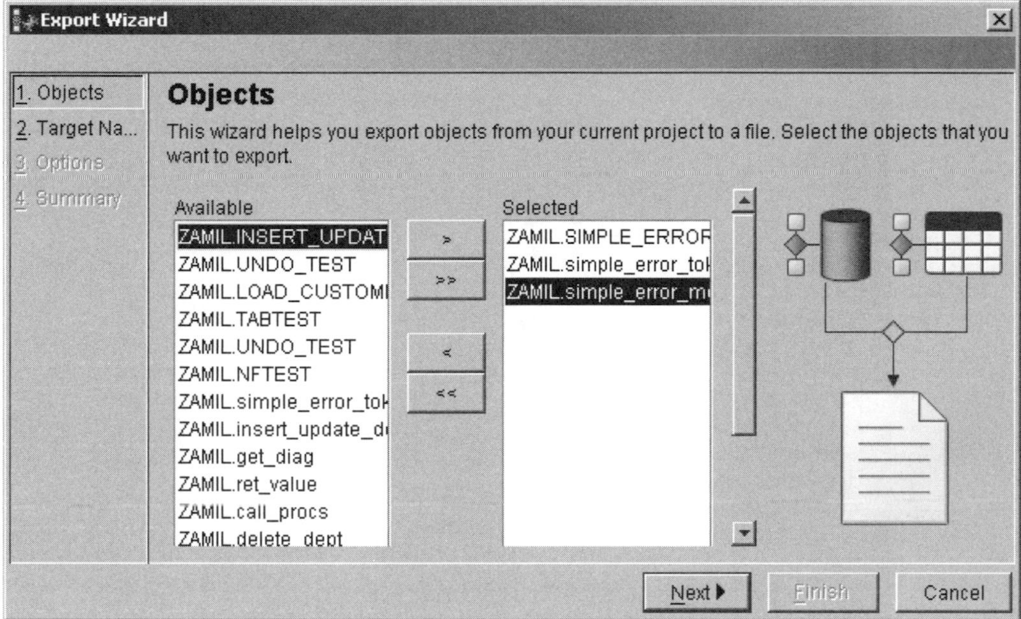


**Figure 9.2** Selecting Stored Procedures for Export

Clicking *Next* will take you to the next screen in the wizard, in which you can specify the location and name of an output file. In the screenshot (Figure 9.3), the target file-name is *sample_proc*. The generated file will be a .DB2 file, contained in a zipped file with the same name.

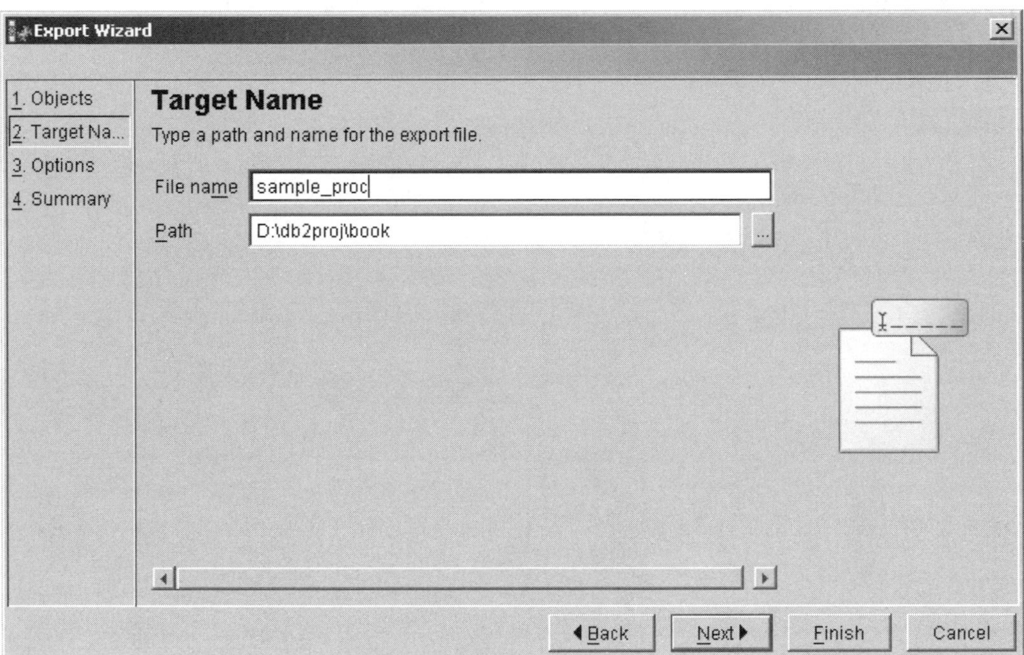


**Figure 9.3** Saving Export File

The next screen (Figure 9.4) offers up some alternatives for the output file. To export in DDL form, you need to select the *Create an export script* radio button. The *Export as project* radio button would be used if you wanted to import as a project. The *Include source files* checkbox can be checked or unchecked. It makes no difference when exporting SQL procedures; it is only used when exporting Java stored procedures.

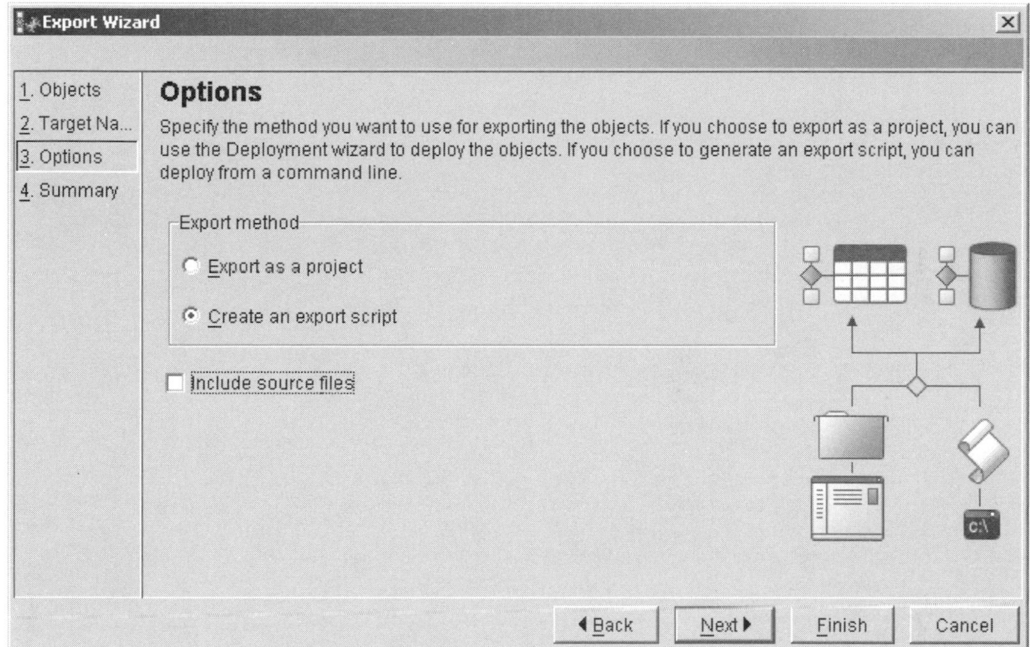


**Figure 9.4** Export Options

The next screen in the wizard just summarizes the options that were selected; clicking *Finish* will generate the file. Figure 9.5 shows the contents of the output file. Notice the first line of the output file is a database CONNECT statement that has been commented out. The file can be modified to remove the comments and specify the values for a different database, user and password. Notice also that the statement termination character is the @ symbol instead of the semi-colon (;). This is done in order to remove ambiguity, since the SQL procedure body contains embedded semi-colons.

**Figure 9.5** Contents of Export File

```
-- connect to SAMPLE user DB2ADMIN using Password
CREATE PROCEDURE simple_error ( IN p_midinit CHAR
                              ,IN p_empno CHAR(6)
                              ,OUT p_sqlstate_out CHAR(5)
                              ,OUT p_sqlcode_out INT )

    SPECIFIC simple_error
```

```
    LANGUAGE SQL
se: BEGIN
   -- Declare return codes
   DECLARE SQLSTATE CHAR(5) DEFAULT '00000';
   DECLARE SQLCODE INT DEFAULT 0;
   -- Declare condition handlers
   DECLARE EXIT HANDLER FOR SQLEXCEPTION
        SELECT SQLSTATE
              ,SQLCODE
          INTO p_sqlstate_out
              ,p_sqlcode_out
          FROM sysibm.sysdummy1;
   DECLARE CONTINUE HANDLER FOR SQLWARNING
        SELECT SQLSTATE
              ,SQLCODE
          INTO p_sqlstate_out
              ,p_sqlcode_out
          FROM sysibm.sysdummy1;
   DECLARE CONTINUE HANDLER FOR NOT FOUND
        SELECT SQLSTATE
              ,SQLCODE
          INTO p_sqlstate_out
              ,p_sqlcode_out
          FROM sysibm.sysdummy1;
   -- Procedure logic
   -- Initialize output parameters with defaults
   VALUES (SQLSTATE, SQLCODE)
     INTO p_sqlstate_out
         ,p_sqlcode_out;
   UPDATE employee                                                    -- (1)
      SET midinit = p_midinit
    WHERE empno = p_empno;
END se
@
CREATE PROCEDURE simple_error_token ( IN p_midinit CHAR
                                     ,IN p_empno CHAR(6)
                                     ,OUT p_sqlcode_out int
                                     ,OUT p_sqlstate_out char(5)
                                     ,OUT p_token_string VARCHAR(100)
                                     ,OUT p_message VARCHAR(500) )
    SPECIFIC simple_error_token
    LANGUAGE SQL
setk: BEGIN
    -- Declare variables
    DECLARE SQLSTATE CHAR(5) DEFAULT '00000';
    DECLARE SQLCODE INT DEFAULT 0;
   -- Declare condition handlers
   DECLARE EXIT HANDLER FOR SQLEXCEPTION
        RETURN 1;
   DECLARE EXIT HANDLER FOR SQLEXCEPTION
      BEGIN
        DECLARE CONTINUE HANDLER FOR SQLEXCEPTION
           GET DIAGNOSTICS EXCEPTION 1 p_message = MESSAGE_TEXT
                                      ,p_token_string = DB2_TOKEN_STRING;
        SELECT SQLCODE
```

```
                ,SQLSTATE
            INTO p_sqlcode_out
                ,p_sqlstate_out
            FROM sysibm.sysdummy1;
          RESIGNAL;
        END;
    DECLARE EXIT HANDLER FOR SQLWARNING
        BEGIN
          DECLARE CONTINUE HANDLER FOR SQLWARNING
             GET DIAGNOSTICS EXCEPTION 1 p_message = MESSAGE_TEXT
                                        ,p_token_string = DB2_TOKEN_STRING;
           SELECT SQLCODE
                ,SQLSTATE
            INTO p_sqlcode_out
                ,p_sqlstate_out
            FROM sysibm.sysdummy1;
          RESIGNAL;
        END;
    DECLARE EXIT HANDLER FOR NOT FOUND
        BEGIN
          DECLARE CONTINUE HANDLER FOR NOT FOUND
             GET DIAGNOSTICS EXCEPTION 1 p_message = MESSAGE_TEXT
                                        ,p_token_string = DB2_TOKEN_STRING;
           SELECT SQLCODE
                ,SQLSTATE
            INTO p_sqlcode_out
                ,p_sqlstate_out
            FROM sysibm.sysdummy1;
          RESIGNAL;
          RETURN 1;
        END;
    -- Procedure logic
    SET p_token_string =  '';
    --SET p_sqlcode_out = SQLCODE;
    --SET p_sqlstate_out = SQLSTATE;
    VALUES (SQLCODE, SQLSTATE)
      INTO p_sqlcode_out, p_sqlstate_out;
    GET DIAGNOSTICS EXCEPTION 1 p_message = MESSAGE_TEXT
                                ,p_token_string = DB2_TOKEN_STRING;
    RETURN 1;
    UPDATE emp                                                             -- (1)
        SET midinit = p_midinit
     WHERE empno = p_empno;
END setk
@
CREATE PROCEDURE simple_error_message ( IN p_midinit CHAR
                                       ,IN p_empno CHAR(6)
                                       ,OUT p_error_message VARCHAR(300) )
    SPECIFIC simple_error_msg
    LANGUAGE SQL
sem: BEGIN
    -- Declare condition handlers
    DECLARE EXIT HANDLER FOR SQLEXCEPTION
         GET DIAGNOSTICS EXCEPTION 1 p_error_message = MESSAGE_TEXT;
    -- Procedure logic
```

```
   SET p_error_message = '';
   UPDATE employee                                               -- (1)
      SET empno = '000020'
    WHERE empno = p_empno;
END sem
@
```

In order to be able to use the script repeatedly against the same database, you can edit the file and insert DROP statements right before the CREATE statements in the script. To avoid ambiguity for over loaded procedures, it is good practice to use the SPECIFIC name of the procedure in the DROP statement.

It's a good idea to remove the comment on the CONNECT statement and insert a CONNECT RESET statement at the end of the file. When un-commenting the CONNECT statement, specify a database and user but remove *using <Password>* altogether. This way, every time the script is invoked, it will prompt you for a password. This will help catch situations in which the script is invoked inadvertently, because it gives you the option of canceling out at the password prompt.

There are other options for exporting SQL procedures. For example, you can SELECT the procedure body text directly from the system catalog tables and pipe the output directly to a file. If you want to have a more robust solution, then you can write a little SQL procedure to extract the procedure body, format the output and generate the corresponding DROP statements. However, since the utility exists in the DB2 Development Center, then why not use it?

Now that you have the SQL procedure in a DDL file, you can apply the script to a target environment. This can be done through the command line. Of course, you will have to make sure that any database objects that are accessed by any of the SQL procedures have been created prior to running the script on the target server. To import (and create the SQL procedures), you can enter the following from the command line:

```
db2 -td@ -f SAMPLE_PROC.db2
```

The *-td@* option specifies that the @ symbol is to be used for the statement termination character and the *-f* option specifies that the input comes from a file. In order for the command to complete successfully, you must already have a supported C/C++ compiler installed and configured at the database server. Refer to Appendix B, "Setting up the Build Environment" for more details.

You may also have noticed while using the DB2 Development Center that there is an option to *Import*. You can use this option to import a SQL procedure, (instead of the command line option described above), however this option has limited use when importing from a file. Only one procedure can be imported at a time, and the input file can only contain CREATE PROCEDURE statements.

## 9.1.2 Using GET ROUTINE and PUT ROUTINE

If a supported compiler does not exist on the target server, the simple method described above of running a DDL script against the target environment will not work.

To help you deal with situations such as this, two CLP commands are available to you, namely GET ROUTINE and PUT ROUTINE. You need to have database administrator (DBADM) or higher authority to execute either of the commands.

GET ROUTINE retrieves necessary information about an SQL procedure from the source environment and places that information in an SQL archive (SAR) file. PUT ROUTINE deploys the SQL procedure to the target environment, taking the SAR file generated from the GET ROUTINE command as input.

Figure 9.6 shows the syntax diagram for the GET ROUTINE command.

**Figure 9.6** Syntax Diagram for GET ROUTINE

```
>>-GET ROUTINE--INTO--file_name--FROM--+----------+------------->
                                       '-SPECIFIC-'

>--PROCEDURE--routine_name--+-----------+---------------------><
                            '-HIDE BODY-'
```

As you can see, the command is self-explanatory. If the SPECIFIC keyword is used, then you must use the specific name of the procedure in place of *routine_name*, otherwise the procedure name must be used.

The HIDE BODY keyword is used in cases where you do not want to expose the content of the procedure when it is deployed. The text of the SQL procedure will not be inserted into the system catalog tables; only the compiled code for the SQL procedure will be transferred. This helps protect your code, since it can be used to hide the business logic contained in it.

Figure 9.7 shows two examples of the command.

**Figure 9.7** Example of GET ROUTINE

```
GET ROUTINE INTO procs/prod_ddl.sar
    FROM SPECIFIC PROCEDURE db2admin.proc_ddl HIDE BODY
GET ROUTINE INTO procs/simple_result_set.sar
    FROM SPECIFIC PROCEDURE db2admin.simple_result_set
```

Observe that you have to run this command once for each procedure that you want to deploy. This can get cumbersome, so Figure 9.8 demonstrates SQL to help you generate a command file for all SQL procedures in a given database. The path to where the SAR files will reside will need to be updated. You also have the option of changing the WHERE clause if you want to be more selective.

**Figure 9.8** Generate GET ROUTINE SQL Script

```
SELECT 'GET ROUTINE INTO procs\'
      || SPECIFICNAME || '.sar FROM SPECIFIC PROCEDURE '
      || RTRIM(PROCSCHEMA) || '.' || SPECIFICNAME
      || ' HIDE BODY' || '@'
  FROM SYSCAT.PROCEDURES
 WHERE LANGUAGE = 'SQL';
```

Assuming that the script is saved in a file called get_routine_script.db2, you can use the following command to direct the output to another file called get_routine_all.db2:

```
db2 -txf get_routine_script.db2 -z get_routine_all.db2
```

The *-x* option suppresses column headings and the *-z* option directs output to a file. Following is a sample of the contents of the get_routine_all.db2 file:

```
GET ROUTINE INTO procs\PROC_DDL.sar
    FROM SPECIFIC PROCEDURE DB2ADMIN.PROC_DDL HIDE BODY@
GET ROUTINE INTO procs\SIMPLE_RESULT_SET.sar
    FROM SPECIFIC PROCEDURE DB2ADMIN.SIMPLE_RESULT_SET HIDE BODY@
```

You can then run the get_routine_all.db2 file against the source database. This will extract all the information on SQL procedures into SAR files.

Create the directory in which you want to store the SAR files, prior to running the script. You may want to give it a descriptive name that indicates the date and time of when the SAR files were generated. Often, you will generate the SAR files, but at a later date, not remember when they were generated.

The SAR files can then be used by the PUT ROUTINE command to deploy the SQL Procedures to the target environment. Figure 9.9 shows the syntax diagram for the PUT ROUTINE command.

**Figure 9.9** Syntax Diagram for PUT ROUTINE

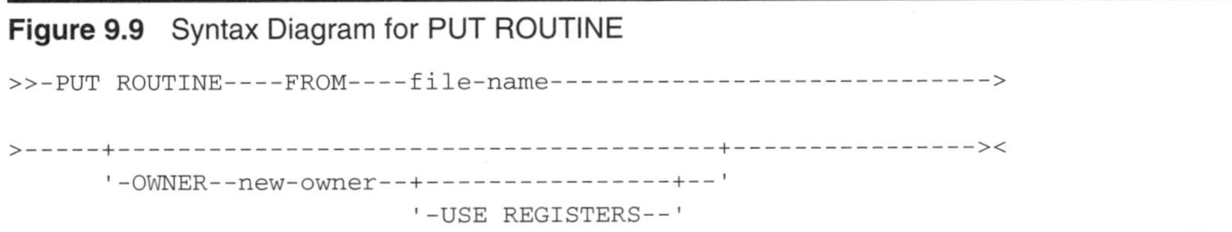

```
>>-PUT ROUTINE----FROM----file-name---------------------------->

>-----+-------------------------------------+---------------><
      '-OWNER--new-owner--+----------------+--'
                          '-USE REGISTERS--'
```

The options for the PUT ROUTINE command may not be as intuitive as the GET ROUTINE. Typically, the owner of the SQL procedure in a development environment is not the same as the owner of the procedure in the production environment. Hence, the PUT ROUTINE command gives you the option of overriding the owner by using the OWNER keyword when deploying. Additionally, the default schema names and the path for function resolution will also likely be different between environments. The register values for CURRENT SCHEMA and CURRENT PATH can be set on the target server, and can be used by the PUT ROUTINE command using the USE REGISTERS keyword.

Figure 9.10 shows two examples of the PUT ROUTINE command. In both of the examples, the OWNER of the SQL procedure on the target system will be the user *db2admin*. To issue this command, the user db2admin must have sufficient authority to create the procedure (user must have SYSADM or DBADM authority, or must have IMPLICIT SCHEMA authority on the database, or CREATEIN privilege on the default schema of the procedure).

**Figure 9.10** Example of PUT ROUTINE

```
PUT ROUTINE FROM procs/proc_ddl.sar OWNER db2admin
PUT ROUTINE FROM procs/simple_result_set.sar OWNER db2admin
```

You can use the sample script shown in Figure 9.11, (against the source database), to generate a script for each of your PUT ROUTINE statements.

**Figure 9.11** Generate PUT ROUTINE SQL Script

```
SELECT 'PUT ROUTINE FROM procs\'
      || SPECIFICNAME || '.sar OWNER db2admin@'
  FROM SYSCAT.PROCEDURES
 WHERE LANGUAGE = 'SQL';
```

Following is a sample of the output generated from this command (which would be run against the target database):

```
PUT ROUTINE FROM procs\PROC_DDL.sar OWNER db2admin@
PUT ROUTINE FROM procs\SIMPLE_RESULT_SET.sar OWNER db2admin@
```

The GET ROUTINE and PUT ROUTINE commands use the pre-installed procedures GET_ROUTINE_SAR() and PUT_ROUTINE_SAR() in schema SYSFUN. These procedures have been externalized, and can be used by you to write your own interface or application to perform the GET ROUTINE and PUT ROUTINE.

There is one limitation with this method of deployment which may not be obvious. SQL procedures get converted to C and are then compiled, so in essence, what these commands enable you to do is to distribute compiled code. It follows then that the operating system (OS) of the source and target environment must be the same.

As you might expect, the DB2 UDB versions of the source and target environments must be the same, although the target version can be at a higher fixpack level than the source.

On UNIX systems, special consideration should be given to the users and the owners of files. The instance owner must belong to the primary group of the fenced user. If these conditions are not met, the commands will not work.

Using GET ROUTINE and PUT ROUTINE is the primary method for SQL procedure distribution in packaged applications. For example, you could be a vendor developing an application that requires stored procedures. GET ROUTINE would be used to create the SAR files, for every OS that is supported by the application. PUT ROUTINE would be then used by the application's install process to deploy the procedures.

The two commands are also used in large organizations consisting of independent branch offices each with their own server. GET ROUTINE and PUT ROUTINE are ideal in this scenario, since they would not require each branch office server to have a supported C/C++ compiler just so SQL procedures can be distributed. Even in cases where a C/C++ compiler is available, the installation using these commands is faster, because the procedure does not have to be recompiled.

The DB2 Development Center can be used for quickly deploying stored procedures. Similar to the *Import* and *Export* options, a *Deploy* option is also available. In cases where you might have separate databases for development and test, the Deploy option allows you to quickly deploy procedures directly from the source database to the target database.

# 9.2 Deployment Considerations

## 9.2.1 Code Page Considerations

When building applications in mixed code-page environments, some thought needs to be given to deployment. For example, if the database server is created with a UNICODE codepage, a client with any codepage can connect to it.

As client applications connect to the database to invoke stored procedures, input character string parameters are converted from the client application's code page to the database server's code page. Since the stored procedure is on the database server, it uses the same code page as the database server, thus no more code page conversion will occur, until the stored procedure completes. At this point, all output character string parameters are converted to the client application's code page and sent back to the caller.

This implies that when building the stored procedure (which will later be deployed using GET ROUTINE or PUT ROUTINE) on a development or test server, the build steps (PREP, COMPILE and BIND) must be executed against a database with the same code page as the code page of the database on the target server.

## 9.2.2 Backup and Recovery Considerations

Although not directly related to deployment, you need to give special consideration to the recovery of a database and its SQL procedures.

Specifically, for databases containing SQL procedures, the RESTORE command or the first connection after the RESTORE command may fail. This will occur if the KEEPDARI DB2 configuration parameter is set to YES, and the DLL associated with the stored procedures are still resident in memory. To get around this, you need to restart the instance, prior to issuing the RESTORE command. Stopping the instance will unload any DLLs associated with the stored procedures from memory.

Always restart the instance prior to issuing a RESTORE, if your database contains SQL procedures.

## 9.3 Chapter Summary

This chapter has described several methods for deploying SQL procedures. One simple method described was exporting the procedure DDL via the DB2 Development Center, and then using the DB2 Command Line Processor to import it into the target database. The CLP commands GET ROUTINE and PUT ROUTINE were also shown as an alternative for deployment, in environments where the existence of a C/C++ compiler cannot be guaranteed on the target database server. Finally some topics that require special attention with respect to deployment, such as code pages and backup and recovery, were presented.

CHAPTER 10

# Working with Triggers and User-Defined Functions

### In this chapter, you will learn:

- how SQL PL for triggers and user-defined functions (UDFs) differ from that used for SQL stored procedures;
- what triggers and UDFs are, and when they should be used;
- how triggers can be used to transparently and consistently enforce logic across all applications that interact with the database;
- how UDFs can be used to simplify your application development efforts.

## 10.1 DB2 Support of SQL PL in Triggers and UDFs

Triggers and UDFs are database objects that help reduce the complexity of database application development. Before looking at any examples, a discussion of how DB2 supports SQL PL logic in these objects is required. Although the language syntax for SQL PL is consistent throughout DB2 from an application development perspective, the language implementation in DB2 to support SQL PL for stored procedures is completely different from that of triggers and UDFs.

When building an SQL procedure, DB2 will convert it into two components: a C language file and a DB2 bind file. The C file contains the procedural logic while the bind file contains the SQL for the procedure. The C code is then compiled into a library file that can be called by DB2 processes and the BIND file is bound to the database where it then becomes a package. When you execute the stored procedure, the library works hand in hand with the database package to execute SQL according to the stored procedure logic.

In contrast, SQL PL in triggers and UDFs are not implemented as libraries and packages. There is no compiled C component, nor is a bind file generated. When you use SQL PL in triggers and UDFs, the code is executed dynamically within the engine as a single dynamic compound statement. There are advantages and disadvantages to both implementations but a discussion of these differences is beyond the scope of this book.

The implementation differences result in some SQL PL elements that are supported in SQL procedures but not in triggers and UDFs. SQL PL support in triggers and UDFs is a subset of that in stored procedures and includes support for the following SQL PL elements:

```
DECLARE <variable>
FOR
GET DIAGNOSTICS
IF
ITERATE
LEAVE
SIGNAL
WHILE
SET
```

Note that although this chapter discusses triggers and UDFs, it is not a complete reference. The intent is simply to show you how to use SQL PL in them. For the full documentation of features and limitations, you should consult the *DB2 SQL Reference*.

## 10.2 Introduction to Triggers

Triggers are database objects associated with a table to define operations that should occur automatically upon an INSERT, UPDATE, or DELETE operation (hereafter called the triggering SQL statement) on that table. There is also another type of trigger, called an INSTEAD OF trigger, that can be defined on database views but are beyond the scope of this book. Operations performed by triggers occur within the database engine and are therefore transparent to the application.

There is often application logic (or rules) that should always be enforced across all applications. These rules may exist because data in one table may be related to data in others. If you have many applications that share a set of tables, it can be cumbersome to ensure that all applications follow and enforce these logic rules consistently and properly. To compound the problem, if the logic or rules change, application code changes are required for all affected applications.

Triggers can solve this problem by moving logic from the application level to the database level so that all applications share the same code which enforces the rules. If there is ever a change in the rules, you only need to change the trigger definitions in the database and all applications will follow the new rules without any additional changes required.

Here are some examples of how triggers might be used:

- When inserting, triggers can be used to supply, validate or manipulate data before allowing an insert operation to occur.
- When updating, triggers can be used to compare the new value (supplied by the UPDATE statement) with the existing value in the table to ensure that the transition from old value to new value follows proper state transitions. (For example, a trigger could be created to allow a column value to change from NO to YES only and not vice versa).
- Upon deletion, triggers can be used to automatically insert logging information into another table for audit trail purposes.

There are three types of triggers: BEFORE, AFTER and INSTEAD OF triggers. When triggers begin doing work (that is, executing your logic) because of a triggering SQL statement, the trigger is said to be activated.

A BEFORE trigger will be activated before any table data is affected by the triggering SQL statement. You would use BEFORE triggers to intercept data provided by the application to validate or supply missing values, for example. If the triggering SQL statement affects more than one row, the BEFORE trigger will be activated for every row that is affected.

AFTER triggers are activated after the triggering SQL statement has executed to completion successfully. In general, you would use AFTER triggers to post-process data.

You would also use AFTER triggers if your logic required doing any INSERT, UPDATE or DELETE operations because these statements are not supported in BEFORE triggers. AFTER triggers also offer additional options in how they can behave. With AFTER triggers, you can optionally define them to be activated on a per statement basis rather than on a per row basis. For example, if a single delete statement results in 1000 rows deleted, an AFTER/FOR EACH STATEMENT trigger defined on that table will activate just once at the end of the entire delete operation. On the other hand, if the trigger were defined as AFTER/FOR EACH ROW, it will activate 1000 times, once for each row affected by the triggering SQL statement.

The last type of trigger, the INSTEAD OF trigger, is defined on a database view and is beyond the scope of this book. However, SQL PL can be used in INSTEAD OF triggers in the same manner that we will soon describe.

The next section will illustrate some simple trigger examples, and then build on them by incorporating the SQL PL elements that you have already seen from previous chapters.

## 10.2.1 Creating Basic Triggers, By Example

Figure 10.1 illustrates the syntax diagram for creating a trigger.

**Figure 10.1** General Syntax Diagram for the CREATE TRIGGER Statement (BEFORE and AFTER Triggers)

```
>>-CREATE TRIGGER--trigger-name--+-NO CASCADE BEFORE-+----------->
                                 '-AFTER-------------'

>--+-INSERT-------------------------+--ON-------table-name------->
   +-DELETE-------------------------+

   '-UPDATE--+--------------------+-'
             |    .-,-----------. |
             |    V             | |
             '-OF---column-name-+-'

>--+----------------------------------------------------------------------+->
   |              .-------------------------------------------------.     |
   |              V                      .-AS-.                     |     |
   '-REFERENCING------------------+-OLD--+----+--correlation-name-+-+-----'
                                  |      .-AS-.                   |
                                  +-NEW--+----+--correlation-name-+
                                  |            .-AS-.             |
                                  +-OLD_TABLE--+----+--identifier-+
                                  |            .-AS-.             |
                                  '-NEW_TABLE--+----+--identifier-'
```

```
>--+-----FOR EACH ROW-------------+--MODE DB2SQL------------------>
   |                              |
   '-----FOR EACH STATEMENT-------'

>--| triggered-action |--------------------------------------><

triggered-action

|--+-----------------------------+--SQL-procedure-statement----|
   '-WHEN--(--search-condition--)-'
```

The syntax diagram may seem fairly complex at first, but after a few concrete examples, you'll see that creating triggers is quite easy. There are a few general rules that apply to all types of triggers that should be highlighted.

- A BEFORE trigger is always defined with the NO CASCADE clause. This means that operations performed within this trigger may not activate other triggers in the database. This has the implicit restriction that no INSERT, UPDATE or DELETE statements are allowed in the body of BEFORE triggers. If you wish to perform INSERT, UPDATE or DELETE statements in a trigger body, you must define them as AFTER triggers.
- If the optional column-name list is not specified in an UPDATE trigger, every column of the table is implied. Omission of the column-name list implies that the trigger will be activated by the update of any column of the table
- Both BEFORE and AFTER triggers support activation FOR EACH ROW. Only AFTER triggers can be defined to activate FOR EACH STATEMENT.
- For update and delete triggers defined with FOR EACH STATEMENT, they will be activated even if no rows are affected by the triggering UPDATE or DELETE statement.
- REFERENCING NEW is used to define a qualifier to reference new values supplied by INSERT and UPDATE statements.
- REFERENCING OLD is used to define a qualifier to reference old data to be discarded by UPDATE and DELETE statements.
- REFERENCING OLD_TABLE specifies a temporary table name which identifies the set of affected rows prior to the triggering SQL operation
- REFERENCING NEW_TABLE specifies a temporary table name which identifies the affected rows as modified by the triggering SQL operation and by any SET statement in a BEFORE trigger that has already executed (AFTER triggers only).

- MODE DB2SQL is simply a clause that must be included as part of the CREATE TRIGGER syntax. DB2SQL is the only mode currently supported.
- The optional WHEN clause defines the conditions for trigger activation. You could, for example, define the trigger to activate only if certain data existed in another table.
- Calling of stored procedures from triggers is not currently supported.

Now, let's start creating triggers.

## 10.2.2 BEFORE Trigger Example

BEFORE triggers are activated before the triggering SQL statement executes. Using a BEFORE trigger, you have the opportunity to supply values, validate data, and even reject the triggering SQL statement according to user-defined rules. In this section, a trigger will be created to activate before an INSERT into a table. Using similar code, you can create triggers to activate before UPDATE and DELETE statements.

In the SAMPLE database, there is a table called *cl_sched* which is used to store data for class schedules. Two columns in *cl_sched*, *starting* and *ending*, define when the class starts and ends, respectively.

A simple rule might be to assume that a class ends one hour after it begins if the ending time is not provided upon INSERT into this table. The trigger shown in Figure 10.2 will enforce this:

**Figure 10.2** General Syntax Diagram for the CREATE TRIGGER Statement (BEFORE and AFTER Triggers)

```
CREATE TRIGGER default_class_end
NO CASCADE BEFORE INSERT ON cl_sched                          --(1)
REFERENCING NEW AS n                                          --(2)
FOR EACH ROW                                                  --(3)
MODE DB2SQL
WHEN (n.ending IS NULL)                                       --(4)
    SET n.ending = n.starting + 1 HOUR                        --(5)
```

The example in Figure 10.2 shows how to create a trigger called *default_class_end* which activates before an insert on table *cl_sched* at (1). To intercept and supply a default ending time, the trigger needs to make reference to values provided by the triggering INSERT statement. The REFERENCING NEW AS *n* clause at (2) associates the new values provided by the insert statement with the qualifier *n*. The ending time of the

INSERT statement can then be checked and/or supplied by referring to *n.ending* at lines (4) and (5).

At line (3), FOR EACH ROW means that this trigger will activate for every row that is inserted. Therefore, if you had executed the following INSERT statement:

```
INSERT INTO cl_sched (class_code, day, starting)
VALUES ('DB20002', 1, '12:00'), ('DB20003', 3, '9:00')
```

The trigger would be activated twice, once for each row inserted, even though only a single INSERT statement was issued.

The trigger is defined to activate only when the ending time is null using the optional WHEN clause at (4), which ensures that the trigger only activates if a value has not been supplied.

Finally, if the trigger is activated, the ending time is supplied automatically and is set to one hour after the starting time at (5).

To test this trigger, execute the following SQL statement:

```
INSERT INTO cl_sched (class_code, day, starting)
VALUES ('DB20001', 1, '10:00')
```

Now, if you select all rows from *cl_sched*, you'll see that the class has been automatically set to have an ending time of 11:00.

```
SELET * FROM cl_sched

CLASS_CODE DAY    STARTING ENDING
---------- ------ -------- --------
DB20001         1 10:00:00 11:00:00
  1 record(s) selected.
```

Similarly, the trigger does not execute if an ending time is supplied:

```
INSERT INTO cl_sched (class_code, day, starting, ending)
VALUES ('DB20002', 2, '12:00', '15:00')
```

Now, selecting from the *cl_sched* will show that the ending time remains at 15:00.

```
SELECT * FROM cl_sched

CLASS_CODE DAY    STARTING ENDING
---------- ------ -------- --------
DB20001         1 10:00:00 11:00:00
DB20002         2 12:00:00 15:00:00
  3 record(s) selected.
```

## 10.2.3 AFTER Trigger Example

As stated earlier, unlike BEFORE triggers, AFTER triggers will allow you to use INSERT, UPDATE or DELETE statements inside the trigger body. This would be useful if you wanted to transparently keep an audit trail of when certain events occurred.

To support the following example, connect to the sample database and execute the following DDL to create a table called *audit*:

```
CREATE TABLE AUDIT (event_time TIMESTAMP, desc VARCHAR(100))
```

Figure 10.3 is an example of a trigger that can be used to keep an audit trail of salary changes with related information such as date and time of the change, as well as the person who made the change.

**Figure 10.3** Example of a Basic AFTER UPDATE Trigger

```
CREATE TRIGGER audit_emp_sal
AFTER UPDATE OF salary ON employee
REFERENCING OLD AS o NEW AS n                                        --(1)
FOR EACH ROW
MODE DB2SQL
INSERT INTO audit VALUES                                             --(2)
(CURRENT TIMESTAMP, ' Employee ' || o.empno ||
' salary changed from ' || CHAR(o.salary) || ' to ' ||
CHAR(n.salary) || ' by ' || USER)
```

In Figure 10.3, the trigger is able to reference both *old* and *new* values because it is defined to activate upon table updates at (1). Upon any change in salary for any employee, the trigger will insert into the *audit* table a record of when the update occurred, what the old and new values are, and who executed the UPDATE statement at (2).(USER is a DB2 special register that holds the connection ID of the application). Also, the WHEN clause in this example has been left out so that this trigger will activate unconditionally.

To test this trigger, update Theodore Spenser's salary since he seems to be underpaid relative to other managers. To see the salaries of current managers, issue the following query:

```
SELECT empno, firstnme, lastname, salary FROM employee
WHERE job='MANAGER'

EMPNO  FIRSTNME     LASTNAME        SALARY
------ ------------ --------------- -----------
000020 MICHAEL      THOMPSON           41250.00
000030 SALLY        KWAN               38250.00
000050 JOHN         GEYER              40175.00
000060 IRVING       STERN              32250.00
000070 EVA          PULASKI            36170.00
000090 EILEEN       HENDERSON          29750.00
000100 THEODORE     SPENSER            26150.00

  7 record(s) selected.
```

To give Theodore a 15% raise, issue the following UPDATE statement:

```
UPDATE employee e SET salary=salary*1.15 WHERE e.empno= '000100';
```

Now you can check the status of the employee table to see Theodore's new salary.

```
SELECT empno, firstnme, lastname, salary FROM employee e
WHERE e.empno='000100'

EMPNO  FIRSTNME     LASTNAME        SALARY
------ ------------ --------------- -----------
000100 THEODORE     SPENSER            30072.50

  1 record(s) selected.
```

Finally, verify that the salary update has been logged in the AUDIT table.

```
SELECT * FROM AUDIT

EVENT_TIME                 DESC
-------------------------- ------------------------------------------
----------------------------------------
2002-04-21-21.26.07.665000 employee 000100 salary changed from
0026150.00  to 0030072.50  by DB2ADMIN

  1 record(s) selected.
```

Now that you've seen some simple triggers, SQL PL can now be introduced.

## 10.2.4 Using SQL PL in Triggers

In the examples presented thus far, the trigger code bodies have only contained single SQL statements. In this section, previous examples will be extended to show you how to incorporate more complex logic using SQL PL elements you've already seen in previous chapters.

Returning to the first example in Figure 10.1, with the default class time, let us say some restrictions have been added with respect to when a class can be scheduled:

- A class cannot end beyond 9 p.m.
- A class cannot be scheduled for weekends.

A trigger could be defined to disallow the INSERT, UPDATE or DELETE on table *cl_sched* that violates the above rules and return a descriptive error to the application.

If you created the trigger from the previous example, drop it before continuing with this example. Note that an ALTER TRIGGER statement does not exist. Therefore, to modify a trigger, you must drop and recreate it:

```
DROP TRIGGER default_class_end
```

Figure 10.4 illustrates the trigger code to enforce the new rules.

**Figure 10.4** Advanced BEFORE INSERT Trigger Using SQL PL

```
CREATE TRIGGER validate_sched
NO CASCADE BEFORE INSERT ON cl_sched
REFERENCING NEW AS n
FOR EACH ROW
MODE DB2SQL
BEGIN ATOMIC                                                    --(1)
-- supply default value for ending time if null
IF (n.ending IS NULL) THEN                                      --(2)
    SET n.ending = n.starting + 1 HOUR;
END IF;

-- ensure that class does not end beyond 9pm
IF (n.ending > '21:00') THEN                                    --(3)
    SIGNAL SQLSTATE '80000'
        SET MESSAGE_TEXT='class ending time is beyond 9pm';     --(4)
ELSEIF (n.DAY=1 or n.DAY=7) THEN                                --(5)
    SIGNAL SQLSTATE '80001'
        SET MESSAGE_TEXT='class cannot be scheduled on a weekend'; --(6)
END IF;
END                                                             --(7)
```

The trigger works by first supplying a default ending time if it has not already been provided at (2). Then, it ensures that the ending time does not exceed 9 p.m. at (3) and has not been scheduled for a weekend at (5).

Here are the highlights of the example in Figure 10.4:

- In order to use multiple statements in the trigger body, the SQL PL statements must be wrapped within an atomic compound statement using BEGIN ATOMIC (1) and END (7).
- Within the atomic compound statement, SQL PL flow control elements like IF at (2), (3), and (5) and SIGNAL at (4) and (6) can be used.
- Note that the maximum length of the error message used with SIGNAL SQLSTATE is 70 characters. If you exceed this limit, the message will be truncated without warning at run-time.

The maximum length of the error message used with SIGNAL SQLSTATE is 70 characters. If you exceed this limit, the message will be truncated without warning at run time.

To test the trigger, execute the following SQL statements:

First, attempt to insert a class where the starting time is 9 p.m. Since the ending time is not supplied, 10 p.m. will be assumed.

```
INSERT INTO CL_SCHED (class_code, day, starting)
    VALUES ('DB20005', 5, '21:00')
```

This insert statement results in the following custom error, as desired:

```
DB21034E  The command was processed as an SQL statement because it was not a
valid Command Line Processor command.  During SQL processing it returned:
SQL0438N  Application raised error with diagnostic text: "class ending time is
beyond 9pm".  SQLSTATE=80000
```

Next, attempt to insert a class where the day of the week is Sunday (the value of DAY starts from Sunday with a value of 1)

```
INSERT INTO CL_SCHED (class_code, day, starting, ending)
    VALUES ('DB20005', 1, '13:00', '15:00')
```

Again, the insert statement results in the following custom error, as expected:

```
DB21034E  The command was processed as an SQL statement because it was not a
valid Command Line Processor command.  During SQL processing it returned:
SQL0438N  Application raised error with diagnostic text: "class cannot be
scheduled on a weekend".  SQLSTATE=80001
```

Finally, insert a valid value into the class schedule table (Thursday, 1 to 3 p.m.).

```
INSERT INTO CL_SCHED (class_code, day, starting, ending)
    VALUES ('DB20005', 5, '13:00', '15:00')
```

By selecting from the *cl_sched* table, you will see the row that was just inserted. (You may see another row, as below, if you attempted the previous example.)

```
SELECT * FROM cl_sched

CLASS_CODE DAY    STARTING ENDING
---------- ------ -------- --------
DB20001         1 10:00:00 11:00:00
DB20005         5 13:00:00 15:00:00
  3 record(s) selected.
```

In summary, triggers are an ideal mechanism to facilitate global enforcement of business logic for all applications and users. Examples of both BEFORE and AFTER triggers were illustrated and the purpose and limitations of using each type were discussed. Using SQL PL for triggers was also demonstrated.

# 10.3 Introduction to DB2 Functions

A function in DB2 is a database object that maps one or many inputs to an output. Out of the box, DB2 provides many useful built-in functions to manipulate strings, dates and data values. For your convenience, a listing of built-in functions has been provided in Appendix E, "Built-In Function Reference." Functions can be used within stored procedures, SQL statements, triggers, and within other functions.

This section will demonstrate how to create customized user-defined functions (UDFs) using SQL PL. UDFs can encapsulate frequently used logic to reduce the complexity of application development.

There are four different types of functions: column, scalar, row and table.

Column functions operate on the values of an entire column such as SUM() and AVG() which return the sum and average values in a column, respectively. There is currently no support to build user-defined column functions.

Scalar functions take input values and return a single value. The built-in function UCASE() is an example of a scalar function which, given a string, returns the same string in upper case form. User-defined scalar functions are supported and will be covered shortly.

Row functions return a row of data. This is a special type of function designed to dismantle a user-defined structured type into a row form. This feature is part of DB2's object relational features, which are beyond the scope of this book. Therefore, row functions will not be discussed here.

Finally, table functions return values in a table format. These functions are called in the FROM clause of a SELECT statement. User-defined table functions are supported and will be covered later in this chapter.

DB2 also supports UDFs written in C and Java. For more information, see the DB2 Application Development Guide.

The CREATE FUNCTION command is used to create UDFs. The best way to learn is to dive right in, so let's begin.

## 10.3.1 Creating a User-Defined Scalar Function

A scalar function returns a single value and is generally valid wherever an SQL expression is valid. The full CREATE FUNCTION syntax as found in the DB2 SQL reference is quite complex. For readability, Figure 10.5 presents a simplified form of the CREATE FUNCTION syntax diagram for scalar functions, which excludes all keywords, clauses, and options not related to scalar UDFs:

**Figure 10.5** The Syntax Diagram for SQL User-Defined Scalar Functions

```
>>-CREATE FUNCTION--function-name------------------------------>

>--(--+--------------------------------+--)--*------------------>
      |  .-,--------------------------.  |
      |  V                            |  |
      '---parameter-name--data-type1-+-'

>--RETURNS--+-data-type2-----------------+--*------------------->

                                        .-LANGUAGE SQL-.
>--+-------------------------+--*--+--------------+--*---------->
   '-SPECIFIC--specific-name-'

>--+-RETURN Statement-----------+------------------------------|
   '-dynamic-compound-statement-'
```

To start with a simple case, let's say that you were migrating an application from Oracle to DB2. Furthermore, the application uses Oracle's NVL() function heavily throughout.

Oracle's NVL() function, in a nutshell, takes two parameters and returns the first non-null parameter. If the first parameter is not null, the first parameter is returned. If the first parameter is null, the second parameter is returned.

DB2's COALESCE() function has similar functionality to NVL(). However, rather than manually editing all SQL statements in the application to use COALESCE() instead of

NVL(), you could create a DB2 UDF called NVL() to call the native COALESCE function, saving you significant SQL migration time. Figure 10.6 depicts the code to create an NVL() function for DB2.

**Figure 10.6** A UDF to Map Oracle's NVL() Function to DB2's COALESCE() Function

```
CREATE FUNCTION NVL (p_var1 VARCHAR(30), p_var2 VARCHAR(30))                --(1)
SPECIFIC NVLVARCHAR30
RETURNS VARCHAR(30)                                                          --(2)
RETURN COALESCE(p_var1, p_var2)                                              --(3)
```

This simple function simply takes two VARCHAR input variables at (1) and routes the parameters to DB2's COALESCE() function at (3). The function is defined with RETURNS VARCHAR(30) at (2) which is a single value and, by definition, is a scalar function.

The above function only allows for VARCHAR parameters. If you required an NVL function for parameters of other data types, you will have to overload the above function with the required types. The SPECIFIC clause specifies that NVLVARCHAR30 will uniquely identify this function in the system catalog tables and is the same as our use of the SPECIFIC clause for SQL stored procedures. Since NVL() may be overloaded, the SPECIFIC name helps us easily differentiate among the different NVL() functions that might be created.

To test the DB2 NVL() function, you can issue the following SQL:

```
SELECT nvl(CAST (NULL AS VARCHAR(10)), 'db2 nvl at work!') FROM sysibm.sysdummy1
1
------------------------------
db2 nvl at work!

  1 record(s) selected.
```

You might have noticed that the null value was CAST as VARCHAR(10), which is different from the parameter definition of the UDF (which uses VARCHAR(30)). This is to show that input values to UDFs do not need to match the parameter definitions in UDFs exactly—the UDF type definition only needs to be as large as the largest string value that may be passed to it.

## 10.3.2 Complex Scalar Function

Now that you've got a feel for UDFs, here is a more complex example. Consider a scenario where your application frequently retrieves the department name to which an employee belongs. The employee table, however, only contains the department code for employees, and you don't want to write your queries to join the employee table and the department table every time the department name is needed. To simplify this task, a UDF can be created which takes the employee number as a parameter and returns the department name. Figure 10.7 presents code for a function that would satisfy these requirements.

**Figure 10.7** A Scalar UDF that Returns a Department Name, Given an Employee Number

```
CREATE FUNCTION deptname(p_empid VARCHAR(6))                              --(1)
RETURNS VARCHAR(30)                                                       --(2)
SPECIFIC deptname                                                         --(3)
BEGIN ATOMIC                                                              --(4)
    DECLARE v_department_name VARCHAR(30);
    DECLARE v_err VARCHAR(70);
    SET v_department_name = (
        SELECT d.deptname FROM department d, employee e                   --(5)
            WHERE e.workdept=d.deptno AND e.empno= p_empid);
    SET v_err = 'Error: employee ' || p_empid || ' was not found';        --(6)
    IF v_department_name IS NULL THEN
        SIGNAL SQLSTATE '80000' SET MESSAGE_TEXT=v_err;                   --(7)
    END IF;
  RETURN v_department_name;
END                                                                       --(8)
```

In Figure 10.7, the function *deptname()* takes an employee ID as its parameter at (1). If you looked at the DDL for the employee table, you would notice that the type for the EMPNO column is actually CHAR(6). The function parameter, however, is defined as VARCHAR(6) because DB2 assumes VARCHAR types to resolve a UDF call. If you were to define the input parameter as CHAR(6), every time you called the function, you would have to cast the input parameter to CHAR(6) as follows (which is highly inconvenient):

```
SELECT * FROM department d WHERE d.deptname=deptname(CAST ('000060' AS CHAR(6)))
```

Use VARCHAR types for character string input in UDF definitions.

At (2), the function is defined to return a single value of type VARCHAR(30) which, by definition, makes it a scalar function.

In our first example, the function body was a single line. As with triggers, to use multiple lines of code in the UDF, the body of the function is wrapped with BEGIN ATOMIC at (4) and END at (8).

To get the department name, the *employee* and *department* tables are joined on the department code (*deptno* and *workdept* columns) at (5) and further filtered by the employee number (which is unique) to guarantee that at most one row will be returned. Note that the SET statement is used to accomplish this rather than SELECT INTO. SELECT INTO is not supported in dynamic compound statements but using the SET statement works just as well.

SELECT INTO is not supported in SQL PL for UDFs. However, the SET statement works just as well. For example, to fetch two columns into two variables, use:

```
SET (var1, var2) = (SELECT C1, C2 FROM T1)
```

There is something that you should be very careful of as well: as a best practice, avoid using variable names that are same as column names within queries. Within a query, DB2 always resolves column names first before evaluating variable and parameter values. Consider what would happen if the input parameter was called *empno* instead of *p_empno* and replaced at (5) in the code sample in Figure 10.7 with the SELECT statement:

```
SELECT d.deptname FROM department d, employee e WHERE e.workdept=d.deptno AND
e.empno= empno
```

Because of the order in which DB2 evaluates column and variable values, the query above is equivalent the query below, which is incorrect:

```
SELECT d.deptname FROM department d, employee e WHERE e.workdept=d.deptno AND 1=1
```

If you use the variable naming scheme that has been used throughout the book, (*p_* prefix for parameter names and *v_* prefix for local variable names), you will not run into this problem.

Looking at the select statement at (5), you'll notice that there is a possibility that an invalid employee number could be passed as a parameter, in which case the SELECT statement will return no values and *v_department_name* will be null. To better handle the scenario, SIGNAL SQLSTATE is used at (7) to throw an error if the employee ID is not found. The SIGNAL SQLSTATE code is optional since, had it been left out, the function would simply return null, which may also be reasonable depending on your needs.

SIGNAL SQLSTATE at (7) was included in the example for other reasons. Notice how dynamic error text was coded. The error message could have been static:

```
SIGNAL SQLSTATE '80000' SET MESSAGE_TEXT='Error: employee was not found';
```

The error text is much more informative, however, if it could provide the employee ID that caused the error. The custom error message cannot be an expression, however. In otherwords, the following would NOT work:

```
SIGNAL SQLSTATE '80000' SET MESSAGE_TEXT='Error: employee ' || p_empid
|| ' was not found';
```

Therefore to work around it, the *v_err* variable was declared to hold the dynamic error message and is modified at (6) before calling SIGNAL SQLSTATE at (7).

Note the variable *v_err* was defined as VARCHAR(70). The limit for custom error text for SIGNAL SQLSTATE is 70 characters. If you have a message that exceeds this limit, the message will be truncated without warning.

The custom error message for SIGNAL SQLSTATE ... SET MESSAGE TEXT=... is limited to 70 characters. If your message exceeds this limit, it will be truncated at run time without warning.

Here are some examples of how this scalar UDF can be used:

1) In a SELECT column list:

```
SELECT e.empno, e.firstnme, e.lastname, deptname(e.empno) department_name
FROM employee e WHERE e.empno='000060'

EMPNO  FIRSTNME     LASTNAME        DEPARTMENT_NAME
------ ------------ --------------- ---------------------------------------------
000060 IRVING       STERN           MANUFACTURING SYSTEMS

  1 record(s) selected.
```

2) In a predicate:

```
SELECT * FROM department d WHERE d.deptname=deptname('000060')

DEPTNO DEPTNAME                             MGRNO  ADMRDEPT LOCATION
------ ------------------------------------ ------ -------- ----------------
D11    MANUFACTURING SYSTEMS                000060 D01      -
```

3) And as part of an expression:

```
VALUES deptname('000060') || ' department'
1
-----------------------------------
MANUFACTURING SYSTEMS Department

  1 record(s) selected.
```

## 10.3.3 Table Functions

Table functions return entire tables and are used in the FROM clause of a SELECT. Suppose you wanted to have a table function that would dynamically enumerate a result set of all employees in a given department. To do the enumeration, two functions from DB2's OLAP function set, called ROW_NUMBER() and OVER(), can be used. The table UDF will take a single parameter that represents the department ID.

To build the table function, the resulting table structure to be returned needs to be determined. In this example, the table to be returned should have the following: an enumeration column, the employee number, last name, and first name of employees. To ensure that you don't encounter type errors, first look at what data types are used for the employee table.

```
DESCRIBE TABLE employee

Column                         Type      Type
name                           schema    name               Length   Scale Null
------------------------------ --------- ------------------ -------- ----- ----
EMPNO                          SYSIBM    CHARACTER                 6     0 No
FIRSTNME                       SYSIBM    VARCHAR                  12     0 No
MIDINIT                        SYSIBM    CHARACTER                 1     0 No
LASTNAME                       SYSIBM    VARCHAR                  15     0 No
WORKDEPT                       SYSIBM    CHARACTER                 3     0 Yes
PHONENO                        SYSIBM    CHARACTER                 4     0 Yes
HIREDATE                       SYSIBM    DATE                      4     0 Yes
JOB                            SYSIBM    CHARACTER                 8     0 Yes
EDLEVEL                        SYSIBM    SMALLINT                  2     0 No
SEX                            SYSIBM    CHARACTER                 1     0 Yes
BIRTHDATE                      SYSIBM    DATE                      4     0 Yes
SALARY                         SYSIBM    DECIMAL                   9     2 Yes
BONUS                          SYSIBM    DECIMAL                   9     2 Yes
COMM                           SYSIBM    DECIMAL                   9     2 Yes

  14 record(s) selected.
```

From the above table description, you can determine that the returned table of our table function will have the following definition:

```
CREATE TABLE  ... (enum INT, empno CHAR(6), lastname VARCHAR(15), firstnme
VARCHAR(20))
```

With this information, the table function can now be created with the code seen in Figure 10.8.

**Figure 10.8** Example of a User-Defined Table Function

```
CREATE FUNCTION getEnumEmployee(p_dept VARCHAR(3))
RETURNS TABLE                                                                    --(1)
    (enum INT, empno VARCHAR(6), lastname VARCHAR(15), firstnme VARCHAR(12)) --(2)
SPECIFIC getEnumEmployee
RETURN                                                                           --(3)
SELECT ROW_NUMBER() OVER(), e.empno, e.lastname, e.firstnme
    FROM employee e
    WHERE e.workdept=p_dept
```

In the above code, the UDF is defined to return a table at (1), and will have the definition previously composed using the column types found in the employee table at (2).

The body of this query is quite simple: the result of a SELECT statement that retrieves all employees for a given department is returned at (3). To generate the enumeration, the ROW_NUMBER() and OVER() scalar functions are used.

Once the above table function has been created, it can be used in queries like the following:

```
SELECT * FROM TABLE(getEnumEmployee('E21')) AS enumEmp
ORDER BY lastname

ENUM        EMPNO  LASTNAME        FIRSTNME
----------- ------ --------------- ------------
          1 000340 GOUNOT          JASON
          2 000330 LEE             WING
          3 000320 MEHTA           RAMLAL
          4 000100 SPENSER         THEODORE

  4 record(s) selected.
```

In the example query, there are a few notable points:

- If you have to order the values returned by the table function, you must specify it in the calling SELECT statement as illustrated above. ORDER BY cannot be specified inside the table function body.
- The enumeration generated by ROW_NUMBER() OVER() is dynamically assigned at the time of function execution. If employee records are added, deleted, or updated between subsequent executions of this function, the resulting order of employees and enumeration may change.

- The function is called in the FROM clause of a SELECT statement, and the table function must be cast to a table type by using the TABLE() function. Furthermore, you must alias the table returned by the table function (such as *enumEmp* above).

## 10.4 Restrictions and Considerations

The following are restrictions and considerations when developing SQL triggers and user-defined functions.

- SQL that modifies table data is not supported in SQL PL for triggers and UDFs
- PREPARE, EXECUTE, and EXECUTE IMMEDIATE statements are not allowed in triggers and UDFs. Trigger and UDF SQL is inherently dynamic.
- Exception handlers are not supported in triggers and UDFs.
- Stored procedure calls from triggers and UDFs are not currently supported.
- Whether you are working with triggers or UDFs, be careful when using DB2's date and time special registers (CURRENT DATE, CURRENT TIME, and CURRENT TIMESTAMP) in multiple locations. Consider the following code:

```
BEGIN ATOMIC
   INSERT INTO hello VALUES (CHAR (CURRENT TIMESTAMP));
   INSERT INTO hello VALUES (CHAR (CURRENT TIMESTAMP));
END
```

- At first glance, you would expect two slightly different *timestamp* values to be inserted into the *hello* table. If you execute it, however, you will find that the same timestamp value is inserted twice because the entire code body is executed as a compound statement.
- If you need to generate a unique timestamps within the same code body, use the built-in GENERATE_UNIQUE() function with the timestamp. For example:

```
BEGIN ATOMIC
   INSERT INTO hello VALUES (CHAR(TIMESTAMP(GENERATE_UNIQUE()) +
CURRENT TIMEZONE));
   INSERT INTO hello VALUES (CHAR(TIMESTAMP(GENERATE_UNIQUE()) +
CURRENT TIMEZONE));
END
```

## 10.5 Chapter Summary

In this chapter, triggers and user-defined functions (UDFs) were discussed. DB2's support for advanced SQL PL logic in triggers and UDFs allows you to encapsulate both simple and complex logic at the database server to simplify application development.

APPENDIX 

# Getting Started with DB2

The objective of this appendix is to get you started with DB2 UDB. If you have not used DB2 before, this appendix is the perfect place to start. It covers DB2 fundamentals and commands that will prepare you to work with the SQL procedure examples demonstrated in this book.

DB2 commands are illustrated to show how to create and manipulate DB2 instances, databases, buffer pools, tablespaces, and tables. A set of DB2 graphical tools is also available to accomplish the same tasks and more information can be found in the *Online Help for the DB2 Administration Tools* manual.

In this appendix, however, we are focusing only on the command line interface to DB2. All of the commands discussed in this appendix are executable from the DB2 Command Window on Windows or a UNIX shell.

## A.1 Launching the DB2 Command Window

The first thing you must learn is how to launch the DB2 Command Window.

From the Windows Start menu, click Programs > IBM DB2 > Command Line Tools and select Command Window, as shown in Figure A.1.

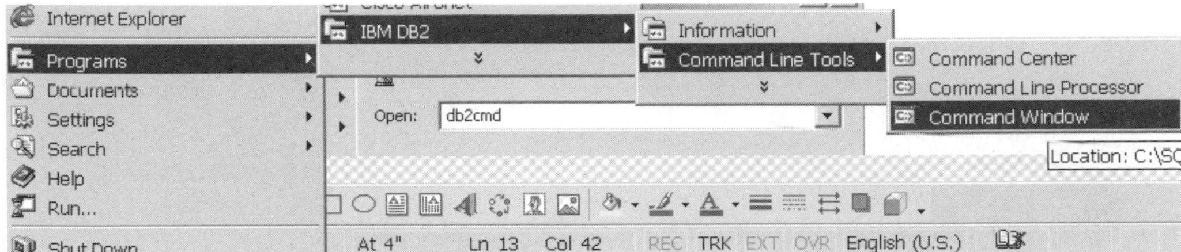


**Figure A.1** Launching the DB2 Command Window Using the Window Start Menu

Another way to launch the Command Window, shown in Figure A.2, is by running *db2cmd* from the Windows Run window.

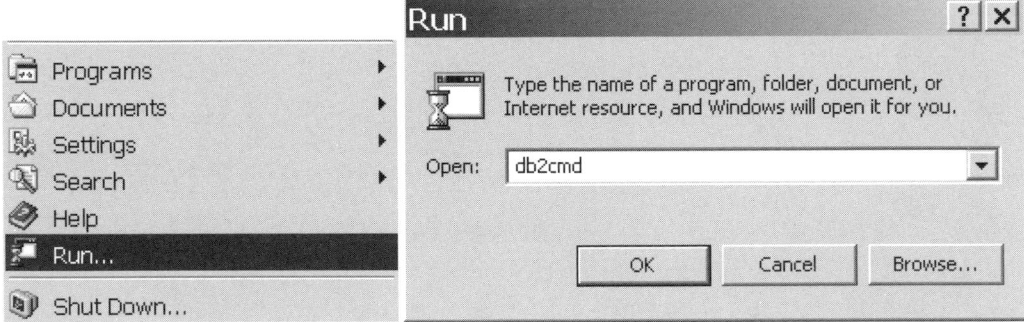


**Figure A.2** Launching the DB2 Command Window Using db2cmd

The DB2 Command Window is the command line interface to DB2. At first glance, it appears exactly the same as the standard Windows DOS prompt, except that the window title says DB2 CLP (Figure A.3). DB2 commands cannot be executed within the normal Windows DOS prompt because the DB2 command line environment has not be initialized. If you have problems executing the commands presented in this appendix, be sure that you are in the DB2 command line environment by verifying that the window title is DB2 CLP.

**Figure A.3** The DB2 Command Window Has DB2 CLP in the Window Title

# A.2 Overview of DB2 Architecture

There is no better place to start describing the DB2 architecture than with a diagram. Figure A.4 shows the basic components of a DB2 environment. We will start from the top at the instance level, and drill down into the details of databases, buffer pools, table spaces and so on.

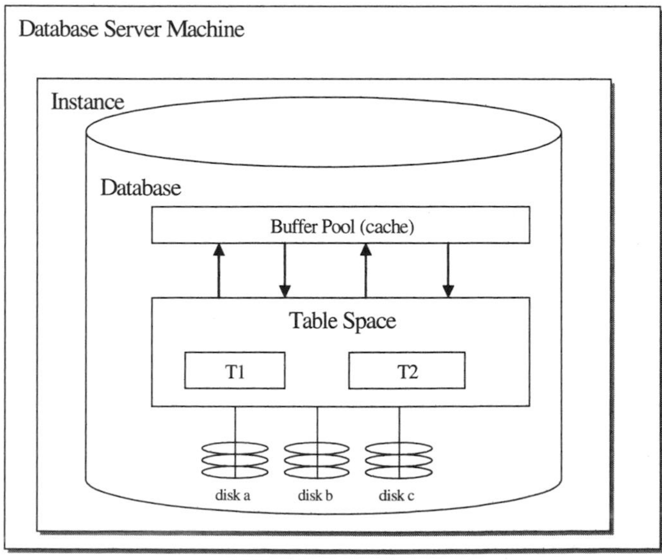


**Figure A.4** Overview of the DB2 Architecture

## A.2.1 DB2 Instances

A DB2 instance is a logical context in which DB2 commands and functions are executed. You can think of an instance as a service or a daemon process that manages access to database files. More than one instance can be defined on a server machine. Each instance is independent of the others, meaning that they can be managed, manipulated, and tuned separately.

With the default installation of DB2 v8.1, one instance is automatically created called *DB2* on Windows and *db2inst1* on UNIX. The default instance is sufficient for creating a database to run the examples contained in this book.

If you wish to list the instances defined on your machine, you can issue the following command:

```
db2ilist
```

## A.2.2 Creating Databases

Each DB2 database is made up of buffer pools, tablespaces, tables, metadata information, database log files, and many other components. Once an instance has been created and started, databases can be created in it.

A SAMPLE database comes with every DB2 server installation but you must manually initiate its creation. The database is used by all the examples illustrated in this book. The command, *db2sampl*, will create the SAMPLE database, create tables in the database, and populate the tables with data. Notice that the command is *db2sampl* without the letter 'e'. Table structures and content for all examples used in this book can be found in Appendix F, "DDL Examples."

If you want to create your own database, use the CREATE DATABASE command. A lot of options are supported by the CREATE DATABASE command which allows for customization such as location of the database, database code page settings, default tablespace characteristics and so on. However, the command for creating a database can be as simple as:

```
db2 CREATE DATABASE <dbname>
```

A complete syntax diagram of the CREATE DATABASE command is available in the *DB2 Command Reference.*

Before you can work with database objects, such as tables, you must first connect to the database. The command to make a database connection is very simple:

```
db2 CONNECT TO <dbname>
```

The above command will connect to the database with the userid currently logged on to the operating system. If you want to connect to the database as a different userid, specify the *USER* option:

```
db2 CONNECT TO <dbname> USER <username>
```

DB2 will then ask for the password and pass it to the operating system for authentication. Figure A.5 illustrates the creation of the sample database and establishment of a connection from the command line.

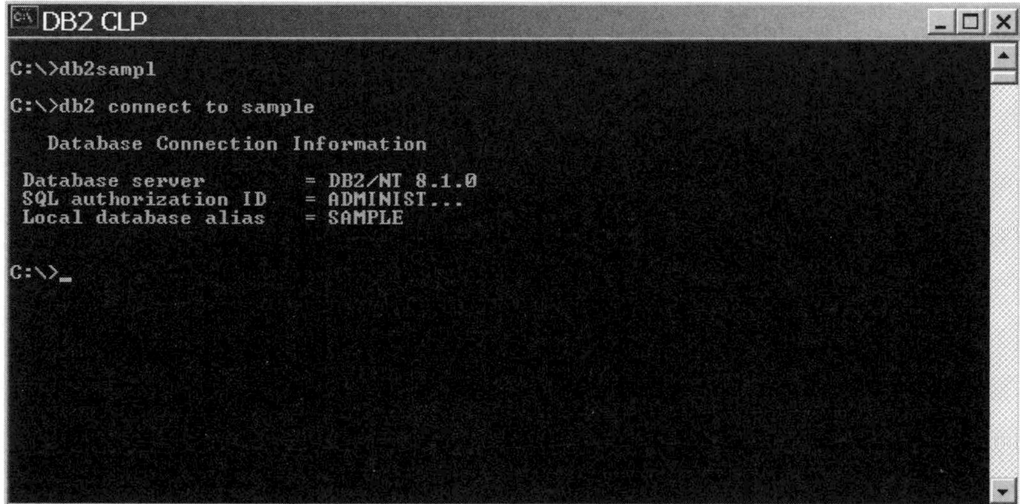


**Figure A.5** Creating the SAMPLE database and Establishing a Connection from the Command Line

To disconnect from a database, use:

```
db2 CONNECT RESET
```

Note that DB2 does not manage and/or authenticate userids and passwords. They are validated by the operating system or other supported external security facilities. Therefore, there is no need to create database users in order to connect to the database.

## A.2.3 Executing SQL in DB2

At this point, you are all set to do some data manipulation. Just like other database management systems, data is manipulated by means of SQL statements. To execute a single SQL statement from the DB2 Command Window, pass the SQL statement as a parameter to the *db2* command:

```
db2 "SELECT * FROM EMPLOYEE"
```

It is often useful to group SQL statements together in a script and execute them using one command. To do this, save the set of SQL statements to a file and use the *db2* command with the *–tf* option. For example, assume you have a file called *sqlstmt.db2* that contains a number of SQL statements as shown in Figure A.6.

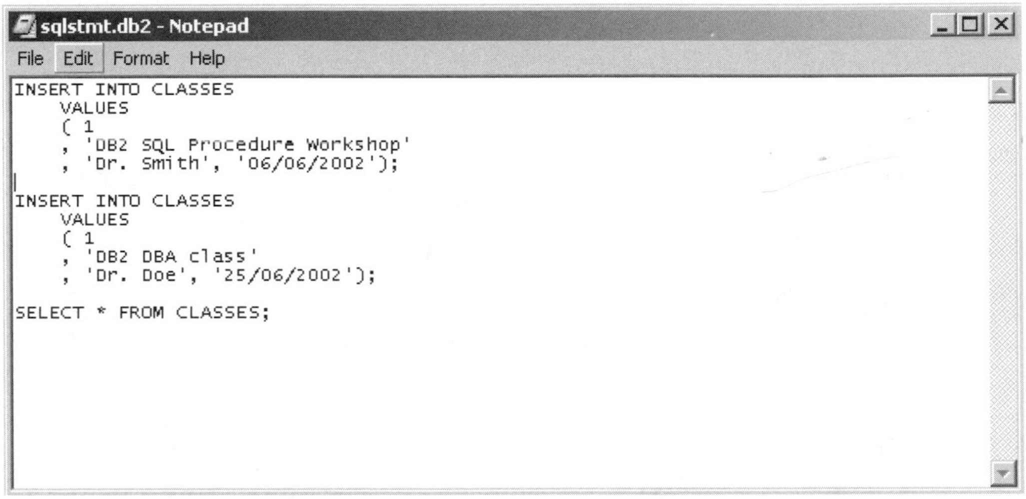

sqlstmt.db2 - Notepad

File Edit Format Help

```
INSERT INTO CLASSES
    VALUES
    ( 1
    , 'DB2 SQL Procedure Workshop'
    , 'Dr. Smith', '06/06/2002');

INSERT INTO CLASSES
    VALUES
    ( 1
    , 'DB2 DBA class'
    , 'Dr. Doe', '25/06/2002');

SELECT * FROM CLASSES;
```

**Figure A.6** Example of a Text File with Multiple SQL Statements

In Figure A.6 each statement is separated by the default statement terminator, the semi colon (;). Use the following command to execute the statements contained in the input file:

```
db2 -tf sqlstmt.db2
```

In some cases the semi colon cannot be used as the statement terminator. For example, scripts containing the CREATE PROCEDURE statement cannot use the default terminator since SQL procedure bodies themselves already use semi colons for statement terminators. An additional option, *-td*, is available to change the termination character. If *sqlstmt.db2*, had instead, used @ as the statement terminator, you would use this command to execute the script:

```
db2 -td@ -f sqlstmt.db2
```

Note that there is no space between the *–td* option and the delimiter character.

To complete this discussion, let's walk through an example of how an SQL procedure presented in this book could be created from the command line. The sample code in Figure A.7 is taken from Figure 6.4 in Chapter 6.

**Figure A.7** Creating an SQL Procedure from the Command Line

```
CREATE PROCEDURE change_bonus( IN p_new_bonus DECIMAL
                             , IN p_where_cond VARCHAR(1000)
                             , OUT p_num_changes INT )
    SPECIFIC change_bonus
    LANGUAGE SQL
cb: BEGIN

    DECLARE v_dynSQL VARCHAR(1000);                                     -- (1)

    SET v_dynSQL = 'UPDATE employee SET BONUS=' ||                      -- (2)
                   CHAR(p_new_bonus) || ' WHERE ' ||
                   p_where_cond;

    EXECUTE IMMEDIATE v_dynSQL;                                         -- (3)

    GET DIAGNOSTICS p_num_changes = row_count;                          -- (4)
END cb
```

First, copy this code into a text file, and add the @ delimiter at the very end of the CREATE PROCEDURE statement as illustrated in Figure A.8.

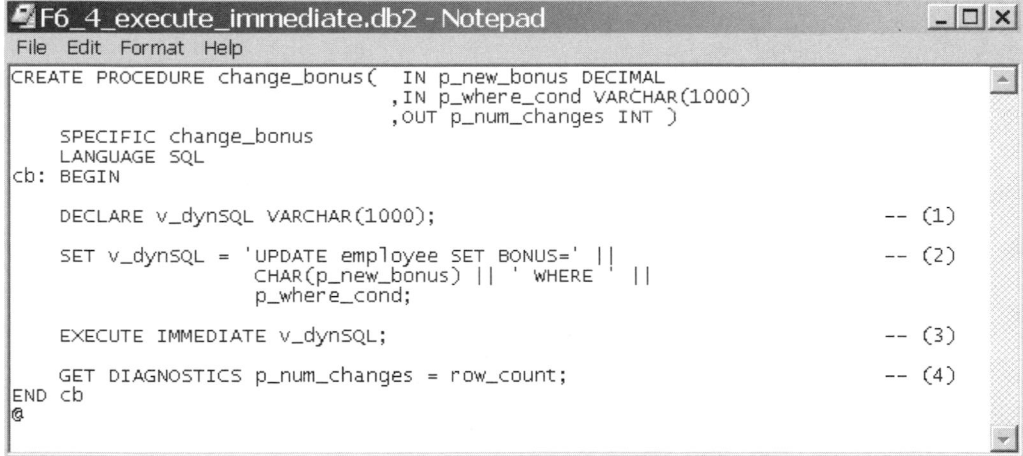


```
CREATE PROCEDURE change_bonus(  IN p_new_bonus DECIMAL
                               ,IN p_where_cond VARCHAR(1000)
                               ,OUT p_num_changes INT )
    SPECIFIC change_bonus
    LANGUAGE SQL
cb: BEGIN
    DECLARE v_dynSQL VARCHAR(1000);                                -- (1)
    SET v_dynSQL = 'UPDATE employee SET BONUS=' ||                 -- (2)
                   CHAR(p_new_bonus) || ' WHERE ' ||
                   p_where_cond;
    EXECUTE IMMEDIATE v_dynSQL;                                    -- (3)
    GET DIAGNOSTICS p_num_changes = row_count;                     -- (4)
END cb
@
```

**Figure A.8** The CREATE PROCEDURE Statement Opened in Windows Notepad

Once you've saved this file (in this case, the filename is F6_4_execute_immedate.db2) you can build the procedure by executing:

```
db2 -td@ -f F6_4_execute_immediate.db2
```

## A.2.4 Configuring the DB2 Environment

Now we'll discuss how to configure the DB2 environment. Proper setup of the DB2 environment is very important because it controls how DB2 operates and functions. It can also be used to customize creation, development, and deployment of SQL procedures. The DB2 configuration parameters, operating system environment variables, and DB2 profile registry variables make up the DB2 environment.

There are instance and database level configuration parameters that you can change which affect the behavior of DB2. With the following commands, you can get the instance (also called database manager) and database configuration parameters:

```
db2 GET DATABASE MANAGER CONFIGURATION
db2 GET DATABASE CONFIGURATION FOR <dbname>
```

To modify database manager or database configuration parameters, use:

```
db2 UPDATE DATABASE MANAGER CONFIGURATION USING <parameter> <new value>
db2 UPDATE DATABASE CONFIGURATION FOR <dbname> USING <parameter> <new value>
```

The majority of the parameters are related to performance and they are not covered here in this book. The *DB2 Administration Guide* provides detailed descriptions of each configuration parameter at both instance and database levels.

Operating system environment variables, as the name implies, are set at the operating system level. The syntax for setting an operating system environment variable depends on the platform and the type of shell you are using. For example, to set the current instance environment to PRODINST on a Windows platform, you use:

```
set DB2INSTANCE=PRODINST
```

On AIX with the korn shell, you use:

```
export DB2INSTANCE=PRODINST
```

## A.2.5 DB2 Profile Registries

DB2 profile registries are DB2-specific variables that affect the management, configuration, and performance of the DB2 system. DB2 profile registries have no relation to the Windows registries. The *db2set* command is used to view and update the variables. To view all available options, you can use:

```
db2set -?
```

To list out the values of the DB2 profile registry variables currently set on the server, use the *-all* option as illustrated in Figure A.9.

**Figure A.9** Usage and Sample Output of db2set –all

```
db2set -all

[e] DB2PATH=C:\SQLLIB
[i] DB2INSTPROF=C:\SQLLIB
[i] DB2COMM=TCPIP,NPIPE                                      -- (1)
[g] DB2SYSTEM=DB2NTSERV
[g] DB2PATH=C:\SQLLIB
[g] DB2INSTDEF=DB2
[g] DB2COMM=TCPIP,NPIPE                                      -- (2)
[g] DB2ADMINSERVER=DB2DAS00
```

The *db2set -all* command displays the settings of the environment. Indicators such as [e], [i], and [g] represent the scope of the setting:

```
[e] represents the setting of the environment
[u] represents the user level registry
[n] represents node level registry
[i] represents instance level registry
[g] represents global level registry
```

In Figure A.9, you may notice that some registry variables appear twice, one at the instance level at (1), and one at the global level at (2). Which one does DB2 use if values are set differently? The instance level profile registry variables take precedence over the same named global level registry variables. Some operating system environment variables that DB2 recognizes may also have the same identifier as the profile registry variables. In this case, the operating system environment variable is used.

Figure A.10 illustrates some options on how to set DB2 profile registry variables.

**Figure A.10** Example of db2set Command

```
db2set VARIABLE=VALUE                                        -- (1)
db2set VARIABLE=VALUE -i <instname>                          -- (2)
db2set VARIABLE=VALUE -g                                     -- (3)
```

Line (1) of Figure A.10 sets the variable for your current instance as defined by the DB2INSTANCE environment variable. Line (2) uses the -i option to set the variable for the *<instname>* instance. Line (3) uses the -g option to set the variable globally for all instances defined on the server.

Changes made to DB2 profile registry variables are not dynamic, meaning that new values do not immediately take effect. To implement the new changes, you need to stop and start the instance.

Before you can use an instance, you must start the instance using the *db2start* command. If you selected the default install options, the default instance is configured to start up automatically. To stop an instance, use *db2stop*.

If there are connections already made to the database and you try to stop the instance, you will receive this error:

```
SQL1025N The database manager was not stopped because databases are still active.
```

All connections made to databases that are defined in an instance must be terminated before that instance can be stopped. To list the applications currently connected to the databases managed by the current instance, you can use the LIST APPLICATIONS command, as illustrated in Figure A.11.

**Figure A.11** Sample Output of the LIST APPLICATIONS Command

```
db2 LIST APPLICATIONS

Auth Id   Application    Appl.      Application Id                DB       # of
          Name           Handle                                   Name     Agents
-------- -------------- ---------- ----------------------------- -------- -----
SQLSPUSER db2bp.exe      5          *LOCAL.DB2.020606173650        EFORMDB  1
DB2ADMIIN db2cc.exe      4          *LOCAL.DB2.020606173635        SAMPLE   1
SQLSPUSER java.exe       6          7F000001.5505.020606173800     SAMPLE   1
SQLSPUSER db2bp.exe      7          *LOCAL.DB2.020606173811        SAMPLE   1
```

Figure A.11 shows a sample output of LIST APPLICATIONS. The *Auth Id* column of the output represents the authentication ID used to connect. The second column is the application name for the connection. Each connection has a unique application handle (*Appl. Handle*) and *Application Id.* The *DB Name* column tells you which database each connection is connected to. The last column is the number of database agent processes working for the connection.

With this information, you can identify and ask the users to log out from the database. Sometimes, counting on users is not feasible. In these circumstances, you can use the FORCE APPLICATION command to terminate their connections. The following command will disconnect every connection from all the databases defined in an instance.

```
db2 FORCE APPLICATION ALL
```

To selectively terminate a single or a number of connections, you specify the application handles obtained from the output of the LIST APPLICATIONS command in the FORCE APPLICATION command.

For example, you might want to terminate every connection made to the SAMPLE database. Using the sample output in Figure A.11, application handles 4, 6, and 7 can be terminated by executing:

```
db2 "FORCE APPLICATION (4, 6, 7)"
```

Internally, this command will terminate the appropriate database processes and rollback any uncommitted changes for the terminated connections asynchronously. Thus, you may not see the effect of the command immediately.

# A.3 Understanding Buffer Pools

Instances and databases have been discussed at a high level and we can now dig deeper into the details of databases, starting with buffer pools.

To reduce the number of I/O operations to the physical disk where data is stored, DB2 uses buffer pools to cache data and index pages in memory. Every database must have at least one buffer pool defined. The default buffer pool created in each database is called IBMDEFAULTBP.

The default buffer pool is sufficiently large for you to work with the examples presented in this book. If you are creating a database for real workloads, however, the default size of IBMDEFAULTBP is typically not sufficient. You should refer to the *DB2 Administration Guide* for a more in-depth discussion on buffer pools.

You can find out what buffer pools are currently defined by connecting to the database and executing the following SQL statement:

```
db2 "SELECT * FROM SYSCAT.BUFFERPOOLS"
```

Creating a buffer pool is also quite easy. To create a buffer pool called BP16K that uses a 16K page size and is 1000 pages large (page size and pages will be discussed shortly), use the CREATE BUFFERPOOL statement:

```
db2 CREATE BUFFERPOOL BP16K size 1000 pagesize 16K
```

You can also change the size of a buffer pool using the ALTER BUFFERPOOL statement. For example, to reduce the size of the buffer pool above to just 500 pages:

```
db2 ALTER BUFFERPOOL BP16K size 500
```

# A.4 Working with Tablespaces

A tablespace can be viewed as a container for tables and its responsibility is to manage how table data is physically stored on disk. In other words, tables are logical objects that are created in tablespaces.

One of the main characteristics of tablespaces is page size. When table data is stored on disk, data is stored on data pages that can range in size. DB2 supports 4K, 8K, 16K and 32K page sizes. If you create a tablespace TS16K that uses a 16K page size and create a table T1 in TS16K, then all data inserted into T1 is stored physically on disk using 16K data pages.

Each tablespace is mapped to a buffer pool and the buffer pool must be the same page size as the tablespace. So naturally, buffer pool page sizes of 4K, 8K, 16K and 32K are also supported. For example, if you want to create a tablespace of 16K page size, a 16K page size buffer pool must exist before the tablespace can be created. The IBMDEFAULTBP buffer pool uses a 4K page size.

Three default tablespaces are created at database creation time. All use a 4K page size and use IBMDEFAULTBP as their buffer pool. They are the SYSCATSPACE (catalog), TEMPSPACE1 (temporary), and USERSPACE1 (user) tablespaces.

The catalog tablespace, SYSCATSPACE, stores tables which contain metadata about the database. These metadata tables are commonly referred to as the system catalog tables. SYSCATSPACE is created during database creation. No user objects can be defined in it.

The temporary tablespace, TEMPSPACE1, is used to store temporary data. Temporary tablespaces are used by DB2 implicitly for tasks such as sorting and can be used explicitly for tasks such as table reorganization. Therefore, you must have at least one temporary tablespace defined in each database.

USERSPACE1 is a user tablespace that stores user-defined objects like tables and indexes. You can create more than one user tablespace with different characteristics in a database.

When creating a tablespace, in addition to page size, you also need to specify one or more tablespace containers which map to actual physical storage such as an operating system directory, file, or raw device. You will also need to specify whether the tablespace will be managed by the database (known as Database Managed Space, or DMS), or by the operating system (known as System Managed Space, or SMS). Containers for SMS tablespaces are operating system directories; whereas containers for

DMS tablespaces can be pre-allocated files or raw devices. If you create a database without any options to the CREATE DATABASE command, the three default tablespaces are created as SMS tablespaces.

Figure A.12 shows some simple examples of how USER, LARGE, and TEMPORARY tablespaces can be created.

**Figure A.12** Examples of Creating USER, LARGE, and TEMPORARY Tablespaces

```
CREATE USER TABLESPACE userdata_ts                                    -- (1)
    MANAGED BY SYSTEM
    USING ( 'c:\userdata1'
          , 'e:\userdata2' );

CREATE LARGE TABLESPACE largedata_ts                                  -- (2)
    MANAGED BY DATABASE
    USING ( file 'c:\largedata\largefile.f1' 3M
          , file 'd:\largedata\largefile.f2' 3M );

CREATE TEMPORARY TABLESPACE temp_ts                                   -- (3)
    MANAGED BY SYSTEM
    USING ( 'c:\tempdata1' );
```

At (1), *userdata_ts* is a USER tablespace. It is MANAGED BY SYSTEM, which means it is an SMS tablespace. User-defined database objects can be stored in it. Data will be striped across two containers and they are operating system directories.

The second tablespace at (2), *largedata_ts,* is a LARGE tablespace. LARGE tablespaces must be defined as DMS with the MANAGED BY DATABASE clause. Notice that two files are defined as the containers for this tablespace and each of them is 3M in size.

The last example at (3) creates an SMS system temporary tablespace with only one container.

Detailed characteristics and differences between SMS and DMS tablespaces are not discussed here. More information can be obtained from the DB2 Administration Guide or references listed in Appendix G, "Additional References" of this book. By using some DB2 commands, you can easily get the list of tablespaces defined in a database, their status, and location of the containers for each tablespace.

To list all the tablespaces of a database, connect to the database and issue:

```
db2 LIST TABLESPACES
```

You will get an output similar to Figure A.13.

**Figure A.13** Sample Output of the LIST TABLESPACES Command

```
           Tablespaces for Current Database

 Tablespace ID                        = 0
 Name                                 = SYSCATSPACE
 Type                                 = System managed space
 Contents                             = Any data
 State                                = 0x0000
   Detailed explanation:
     Normal

 Tablespace ID                        = 1
 Name                                 = TEMPSPACE1
 Type                                 = System managed space
 Contents                             = System Temporary data
 State                                = 0x0000
   Detailed explanation:
     Normal

 Tablespace ID                        = 2
 Name                                 = USERSPACE1
 Type                                 = System managed space
 Contents                             = Any data
 State                                = 0x0000
   Detailed explanation:
     Normal

 Tablespace ID                        = 3
 Name                                 = LARGEDATATS
 Type                                 = Database managed space
 Contents                             = Any data
 State                                = 0x0000
   Detailed explanation:
     Normal
```

The output provides the unique tablespace ID, tablespace name, type of the tablespace (i.e., SMS or DMS), and status of the tablespace.

To get information about the containers used for a specific tablespace, execute:

```
db2 LIST TABLESPACE CONTAINERS FOR <table-space-id>
```

You need to provide the tablespace ID in this command and this information is available from the output of the LIST TABLESPACES command. An example of using this command and the result is shown in Figure A.14.

**Figure A.14** Example of the LIST TABLESPACE CONTAINERS Command

```
db2 LIST TABLESPACE CONTAINERS FOR 3

            Tablespace Containers for Tablespace 3

 Container ID                         = 0
 Name                                 = c:\largedata\largefile.f1
 Type                                 = File

 Container ID                         = 1
 Name                                 = d:\largedata\largefile.f2
 Type                                 = File
```

## A.5 Working with Tables

Now it's time to learn how to create some tables. Again, tables are created within tablespaces. A default tablespace called USERSPACE1 (Figure A.15) is created for you upon database creation so that you can begin creating tables right away.

**Figure A.15** Example of Table Creation

```
CREATE TABLE classes
    ( classid      INTEGER NOT NULL
    , classname    VARCHAR(50) NOT NULL
    , instructor   VARCHAR(50)
    , classdate    DATE
    , PRIMARY KEY ( classid ) )                                        -- (1)
    IN userdata_ts                                                     -- (2)
```

Figure A.15 shows an example of creating a table with a primary key defined on the *classid* column at (1).

To explicitly specify which tablespace you want this table to be created in, use the IN *<table-space-name>* clause as illustrated at (2). If the IN clause is not specified, the table will be created in a tablespace that has a sufficiently large page size, given the row size of the table, and where the user has privileges to do so. Every user object in DB2 must belong to a schema. A schema is a logical grouping of database objects, like tables and stored procedures. It is possible to have tables with the same name but in different schemas. You can explicitly reference a database object by its schema and object name using *<schema-name>.<db-object>*. Notice that schema is not specified as part of the statement in Figure A.15. In such cases, the authorization ID used to connect and execute the CREATE TABLE statement will be used for the schema.

In some situations, you may want to create tables in a schema other than your authorization ID, but don't want to fully qualify all the object names. There is a register called CURRENT SCHEMA that can be used to obtain or set the current schema. To get the current schema, simply do this:

```
db2 VALUES CURRENT SCHEMA
```

The default value of the CURRENT SCHEMA is the authorization ID used to connect to the database.

To change the current schema, use this command:

```
db2 SET CURRENT SCHEMA = NEWSCHEMA
```

Once the new schema is set, any references to database objects that are not explicitly qualified with a schema will implicitly use this new schema for the duration of the session.

To list out tables defined in a database, you can use the LIST TABLES command. This command has several options.

```
db2 LIST TABLES
```

This command lists tables that belong to the schema assigned to the CURRENT SCHEMA register mentioned above.

If you want to list all the tables under a specific schema, you can extend the previous command to:

```
db2 LIST TABLES FOR SCHEMA <schema-name>
```

The FOR ALL option shown below will then list all the tables under every schema defined in the database.

```
db2 LIST TABLES FOR ALL
```

One other useful thing to know is how to easily find out the structure of a table. For example, you may want to insert a row in a table for which you do not know the data type for a specific column. This command will definitely save you time in searching for the answer:

```
db2 DESCRIBE TABLE <table-name>
```

To *describe* the STAFF table of the SAMPLE database, you can issue:

```
db2 DESCRIBE TABLE staff
```

You should get output similar to Figure A.16:

**Figure A.16** Example Output of the DESCRIBE TABLE Command

```
Column                         Type      Type
name                           schema    name               Length   Scale Nulls
------------------------------ --------- ------------------ -------- ----- -----
ID                             SYSIBM    SMALLINT                  2     0 No
NAME                           SYSIBM    VARCHAR                   9     0 Yes
DEPT                           SYSIBM    SMALLINT                  2     0 Yes
JOB                            SYSIBM    CHARACTER                 5     0 Yes
YEARS                          SYSIBM    SMALLINT                  2     0 Yes
SALARY                         SYSIBM    DECIMAL                   7     2 Yes
COMM                           SYSIBM    DECIMAL                   7     2 Yes

  7 record(s) selected.
```

## A.5.1 Introducing the System Catalog Tables

Most commands demonstrated in this appendix so far obtain information about the database. For example, the LIST TABLESPACES and LIST TABLES commands list the tablespaces and tables defined in a database, respectively. Where is the information actually stored? The information about data (also known as metadata) is contained in the system catalog tables. These tables are defined under the SYSIBM schema. Since the amount of information stored in the SYSIBM tables is usually more than what database administrators or users want to know, filtered information is extracted through the use of views. They are defined under the SYSCAT schema. Table A.1 shows some common SYSCAT views that may be useful when developing your SQL procedures. For a complete list, refer to the *DB2 SQL Reference Guide.*

**Table A.1** Common System Catalog Views

| Catalog Views | Descriptions |
|---|---|
| SYSCAT.BUFFERPOOLS | Buffer Pool configuration |
| SYSCAT.COLUMNS | Columns |
| SYSCAT.FUNCTIONS | Functions |
| SYSCAT.PACKAGES | Packages |
| SYSCAT.PROCEDURES | Stored Procedures |
| SYSCAT.TABLES | Tables |
| SYSCAT.TABLESPACES | Tablespaces |
| SYSCAT.TRIGGERS | Triggers |

## A.6 Summary

This appendix introduced some basic commands to get you started with a DB2 database. Creation and manipulation of DB2 instances, databases, buffer pools, tablespaces, and tables were demonstrated. Some basic scripting and command options were also discussed. At this point, you should be able to set up a DB2 database to work with the examples shown in this book.

A P P E N D I X 

# Setting up the Build Environment

This appendix outlines DB2 install requirements and steps to set up an environment for building SQL stored procedures.

## B.1 DB2 Installation

The version of DB2 included with this book is DB2 Personal Edition v8.1 for Windows and is a full-featured version of DB2 for the purpose of single server development and education. SQL procedures developed on Personal Edition (PE) will also work on Workgroup Server Edition (WSE) and Enterprise Server Edition (ESE).

A DB2 installation can be divided into four components:

- Administration Client
- Application Development Client
- Runtime Client
- Database Server

You have the option to install only the components that you need. Be aware that even though SQL procedures are server-side objects, you are not limited to developing them directly on the machine. You can just as easily develop SQL procedures using only the DB2 Development Center (or even just the command line) from a remote client machine as long as DB2 client software is installed. To illustrate, here are some sample scenarios and their installation requirements.

## B.1.1 Local Database Development

Developing on a local database means that the database and stored procedure development occurs on the same machine. This is the simplest scenario and is illustrated in Figure B.1.

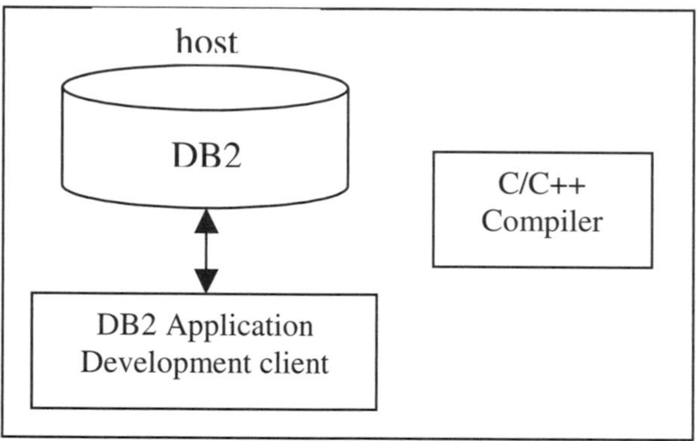


**Figure B.1** Local Database Development Configuration

In this setup, the following DB2 components are required:

- DB2 Personal, Workgroup, or Enterprise Server Edition
- DB2 Application Development Client

The Application Development Client will provide the DB2 Development Center tool for writing stored procedures and the required libraries for building them. In addition, you will also need to install a supported C compiler for your platform. See the Compiler Requirements section below for details.

DB2 for Linux supports the GNU gcc and g++ compilers which are available for free. If you do not have access to a C compiler, consider trying DB2 for Linux which is available for free trial download at http://www.ibm.com/db2.

## B.1.2 Remote Database Development

Remote database development means that stored procedures are developed from a machine which is different from that which hosts data, database objects, and stored procedures. For example, you may have a DB2 database server which resides on Linux, but have a team of developers who develop against the same database from various remote Windows clients. Figure B.2 illustrates this configuration.



**Figure B.2** Remote Database Development Configuration

To support remote database development, the following components must be installed on the database server machine:

- DB2 Personal, Workgroup or Enterprise Server Edition
- DB2 Application Development Client

In addition, you will also need to install a supported C compiler on the server to compile stored procedures. See the Compiler Requirements section below for details.

On the client machine, because stored procedures are built and persisted at the server, you only need to install one of the above mentioned DB2 clients for database connectivity. Once you have established connectivity to the server, you will be able to build SQL procedures using the command line.

It is recommended that you install the DB2 Application Development Client, however, as it provides the DB2 Development Center tool for easier stored procedure development and other useful GUI tools such as the DB2 Control Center. A C compiler is not required on the client machine in this configuration.

As a final step, at each client machine, establish connectivity to the database server using the CATALOG command or the DB2 Configuration Assistant. Consult the product documentation for more details.

## B.1.3 Compiler Requirements

A supported C compiler must be installed on the machine where SQL procedures will be built. Note that a compiler is not needed for deploying stored procedures from one database to another—it is required only for building them. Please see Chapter 9, "Deploying SQL Procedures" for details.

Table B.1 lists the supported compilers for DB2 v8.1 for various platforms.

**Table B.1** Compilers Supported for DB2 v8.1 by Platform

| Platform | Compiler |
|---|---|
| AIX | IBM VisualAge C++ 5.0 (*)<br>IBM C for AIX Version 5.0 |
| HP-UX | HP aC++ Version A.03.31 (*)<br>HP C Compiler Version B.11.11.02 |
| Linux | GNU/Linux g++ (*)<br>GNU/Linux gcc |
| Solaris | Forte C++ Version 5.0 (*)<br>Forte C Version 5.0 |
| Windows | Visual C++ 5.0, 6.0, and .NET |

By default, DB2's registry variables are preconfigured to use the compliers marked with a star (*). If you are using one of these compilers, no further action is necessary and you can proceed directly to Verifying Your Build Environment below.

# B.2 Setting up the SQL Procedure Build Environment

On all platforms, if you modify DB2 registry variables, you must stop and restart the instance for changes to take effect (using db2stop and db2start).

You may notice that these settings differ slightly from the initial release of DB2 v8 documentation. The settings described here are correct.

## B.2.1 AIX

By default, DB2 supports the VisualAge C++ version 5.0 compiler. If you are using this compiler, no additional configuration is necessary.

To configure DB2 to use IBM C for AIX Version 5.0:

```
db2set DB2_SQLROUTINE_COMPILE_COMMAND=xlc_r -I$HOME/sqllib/include \
   SQLROUTINE_FILENAME.c -bE:SQLROUTINE_FILENAME.exp \
   -e SQLROUTINE_ENTRY -o SQLROUTINE_FILENAME -L$HOME/sqllib/lib -ldb2
```

## B.2.2 HP-UX

By default, DB2 supports the HP aC++ Version A.03.31 compiler. If you are using this compiler, no additional configuration is necessary.

To configure DB2 to use the HP C Compiler Version B.11.11.02, issue the following as a DB2 SYSADM user:

```
db2set DB2_SQLROUTINE_COMPILE_COMMAND=cc +DAportable +ul -Aa +z \
   -D_POSIX_C_SOURCE=199506L \
   -I$HOME/sqllib/include -c SQLROUTINE_FILENAME.c; \
   ld -b -lpthread -o SQLROUTINE_FILENAME SQLROUTINE_FILENAME.o \
   -L$HOME/sqllib/lib -ldb2
```

## B.2.3 Linux

By default, DB2 supports the GNU/g++ compiler. If you are using this compiler, no additional configuration is necessary.

To configure DB2 to use the GNU/gcc compiler, issue the following command as a DB2 SYSADM user:

```
db2set DB2_SQLROUTINE_COMPILE_COMMAND=cc -fpic  -D_REENTRANT \
   -I$HOME/sqllib/include SQLROUTINE_FILENAME.c \
   -shared -lpthread -o SQLROUTINE_FILENAME -L$HOME/sqllib/lib -ldb2
```

## B.2.4 Solaris

By default, DB2 supports the Forte C++ Version 5.0 compiler. If you are using this compiler, no additional configuration will be necessary.

To configure DB2 to use the Forte C Version 5.0 compiler, issue the following command as a DB2 SYSDM user:

```
db2set DB2_SQLROUTINE_COMPILE_COMMAND=cc -xarch=v8plusa -Kpic  -mt \
   -I$HOME/sqllib/include SQLROUTINE_FILENAME.c \
   -G -o SQLROUTINE_FILENAME -L$HOME/sqllib/lib \
   -R$HOME/sqllib/lib -ldb2
```

## B.2.5 Windows

DB2 v8.1 is supported on Windows NT, Windows 2000, Windows XP, and Windows .NET Server. By default, DB2 supports the Microsoft Visual C++ compiler. During installation of Visual Studio, the install process will ask if you wish to have the compiler environment added to your system variables. If you answered YES to this question, no additional configuration is needed and you can proceed to the next section.

If you do not have the compiler environment added to your system variables, you can set up DB2 to automatically call vcvars32.bat (provided by the Visual C++ install) to set up the compiler environment. Assuming the C++ compiler is installed on the C: drive, set the DB2_SQLROUTINE_COMPILER_PATH DB2 registry variable as follows (substitute the appropriate install path as necessary):

For Microsoft Visual C++ Version 5.0:

```
db2set DB2_SQLROUTINE_COMPILER_PATH="c:\devstudio\vc\bin\vcvars32.bat"
```

For Microsoft Visual C++ Version 6.0:

```
db2set DB2_SQLROUTINE_COMPILER_PATH="c:\Micros~1\vc98\bin\vcvars32.bat"
```

For Microsoft Visual C++ .NET

```
db2set DB2_SQLROUTINE_COMPILER_PATH=
"D:\Program Files\Microsoft Visual Studio .NET\Common7\Tools\vsvars32.bat"
```

If you have problems with configuring the Windows environment, ensure that the value of the DB2_SQLROUTINE_COMPILER_PATH registry variable effectively points to VCVARS32.bat (for MSVC++ Version 5.0 or 6.0) or to VSVARS32.bat (for .NET). If you update the value of this variable, remember that you have to restart the DB2 instance for the new value to become effective.

## B.2.6 Verifying Your Build Environment

This section describes the steps to verify that your system is set up correctly for building SQL procedures.

First, if you have not already done so, create the sample database that is used for all examples presented in this book.

To do this, from the command line, type:

```
db2sampl
```

Then, connect to the database:

```
db2 "connect to sample user <userid> using <password>"
```

Once connected, create a stored procedure called P1() which does nothing.

```
db2 "create procedure p1() language sql begin end"
```

Finally, call the stored procedure from the command line:

```
db2 "call p1()"
```

You should see the following output which means that your environment is working properly:

```
RETURN_STATUS: "0"
```

Once you have verified your build environment, your system is ready to build stored procedures.

APPENDIX 

# Using the DB2 Development Center

## C.1 What is the Development Center?

The DB2 Development Center (DC) is an integrated development environment (IDE) that is included with DB2 UDB V8. This application is included to offer developers and database administrators (DBAs) an easy interface to create and build SQL procedures and user-defined functions. The IDE also includes a debugger for SQL procedures. It can be used to develop both Java and SQL procedures but this appendix will only cover the latter. There is a full set of online help pages included with the application that offer detailed information. The help pages can be used to assist the reader if the following sections are not detailed enough or further information is required.

### C.1.1 How Do I Install It?

When installing DB2, there is an option for *Application Development* tools (that includes the Development Center) and will be selected by default for a typical installation. If you perform a custom installation of DB2, ensure that the *Development Center* option is selected as illustrated in Figure C.1.

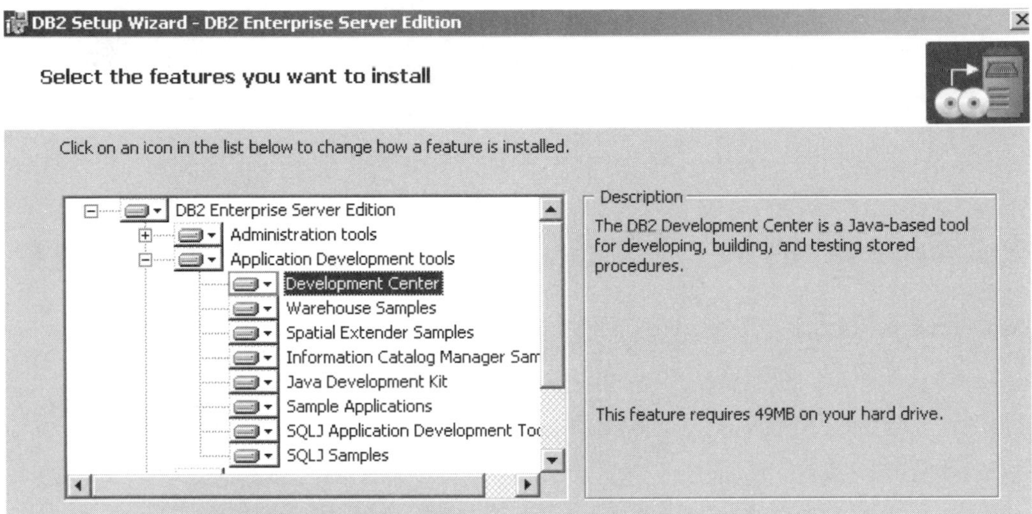


**Figure C.1** Selecting the Installation of the DC

## C.1.2 How Do I Run It?

### *Windows*

The Development Center is launched from the DB2 Development Tools menu listed in the Windows Start menu (Figure C.2). The program is Java based and is available to run on all platforms supported by DB2 UDB V8. The program can also be run as an integrated component of IBM WebSphere Studio Application Developer (WSAD) or Microsoft Visual Studio.

**Figure C.2** Development Center Menu Location in Windows

### *UNIX and Linux*

The Development Center is found in the $DB2INSTHOME/sqllib/bin directory and is called *db2dc*. The program is included in the path of any user who sources the $DB2INSTHOME/sqllib/db2profile DB2 environment script. The program will run in any system that supports a graphical user interface. The program, therefore, cannot be run in an interface that supports only text such as a Telnet connection without X-Windows or similar products running.

## C.2 Using the Development Center

There are two major interfaces used in the DC: the main window and the editor window. The main interface contains information about all the stored procedures, user-defined functions and structured types for the databases used by the projects currently open. A whole range of actions can be performed by right clicking on the project folder or stored procedure icons (Figure C.3). These actions include:

- Creating a project
- Saving a project
- Building a stored procedure
- Debugging a stored procedure
- Importing a stored procedure
- Editing a stored procedure
- Dropping a stored procedure from the database

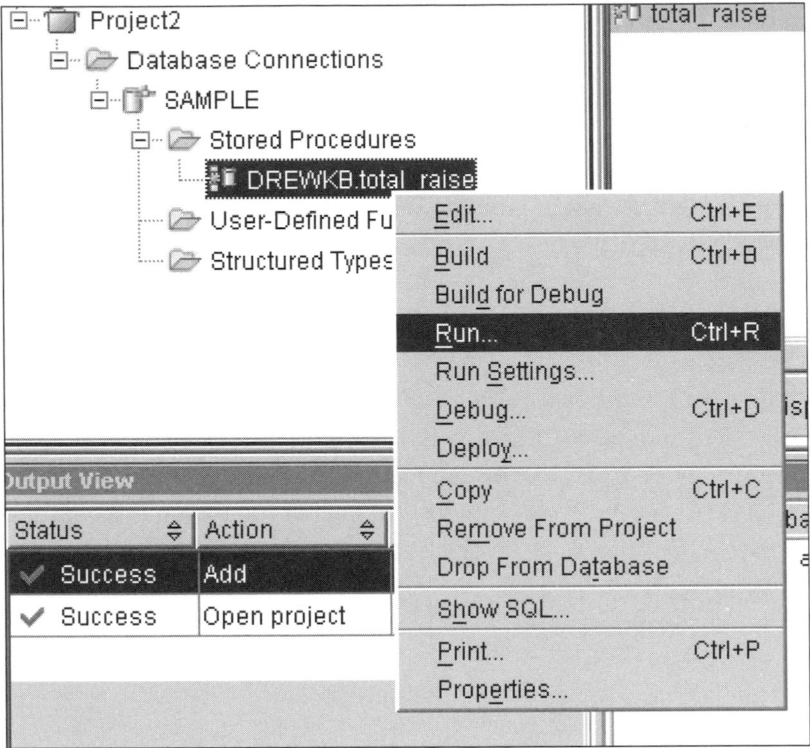


**Figure C.3** Stored Procedure Options

The main interface, as shown in Figure C.4, is used for the actual building, execution and testing of stored procedures and is used in conjunction with the editor window during debugging and editing.

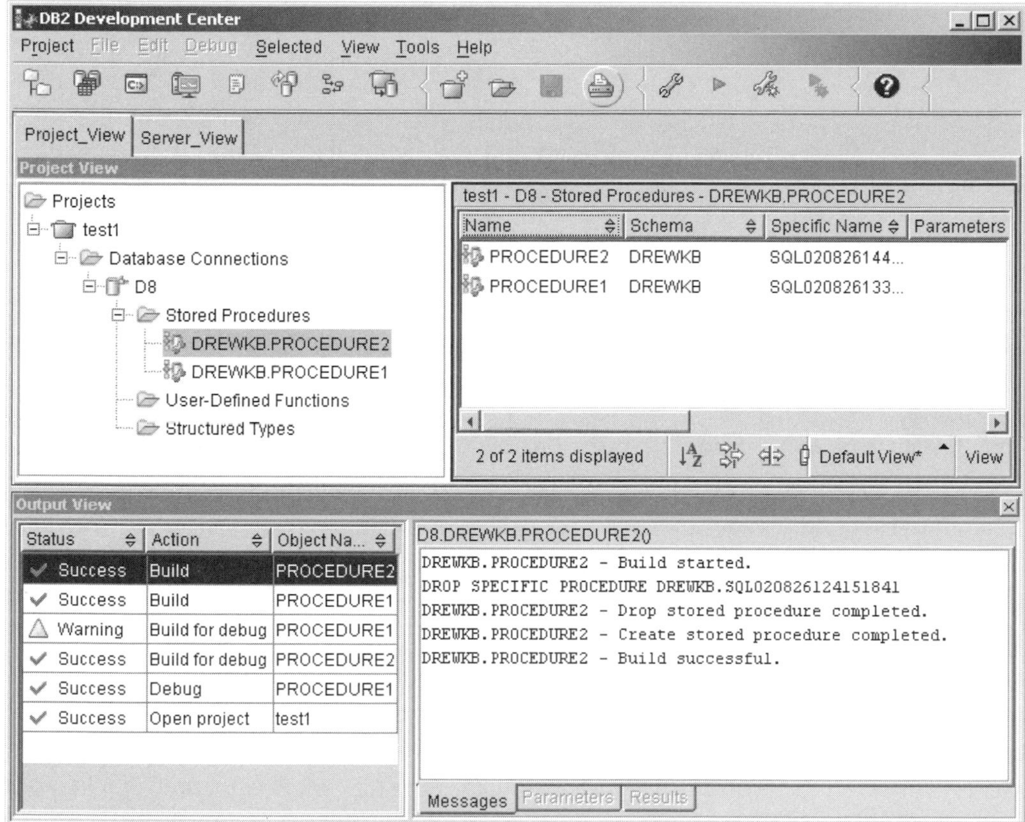


**Figure C.4** Development Center Main Window

The source code for a procedure can be retrieved by double-clicking the icon of any stored procedure in a project, pressing ***CTRL-E*** while highlighting a stored procedure, or by right-clicking it and selecting the ***Edit*** menu item. This will open the ***editor*** interface.

## C.2.1 Working with Projects

The Development Center uses ***projects*** to keep track of all stored procedures, UDFs and structured types that are relevant to a project. A project can even reference application objects from multiple databases. There can also be multiple and varying copies of the same procedure open in different projects. Each project will have its own copy of all its procedures. This code can be saved and it will not overwrite copies from other projects. The procedure code will be saved into the database when it is built. If a different copy of the procedure from another project is built, the new code from the second project will overwrite the code from the first project at the database server. Example 1 illustrates this concept.

**Example 1:**

> There are two projects, projectA and projectB, which both contain a copy of procedure procTest from the same database.
>
> User1 opens up projectA and edits its copy of procTest to have a return code of 4.
>
> User2 opens up projectB and also edits its copy of procTest to have a return code of 3. There are now two versions of the procedure open.
>
> User1 then builds procTest. If the procedure is now run, the return code will be 4. The code for procTest that User2 has open is not affected by User1's actions.
>
> User2 then builds her copy of procTest. User2 will be asked if she wants to drop the old copy of the procedure (built by User1) and build a new one. If she chooses to build the procedure, then the return code of the procedure will be 3.

New projects can be created by selecting *New Project* from the *Project* pull down menu. The properties of the project, such as which database(s) it connects to, are set when the project is first opened. Projects can also be created by using the *Development Center Launchpad* which will step you through setting each property of the project. The *Launchpad* automatically starts by default when the DC is started up. The *Launchpad* can be opened after the DC has started by selecting the *Launchpad* option from the Project pull down menu as illustrated in Figure C.5.

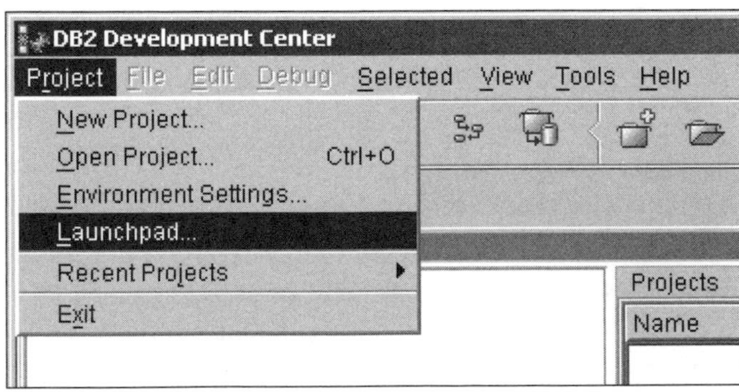


**Figure C.5** Launchpad Screen

Multiple projects can be open in the DC at the same time. Projects can be opened from the *Project* pull down menu by selecting the ***Open*** option. The *Remove Project* option will delete the project from memory but will not delete the application objects that were successfully built on the database. Be sure to save all your projects to ensure that all your changes to the project are kept. If you do not save the project and have not built the stored procedure, then your changes will be lost. Procedure changes will not take effect on the database until they are built, despite the project having been saved.

## C.2.2 Creating New Stored Procedures

Creating an SQL procedure is easy using the DC since there is a wizard (Figure C.6) that can walk you through each step. The wizard will ask you questions about:

- Input and output parameters
- Number of result sets being returned
- Type of SQL being used
- Types of exceptions being returned
- Code fragments used from other stored procedures

Experienced users can also create new procedures without using the wizard. The procedure is created by right-clicking the *Stored Procedure* folder icon, selecting New, and then SQL Stored Procedure as illustrated in Figure C.7.

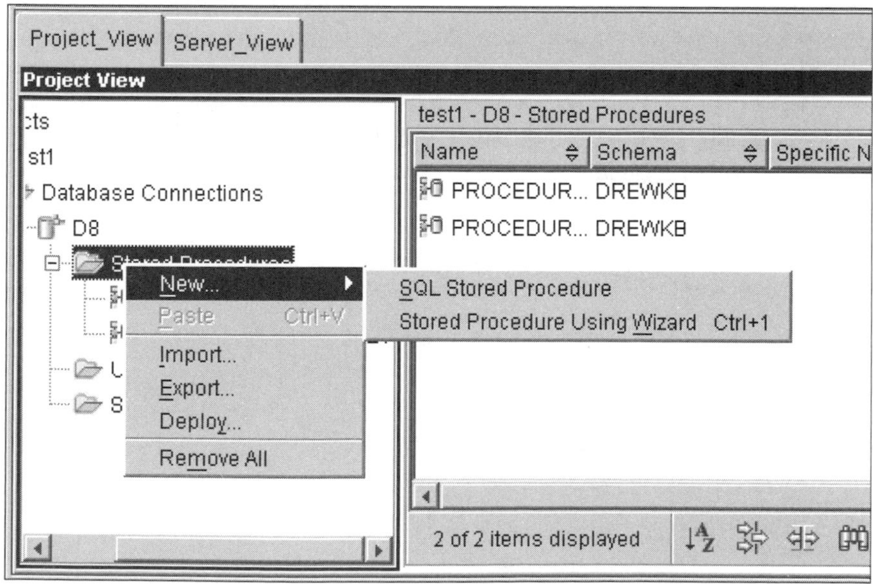


**Figure C.6** Creating a New SQL Stored Procedure

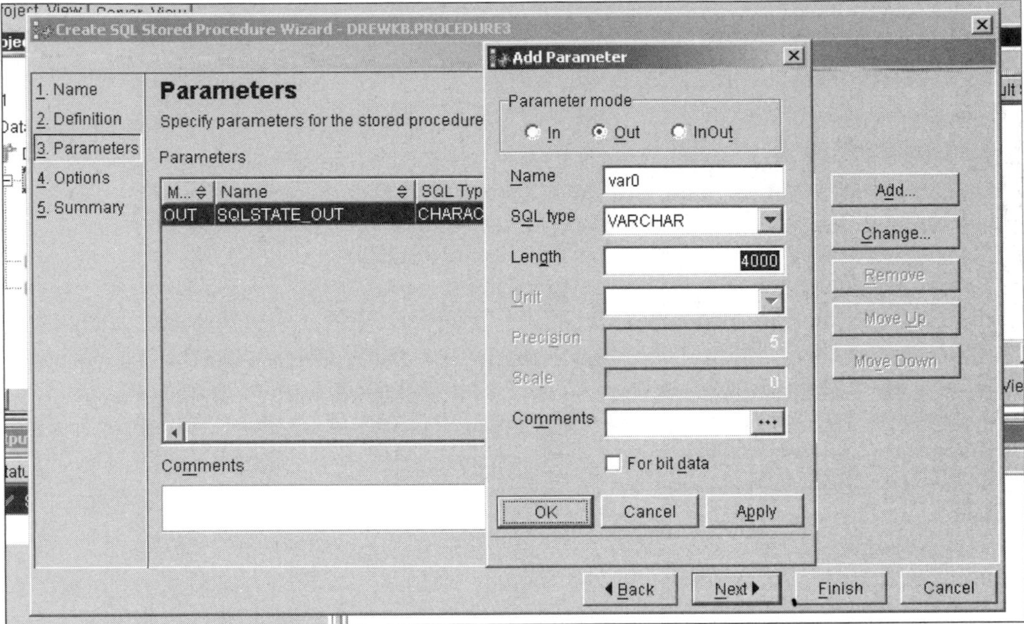


**Figure C.7** SQL Stored Procedure Creation Wizard

## C.2.3 Importing Stored Procedures

Often, an SQL procedure that you wish to work with has already been written by someone else or exists in another project. The Development Center allows you to quickly create a new procedure from code that is saved elsewhere.

Once you have opened up a project, you can import a procedure by right-clicking on the stored procedure folder icon and selecting ***Import***, as illustrated in Figure C.8.

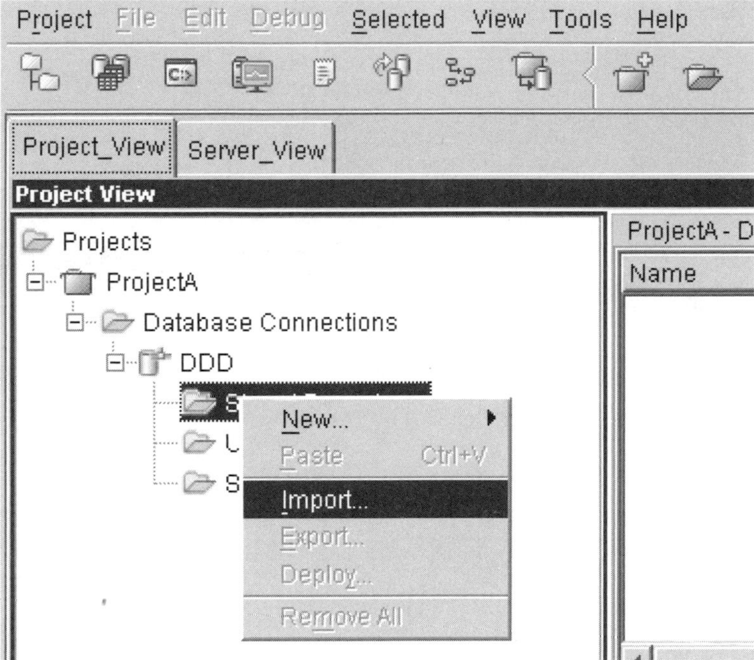


**Figure C.8** Importing a Stored Procedure

There are two sources from which a procedure can be imported. The procedure can be directly extracted from a database or it can be read in from a file. The database import option allows you to use filters to limit the search for procedures that may exist in a database. The file system option will allow you to either import a procedure from a file or from another project. These two options are shown in Figure C.9.

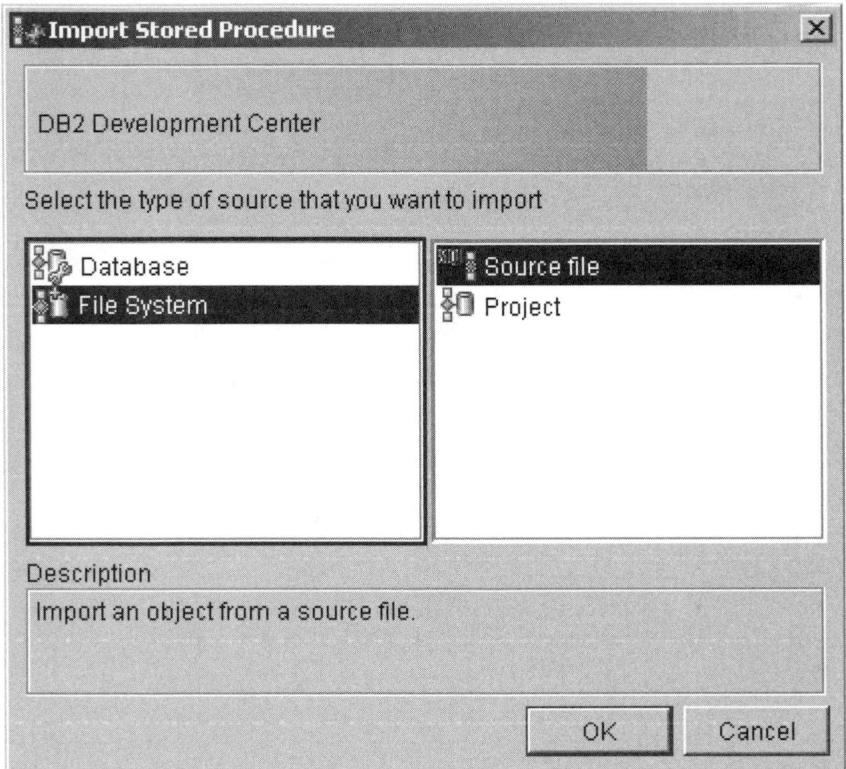


**Figure C.9** The Import Operation Allows You to Import From a Database or a File

All of the SQL procedures used in this book are included in files on the book's CD and are named based on chapter and figure numbers. When you import a procedure, there are a number of options available that allow you to alter the properties and specifics of the procedure (Figure C.10). These options should not be altered when you are initially working with the sample procedures but you are free to experiment with them as you become more comfortable with DB2 and SQL PL.

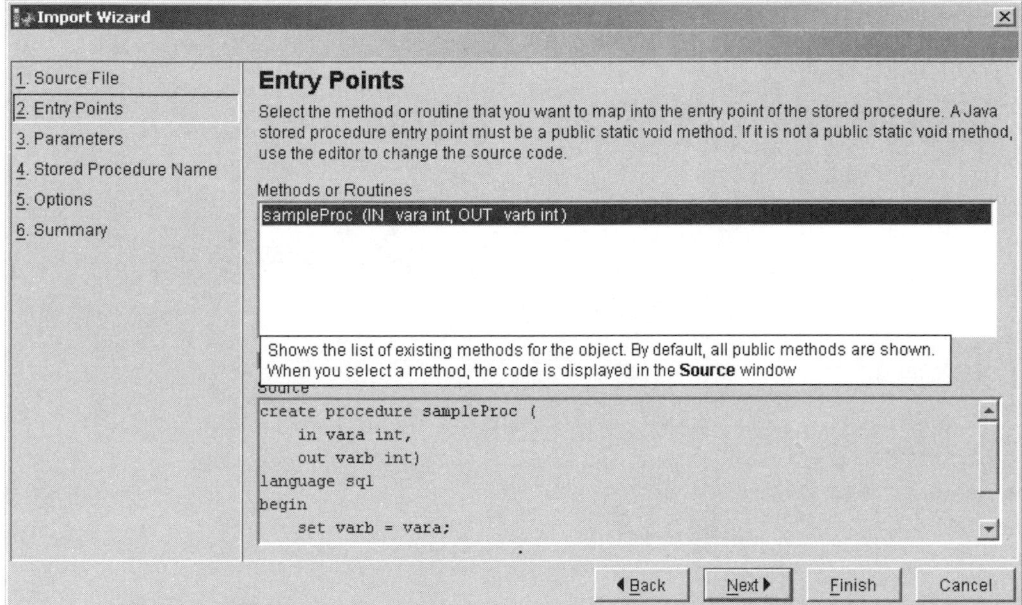


**Figure C.10** Import Options when Importing from a File

## C.2.4 Editing Stored Procedures

Each procedure opened for editing will have its own window from which it can be modified and debugged (Figure C.11). The text is displayed in the editor window with a number of debugging options listed above it. The editor interface offers a full range of functions to manipulate and search through the procedure text. All SQL keywords are highlighted in blue, which will make editing easier. When a procedure is built, run, or debugged, the results and output will not appear in the edit window. Instead, they will be displayed in the main DC interface at the bottom of the window.

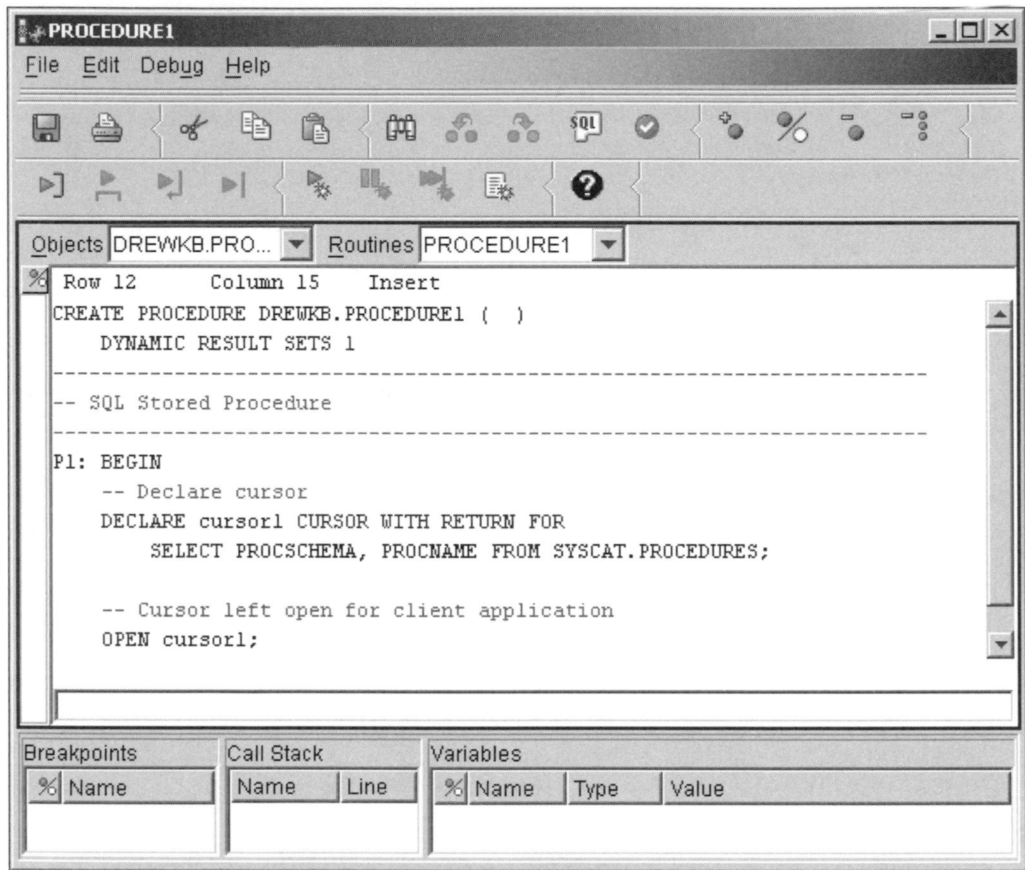


**Figure C.11** Stored Procedure Editing Window

## C.2.5 Building Stored Procedures

DB2 UDB V8.1 requires that a supported C compiler be installed on the system for building SQL stored procedures. The C compiler is used to convert the SQL procedures to C compiled code which is then run by the database engine. See Appendix B, "Setting Up the Build Environment" for the supported compilers and the steps required to configure a compiler for DB2.

SQL procedures are edited in the editor window, but are built by clicking *build* in the main DC window. Right-clicking the specific procedure will give you a list of different build options. The two main options, shown in Figure C.12, are *Build* and *Build* for *Debug*. The Build option will first drop the stored procedure if it already exists at the database and then rebuild it. If the build fails, then the stored procedure cannot be executed until the code or compilation problem is fixed and rebuilt.

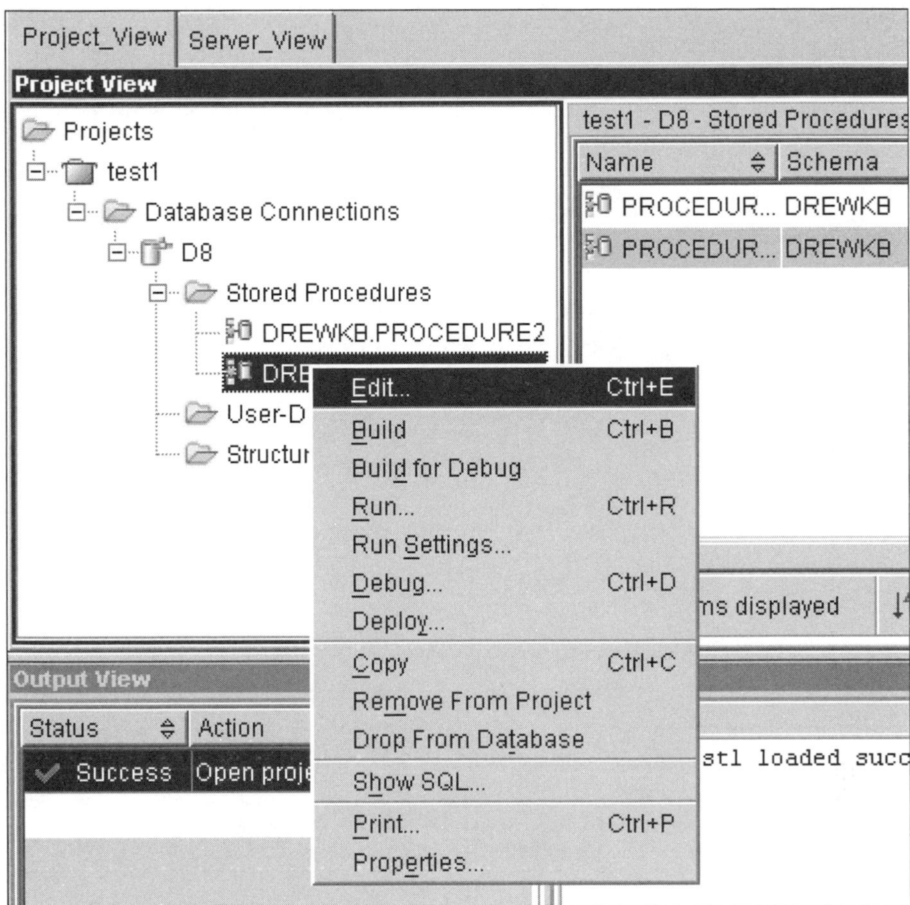


**Figure C.12** Build Options with SQL Stored Procedures

## C.2.6 Debugging Stored Procedures

The DC offers a complete range of debugging tools for stepping through a procedure. The debugger is integrated into the edit window. When a debug session is started, DC will either open up a window for the current procedure or use an existing window if the procedure is already being edited.

A procedure must be built in debug mode in order for the debugging capabilities to be used. If a procedure is built in regular mode, attempts to run it in debug mode will result in the procedure simply being run normally. The *build for debug* option is listed with the other procedure options as shown in Figure C.13.

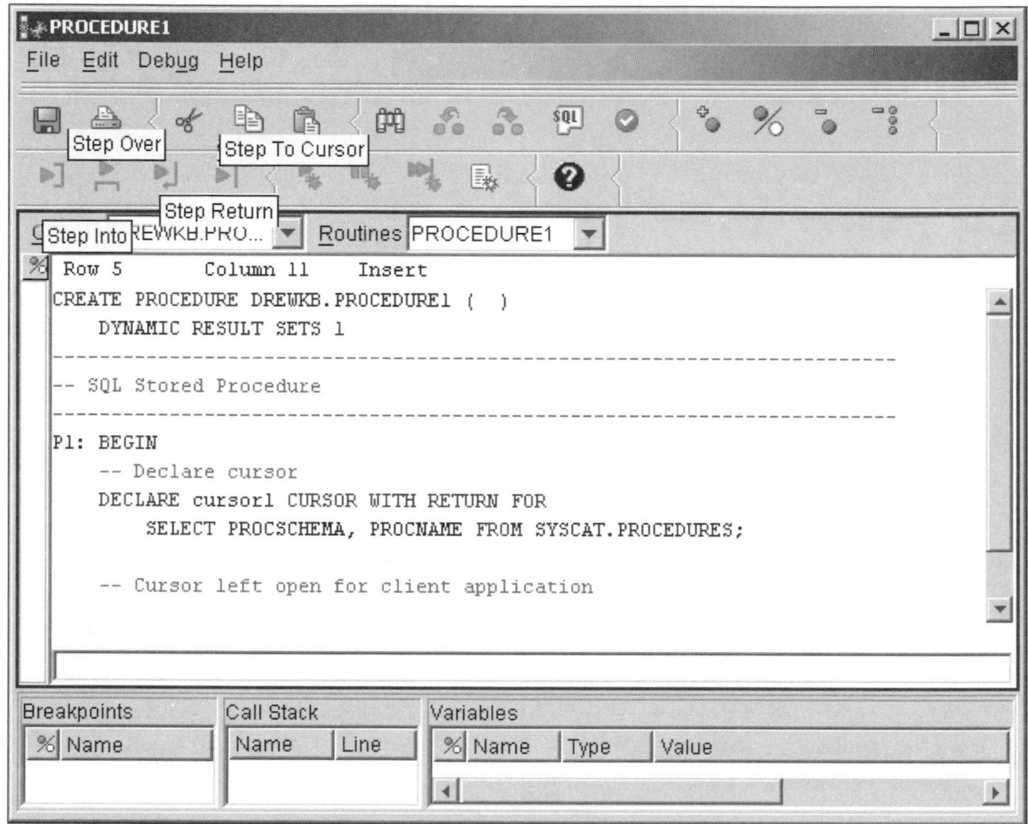


**Figure C.13** Debugging Options

A procedure can be traced through line by line by selecting the *Step Into* icon. The procedure will be run one line at a time and its progress is controlled by continuing to click on the *Step Into* icon.

The *Step Over* icon will cause a block of code or a called procedure to be executed without stepping through every line. This allows you to avoid tracing entire blocks of code that you are not interested in or have already fixed. The *Step To Cursor* icon allows you to run all of the applicable code up to the point of the desired statement in non-debug mode. This is quite useful if you have already debugged a large section of a procedure and want to resume your debugging deep inside the code. The *Step Return* icon can be clicked to cause the procedure to exit immediately from the current point in the code.

A procedure can often be quite long and having to step through all the lines to reach a section with a possible error in it can be quite tedious. A breakpoint can be added to the code which will halt the execution of a procedure when that point is reached by the debugger (see Figure C.14). A breakpoint is added in a procedure by clicking in the left-most column of the edit window while the arrow is on the line of code where the break should occur. Multiple breakpoints can be added to a procedure and each breakpoint will be indicated by a red dot. A breakpoint is useful if you want to check the current values of a variable at a particular point in the code to ensure that the procedure is performing as expected. A breakpoint can be removed as easily as it is added, returning the code to normal execution.

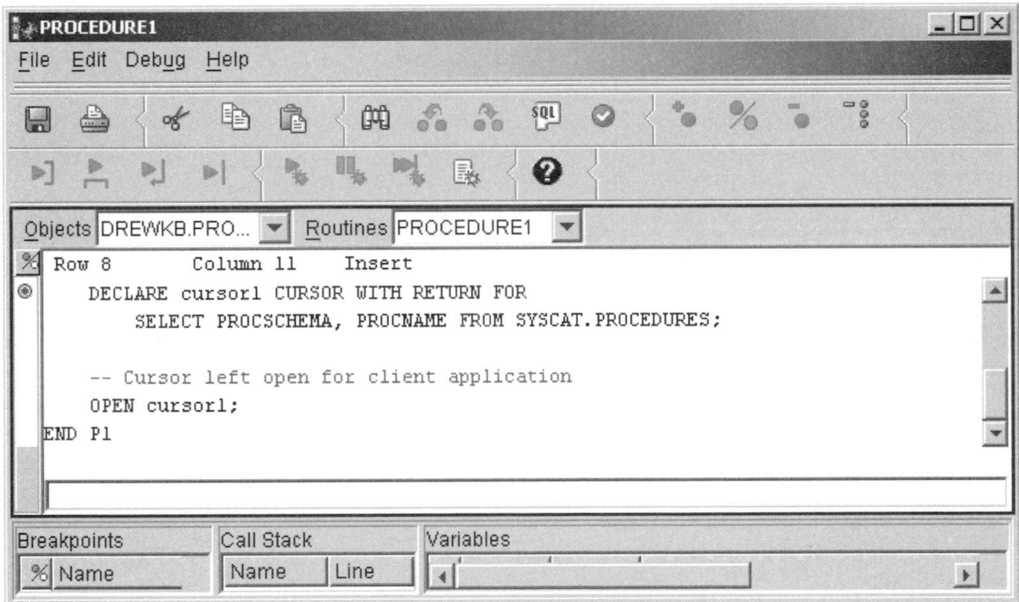


**Figure C.14** Adding a Breakpoint

A breakpoint in a procedure can be reached by initially stepping through the code and then clicking the *Step to Cursor* icon. The code will execute in normal mode until the first breakpoint is reached. The debugger will then return to debug mode and the procedure can continue to be stepped through.

## C.2.7 Debugging Nested Stored Procedures

A stored procedure may call additional procedures as they execute which can make debugging complicated. The DC debugger has been designed to simplify this task. The parent stored procedure from which the debugger is initially started in must be built in debug mode. When another procedure is called, at each nested level, it is checked to see if it is also in debug mode. If the nested procedure has not been built in debug mode, it will be executed normally until it completes. If the nested procedure is in debug mode, an edit window will be opened for it and the debugger will begin to step through it. Consider the example shown in Table C.1.

**Table C.1** Example of Debugging a Nested Stored Procedure

| Procedure | Debug Mode | Procedure Called |
|---|---|---|
| Proc1 | Debug | Proc2 |
| Proc2 | Debug | Proc3 |
| Proc3 | Normal | Proc4 |
| Proc4 | Debug | |

In Table C.1, a developer initially debugs *Proc1* by stepping through it. The debugger will execute the procedure one line at a time until the call to *Proc2* is reached. An edit window for *Proc2* will then be opened and it will be stepped through because it was built in debug mode. The debugger will stop when the call to *Proc3* is reached and will run the procedure normally. The debugger will renew stepping through the code when the call by *Proc3* to *Proc4* is reached.

Upon the completion of *Proc4*, the debugger will return to running *Proc3* normally without any debugging options. At the completion of *Proc3* the debugger will resume stepping through the procedure in *Proc2's* edit window. Upon completion of *Proc2*, the debugger will return to the original calling *Proc1*. Debugging will finish once *Proc1* completes.

More complex debugging tasks can also be done by adding breakpoints in nested procedures, as shown in Table C.2. The initial procedure will run normally until the breakpoint is reached in a nested procedure. The nested procedure with the breakpoint must be built in debug mode to allow the procedure to be stepped through once the breakpoint is reached. The nested break points can be reached by using the *Step to Cursor* icon. If multiple breakpoints are embedded in the procedures, then clicking on the icon again will cause the program to execute until the next breakpoint is reached.

**Table C.2** Example of Debugging a Nested Stored Procedure Using Breakpoints

| Procedure | Debug Mode | Procedure Called |
|---|---|---|
| ProcA | Debug | ProcB |
| ProcB | Normal | ProcC |
| ProcC | Debug<br>(with breakpoint) | |

In Table C.2, procedure *ProcA* is run in debug mode. The *Step to Cursor* icon is then clicked. *ProcA* makes a call to *ProcB*, which will be executed normally and the code will not be debugged. The execution will continue until *ProcB* calls *procC* and the breakpoint in *ProcC* is reached. You can then step through *ProcC* starting from the breakpoint. Upon completion of *ProcC*, the debugger will return to executing *ProcB* normally until its completion. Finally, *ProcA* will be stepped through until it is completed.

Combining the mixture of debugged and non-debugged procedures with breakpoints allows problems that may be buried many levels down in a nested procedure to be found and tested easily. The procedures can be tested for correctness by ensuring that the top level procedure is performing correctly until the first nested procedure call. A breakpoint can then be added just after the call so that earlier tested code does not have to be stepped through. As each layer of procedure is fully tested, the breakpoint can be moved or the procedure can be removed from being debugged completely by building it in normal mode. Stored procedures that call dozens of other procedures or are thousands of lines long can then be tested on a component or sectional basis without having to re-test code.

## C.2.8 Stored Procedure Run Settings

There are also advanced debugging options that are available in the Development Center. By changing the *Run Settings* of a procedure, as shown in Figure C.15 and Figure C.16, you have the option of not having any changes committed. With this option, after a procedure has finished executing, all changes will be automatically rolled back. This is useful for keeping the state of the database consistent while you debug your code. Scripts can also be set to run before or after the procedure executes. This gives you greater control over the testing environment of stored procedures.

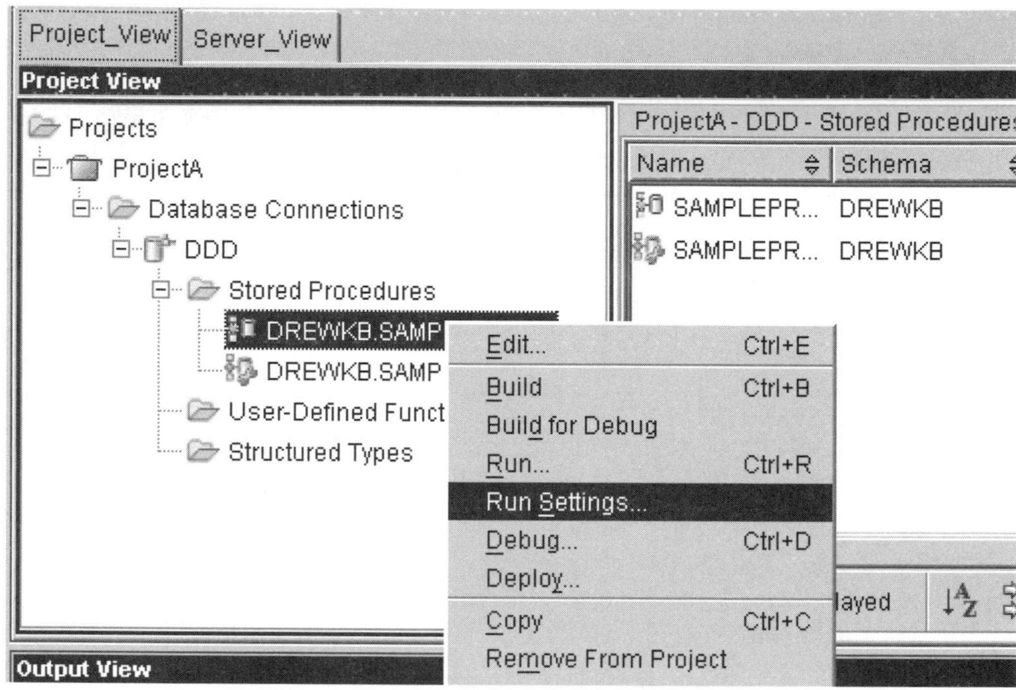


**Figure C.15** Setting Stored Procedure settings

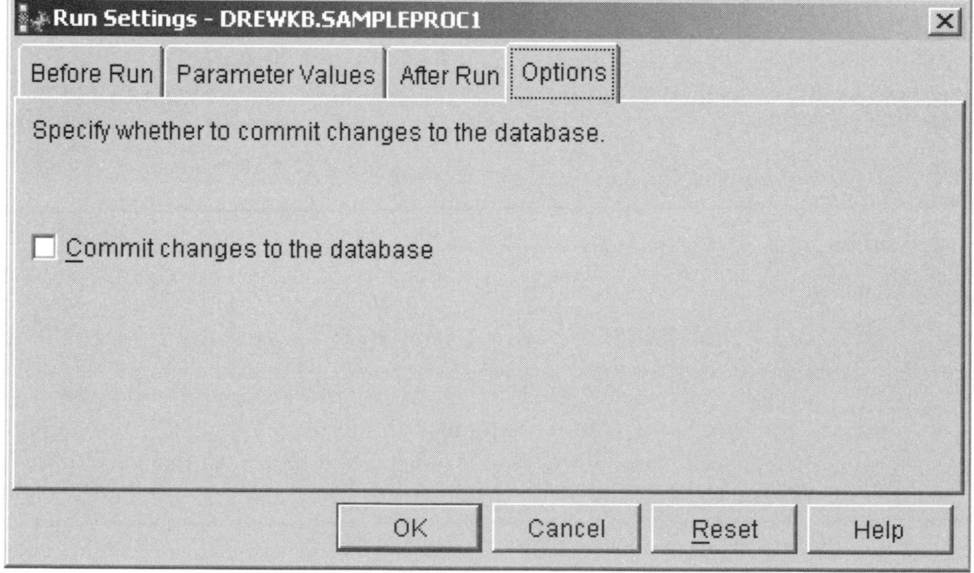


**Figure C.16** Setting Stored Procedure Run options

## C.2.9 Additional Help

There is a thorough set of help menus and documents included with the DC. The help files can be opened by clicking on the question mark icon or by selecting *Help Index* from the Help pull down menu (Figure C.17).

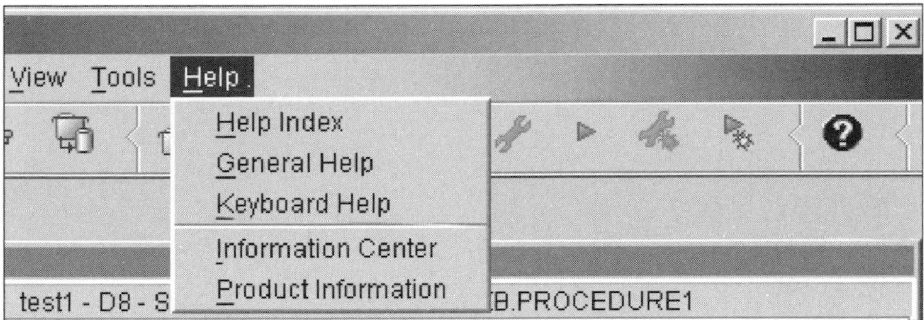


**Figure C.17** Help menu options

# C.3 Summary

The DB2 Development Center is a powerful IDE for developing stored procedures and user-defined functions. By defining multiple projects (which may share the same database), you can manage related database application objects with ease. The integrated debugger allows you to debug complex SQL procedures, even if they make nested procedure calls. Debugging concepts and strategies were highlighted and more help on the Development Center is available from the documentation provided with the product.

APPENDIX 

# Security Considerations in SQL Procedures

Controlling data access is very important in every database implementation unless you do not care who can access, change, or delete data. Different privileges are used to control access to different database objects. For example, to select from a table, you need the SELECT privilege. To create an index, you need the INDEX privilege. Since SQL procedures may contain SQL and DDL statements that reference other database objects, an understanding of security is important when developing your stored procedures. Before jumping into the privileges discussion, you should know what happens behind the scenes when an SQL procedure is created.

## D.1 DB2 Packages

When an SQL procedure is created, its procedure body is converted into an embedded SQL C program. Then, three operations are performed against the converted embedded SQL program.

In the first step, the program is pre-compiled so that a C source file (*.c) and a bind file (*.bnd) are generated. The C code contains the application logic and the bind file contains the embedded SQL statements in a form that the database manager can use.

Next, the C file is compiled and linked to become a library. For example, on Windows, a dynamically linked library (*.dll) would result.

The last step is called binding. The bind file from step one is said to be "bound to the database" by converting the .bnd file into a DB2 package. A package is a database object that contains the data access plan of how SQL statements will be executed.

All of the above steps are performed automatically when an SQL procedure is created (see Figure D.1). Upon successful execution of CREATE PROCEDURE, five generated files are kept by the database server. They are the C source file (*.c), the library file (*.dll), the embedded SQL program file (*.sqc), the bind file (*.bnd), and the message file (*.txt) that records errors, warnings and messages of the whole procedure creation process. The path to these files varies, depending on whether you are using Windows or UNIX.

On Windows:

```
<db2 install path>/sqllib/function/routine/sqlproc/<dbname>/<proc schema name>/
```

On UNIX:

```
<instance home directory>/sqllib/function/routine/sqlproc/<dbname>/proc schema
name>/
```

If you look at the generated files, you'll notice that the file names are in the format of Pxxxxxxx where xxxxxxx are numbers. The numbers are system generated and they are the actual package names. For example, the associated package name of stored procedure may be P0630080. Every package name generated by DB2 is unique. Do not remove these files.

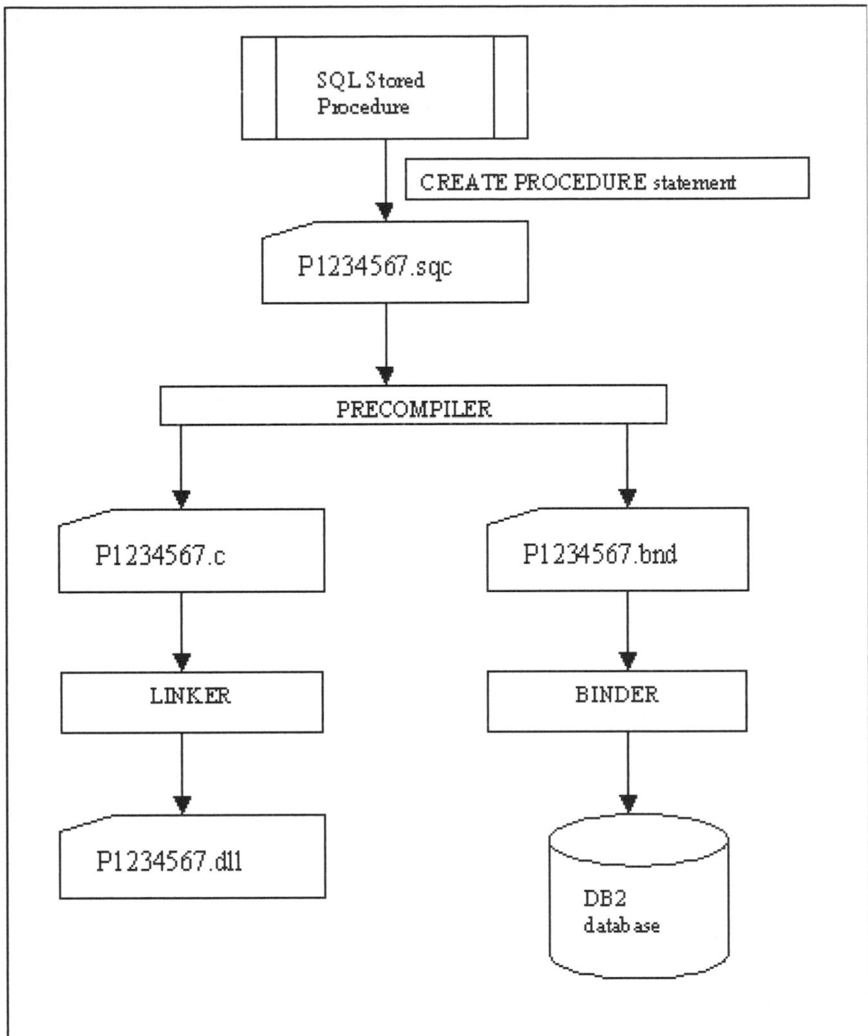


**Figure D.1** Creation of a SQL Procedure

# D.2 Privileges

Now that you understand that SQL procedures are actually database packages, let's talk about what privileges are required to create and execute them. There are basically two groups of users who need some kind of privileges to work with SQL procedures.

## D.2.1 Privileges Required by Developers

The first group is development, which includes developers who write and create the procedures. Among the three steps of creating a procedure, only the last step requires access to the database. The developers need to be able to bind the bind file and create a package in the database. They need the BINDADD privilege, which is a database level privilege that allows them to add a new package to a database. Refer to the *SQL Reference Guide* for complete syntax for the GRANT statement. Here is an example of how to grant the BINDADD privilege to a user:

```
DB2 GRANT BINDADD ON dbname TO USER db2dev
```

Besides the BINDADD privilege, the developers also need proper privileges to access database objects referenced within the procedures. Privileges can be granted to each developer individually or to the developer group. For example:

```
DB2 GRANT SELECT, DELETE ON TABLE employee TO USER db2dev
DB2 GRANT SELECT, DELETE ON TABLE employee TO GROUP db2dgrp
```

In DB2, table privileges granted to groups only apply to dynamic statements. This means that if the procedure contains static SQL statements, table privileges must be granted to each developer individually or to PUBLIC. Otherwise, creation of such an SQL procedure will fail with insufficient privileges. For example:

```
DB2 GRANT SELECT, DELETE ON TABLE employee TO USER db2dev
DB2 GRANT SELECT, DELETE ON TABLE employee TO PUBLIC
```

PUBLIC is not considered as a group, it represents every user that accesses the database.

## D.2.2 Privileges Required by Users

The other group is the user group - users who execute the procedure. They need EXECUTE privilege on the procedure. It is a routine level privilege. The GRANT statement is very straight forward:

```
DB2 GRANT EXECUTE
    ON PROCEDURE seqnextval ( VARCHAR(50), INT )
    TO USER db2user
```

The only thing to be aware is that the procedure name and its signature have to be specified. You can avoid specifying the complete signature of the procedure by using the procedure's specific name like this:

```
DB2 GRANT EXECUTE
    ON SPECIFIC PROCEDURE seqnextval
    TO USER db2user
```

Routine privilege is newly introduced in DB2 UDB Version 8. In Version 7, EXECUTE privilege of the package is required to execute a SQL procedure. It is not very obvious on how to obtain the package name for the SQL procedure. The process of associating the package name with the procedure is briefly described here for your reference.

As discussed above, the procedure name is different from the package name. You can look at the Pxxxxxxx.txt message file generated at procedure creation time to get the package name. See sub-section DB2 PACKAGES for file location. The procedure name is listed in the beginning of the file. This method is not very feasible if there are hundreds of stored procedures. Another method is to query the IMPLEMENTATION column from the SYSCAT.PROCEDURES table. For example you want to find the package name of the procedure *crtnewproj*, use this command:

```
DB2 SELECT implementation
    FROM syscat.procedures
    WHERE procname='CRTNEWPROJ'
```

You should get a similar result as:

```
IMPLEMENTATION
------------------
P1359830!pgsjmp

  1 record(s) selected.
```

In this example, the package is P1359830.

Once package name is located, you can GRANT EXECUTE on the package to the users. For example:

```
DB2 GRANT EXECUTE ON PACKAGE P1359830 TO USER db2user
DB2 GRANT EXECUTE ON PACKAGE P1359830 TO GROUP db2ugrp
```

Notice that we have not mentioned anything about altering stored procedures. Stored procedures are one of the few database objects that cannot be altered. If a procedure requires code changes, it has to be dropped and created. All the privileges associated with the procedure (or for V7, package) are also dropped. In other words, if you rebuild a stored procedure, you will need to once again grant EXECUTE privilege on the procedure (for V7, the new package name) to the users.

Privilege considerations for users on dynamic and static SQL statements are much simpler. For static SQL statements, EXECUTE is the only privilege required by the users. With dynamic SQL statements, users also need table privileges granted to each user individually or to the user group in addition to the EXECUTE privilege. For example:

```
DB2 GRANT SELECT, DELETE ON TABLE employee TO USER db2user
DB2 GRANT SELECT, DELETE ON TABLE employee TO GROUP db2ugrp
```

# D.3 Summary

Table D.1 summarizes the privileges required by the developers and users when different types of SQL statements are used.

**Table D.1** Summary of Privileges Required

| | Dynamic SQL | Static SQL |
|---|---|---|
| DEVELOPERS | BINDADD +<br>Table privileges granted to individual developer or to developer group | BINDADD +<br>Table privileges granted to individual developer or to PUBLIC |
| USERS | EXECUTE +<br>Table privileges granted to individual developer or to developer group | EXECUTE |

APPENDIX 

# Built-in Function Reference

This appendix is a brief description of built-in functions available in DB2. The intention of this appendix is to help you find the function you need quickly. Once you have found a function that suits your needs, you can refer to the *SQL Reference* for more details about the parameters and functionality.

DB2 built-in functions are organized under various schemas. Most functions are under either SYSIBM or SYSFUN schema. Functions supporting MQ Series are under MQDB2 or DB2MQ schemas. Functions supporting snapshot monitoring are under SYSPROC schema. A few functions are under both SYSIBM and SYSFUN schemas and have different functionality under each schema. Except for these functions, when the built-in functions are invoked, the schemas can be omitted.

## E.1 Column/Aggregate Functions

A column function takes as argument a set of values derived from an expression. These functions are described in Table E.1.

**Table E.1** Column/Aggregate Functions

| Function Name | Description |
|---|---|
| AVG | Returns the average of a set of numbers. |
| CORRELATION | Returns the coefficient of correlation of a set of number pairs. |
| COUNT | Returns the number of rows or values in a set of rows or values. |
| COUNT_BIG | Returns the number of rows or values in a set of rows or values. The result can be up to the limit of a bigint. |
| COVARIANCE | Returns the (population) covariance of a set of number pairs. |
| GROUPING | Returns either 0 or 1 indicating whether or not a row returned in a GROUP BY answer set is generated by the super-group. Used in conjunction with grouping-sets and super-groups. |
| MAX | Returns the maximum value in a set of values. |
| MIN | Returns the minimum value in a set of values. |
| REGRESSION Functions<br>REGR_AVGX<br>REGR_AVGY<br>REGR_COUNT<br>REGR_INTERCEPT<br>or REGR_ICPT<br>REGR_R2<br>REGR_SLOPE<br>REGR_SXX<br>REGR_SXY<br>REGR_SYY | Support the fitting of an ordinary-least-squares regression line of the form y = a * x + b to a set of number pairs. |
| STDDEV | Returns the standard deviation of a set of numbers. |
| SUM | Returns the sum of a set of numbers. |
| VARIANCE | Returns the variance of a set of numbers. |

## E.2 Scalar Functions

A scalar function applies to a single row of data rather than a set of rows. Scalar functions are listed in Table E.2.

**Table E.2** Scalar Functions

| Function Name | Description |
|---|---|
| ABS<br>or ABSVAL | Returns the absolute value of the argument. |
| ACOS | Returns the arccosine of the argument as an angle expressed in radians. |
| ASCII | Returns the ASCII code value of the left-most character of the argument as an integer. |
| ASIN | Returns the arcsine on the argument as an angle expressed in radians. |
| ATAN | Returns the arctangent of the argument as an angle expressed in radians. |
| ATANH | Returns the hyperbolic arctangent of the argument, where the argument is an angle expressed in radians. |
| ATAN2 | Returns the arctangent of x and y coordinates as an angle expressed in radians. |
| BIGINT | Returns a 64-bit integer representation of a number, character string, date, time, or timestamp in the form of an integer constant. |
| BLOB | Returns a BLOB representation of a string of any type. |
| CEILING<br>or CEIL | Returns the smallest integer value greater than or equal to the argument. |
| CHAR | Returns a fixed-length character string representation of the first argument. |
| CHR | Returns the character that has the ASCII code value specified by the argument. |
| CLOB | Returns a CLOB representation of a character string type. |
| COALESCE | Returns the first argument that is not null. |
| CONCAT | Returns the concatenation of two string arguments. |
| COS | Returns the cosine of the argument, where the argument is an angle expressed in radians. |
| COSH | Returns the hyperbolic cosine of the argument, where the argument is an angle expressed in radians. |

**Table E.2** Scalar Functions

| Function Name | Description |
| --- | --- |
| COT | Returns the cotangent of the argument, where the argument is an angle expressed in radians. |
| DATE | Returns a date from a value. |
| DAY | Returns the day part of a value. |
| DAYNAME | Returns a mixed case character string containing the name of the day (e.g., Friday) for the day portion of the argument. |
| DAYOFWEEK | Returns the day of the week in the argument as an integer value in the range 1-7, where 1 represents Sunday. |
| DAYOFWEEK_ISO | Returns the day of the week in the argument as an integer value in the range 1-7, where 1 represents Monday. |
| DAYOFYEAR | Returns the day of the year in the argument as an integer value in the range 1-366. |
| DAYS | Returns an integer representation of a date. |
| DBCLOB | Returns a DBCLOB representation of a graphic string type. |
| DECIMAL | Returns a decimal representation of the argument. |
| DECRYPT_BIN<br>DECRYPT_CHAR | Both return a value that is the result of decrypting encrypted-data. |
| DEGREES | Returns the number of degrees converted from the argument expressed in radians. |
| DEREF | Returns an instance of the target type of the argument. |
| DIFFERENCE | Returns a value from 0 to 4 representing the difference between the sounds of two strings based on applying the SOUNDEX function to the strings. A value of 4 is the best possible sound match. |
| DIGITS | Returns a character-string representation of a number. |
| DLCOMMENT | Returns the comment value, if it exists, from a DATALINK value. |
| DLLINKTYPE | Returns the linktype value from a DATALINK value. |
| DLNEWCOPY | Returns a DATALINK value which has an attribute indicating that the referenced file has changed. |
| DLPREVIOUSCOPY | Returns a DATALINK value which has an attribute indicating that the previous version of the file should be restored. |

**Table E.2** Scalar Functions

| Function Name | Description |
|---|---|
| DLREPLACECONTENT | Returns a DATALINK value. |
| DLURLCOMPLETE | Returns the data location attribute from a DATALINK value with a link type of URL. When the DATALINK column is defined with the attribute READ PERMISSION DB, the value includes a file access token. |
| DLURLCOMPLETEONLY | Returns the data location attribute from a DATALINK value with a link type of URL. The value returned never includes a file access token. |
| DLURLCOMPLETEWRITE | Returns the complete URL value from a DATALINK value with a link type of URL. If the DATALINK column is defined with WRITE PERMISSION ADMIN, a write token is included in the return value. |
| DLURLPATH | Returns the path and file name necessary to access a file within a given server from a DATALINK value with a linktype of URL. When a DATALINK column defined with the attribute READ PERMISSION DB, the value includes a file access token. |
| DLURLPATHONLY | Returns the path and file name necessary to access a file within a given server from a DATALINK value with a linktype of URL. The value returned NEVER includes a file access token. |
| DLURLPATHWRITE | Returns the path and file name necessary to access a file within a given server from a DATALINK value with a linktype of URL. The value returned includes a write token if the DATALINK column is defined with WRITE PERMISSION ADMIN. |
| DLURLSCHEME | Returns the scheme from a DATALINK value with a linktype of URL. |
| DLURLSERVER | Returns the file server from a DATALINK value with a linktype of URL. |
| DLVALUE | Returns a DATALINK value. |
| DOUBLE | Returns a floating-point number corresponding to the argument. |
| ENCRYPT | Returns a value that is the result of encrypting. |
| EVENT_MON_STATE | Returns the current state of an event monitor. |
| EXP | Returns the exponential function of the argument. |
| FLOAT | Returns a floating-point representation of a number. |

**Table E.2** Scalar Functions

| Function Name | Description |
|---|---|
| FLOOR | Returns the largest integer value less than or equal to the argument. |
| GETHINT | Return the password hint if one is found in the encrypted data. |
| GENERATE_UNIQUE | Returns a bit data character string 13 bytes long (CHAR(13) FOR BIT DATA) that is unique compared to any other execution of the same function. |
| GRAPHIC | Returns a fixed-length graphic string representation of the argument. |
| HEX | Returns a hexadecimal representation of a value as a character string. |
| HOUR | Returns the hour part of a value. |
| IDENTITY_VAL_LOCAL | A non-deterministic function that returns the most recently assigned value for an identity column, where the assignment occurred as a result of a single row INSERT statement using a VALUES clause. |
| INSERT | Returns a modified string after delete or insert of a specified string into the input string. |
| INTEGER | Returns an integer representation of the argument. |
| JULIAN_DAY | Returns an integer value representing the number of days from January 1, 4712 B.C. (the start of Julian date calendar) to the date value specified in the argument. |
| LCASE (SYSIBM schema) or LOWER | Returns a string in which all the SBCS characters have been converted to lowercase characters. That is, the characters A-Z will be translated to the characters a-z, and characters with diacritical marks will be translated to their lower case equivalents if they exist. |
| LCASE (SYSFUN schema) | Returns a string in which all the characters A-Z have been converted to the characters a-z, but characters with diacritical marks are not converted. |
| LEFT | Returns a string consisting of the leftmost argument2 bytes in argument1. |
| LENGTH | Returns the length of a value. |
| LN | Returns the natural logarithm of the argument (same as LOG). |
| LOCATE | Returns the starting position of the first occurrence of argument1 within argument2. |

**Table E.2** Scalar Functions

| Function Name | Description |
|---|---|
| LOG | Returns the natural logarithm of the argument (same as LN). |
| LOG10 | Returns the base 10 logarithm of the argument. |
| LONG_VARCHAR | Returns a LONG VARCHAR representation of a character string data type. |
| LONG_VARGRAPHIC | Returns a LONG VARGRAPHIC representation of a double-byte character string. |
| LTRIM (SYSIBM schema) | Returns the characters of the argument with leading blanks removed. The argument can be a CHAR, VARCHAR, GRAPHIC, or VARGRAPHIC data type. |
| LTRIM (SYSFUN schema) | Returns the characters of the argument with leading blanks removed. The argument can be of any built-in character string type. |
| MICROSECOND | Returns the microsecond part of a value. |
| MIDNIGHT_SECONDS | Returns an integer value in the range 0 to 86 400 representing the number of seconds between midnight and the time value specified in the argument. |
| MINUTE | Returns the minute part of a value. |
| MOD | Returns the remainder of the first argument divided by the second argument. |
| MONTH | Returns the month part of a value. |
| MONTHNAME | Returns a mixed case character string containing the name of month (e.g., January) for the month portion of the argument. |
| MQPUBLISH | Publishes data to MQSeries. |
| MQREAD | Returns a message from the MQSeries location specified by receive-service, using the quality of service policy defined in service-policy. Executing this operation does not remove the message from the queue associated with receive-service, but instead returns the message at the head of the queue. The result of the function is VARCHAR(4000). |
| MQREADCLOB | Returns a message from the MQSeries location specified by receive-service, using the quality of service policy defined in service-policy. Executing this operation does not remove the message from the queue associated with receive-service, but instead returns the message at the head of the queue. The return value is a CLOB of 1MB maximum length. |

**Table E.2** Scalar Functions

| Function Name | Description |
|---|---|
| MQRECEIVE | Returns a message from the MQSeries location specified by receive-service, using the quality of service policy service-policy. Performing this operation removes the message from the queue associated with receive-service. The result of the function is VARCHAR(4000). |
| MQRECEIVECLOB | Returns a message from the MQSeries location specified by receive-service, using the quality of service policy service-policy. Performing this operation removes the message from the queue associated with receive-service. The return value is a CLOB of 1MB maximum length. |
| MQSEND | Sends the data contained in msg-data to the MQSeries location specified by send-service, using the quality of service policy defined by service-policy. Returns a value of '1' if successful or a '0' if unsuccessful. |
| MQSUBSCRIBE | Registers interest in MQSeries messages published on a specified topic. |
| MQUNSUBSCRIBE | Unregisters an existing message subscription. |
| MULTIPLY_ALT | Returns the product of the two arguments as a decimal value. It is provided as an alternative to the multiplication operator, especially when the sum of the precisions of the arguments exceeds 31. |
| NODENUMBER or DBPARTITIONNUM | Returns the partition number of the row. |
| NULLIF | Returns a null value if the arguments are equal, otherwise it returns the value of the first argument. |
| PARTITION or HASHEDVALUE | Returns the partitioning map index of the row obtained by applying the partitioning function on the partitioning key value of the row. |
| POSSTR | Returns the starting position of the first occurrence of one string within another string. |
| POWER | Returns the value of expression1 to the power of expression2. |
| QUARTER | Returns an integer value in the range 1 to 4 representing the quarter of the year for the date specified in the argument. |
| RADIANS | Returns the number of radians converted from argument which is expressed in degrees. |

**Table E.2** Scalar Functions

| Function Name | Description |
|---|---|
| RAISE_ERROR | Causes the statement that includes the function to return an error with the specified SQLSTATE. |
| RAND | Returns a random floating point value between 0 and 1 using the argument as the optional seed value. |
| REAL | Returns a single-precision floating-point representation of a number. |
| REC2XML | Returns a string formatted with XML tags and containing column names and column data. |
| REPEAT | Returns a character string composed of the first argument repeated the number of times specified by the second argument. |
| REPLACE | Replaces all occurrences of expression2 in expression1 with expression3. |
| RIGHT | Returns a string consisting of the rightmost expression2 bytes in expression1. |
| ROUND | Returns expression1 rounded to expression2 places to the right of the decimal point if expression2 is positive, or to the left of the decimal point if expression2 is zero or negative. |
| RTRIM (SYSIBM schema) | Returns the characters of the argument with trailing blanks removed. The argument can be a CHAR, VARCHAR, GRAPHIC, or VARGRAPHIC data type. |
| RTRIM (SYSFUN schema) | Returns the characters of the argument with trailing blanks removed. The argument can be of any built-in character string data types. |
| SECOND | Returns the seconds part of a value. |
| SIGN | Returns an indicator of the sign of the argument. If the argument is less than zero, -1 is returned. If argument equals zero, 0 is returned. If argument is greater than zero, 1 is returned. |
| SIN | Returns the sine of the argument, where the argument is an angle expressed in radians. |
| SINH | Returns the hyperbolic sine of the argument, where the argument is an angle expressed in radians. |
| SMALLINT | Returns a small integer representation of a number or character string in the form of a small integer constant. |

**Table E.2** Scalar Functions

| Function Name | Description |
|---|---|
| SOUNDEX | Returns a 4 character code representing the sound of the words in the argument. |
| SPACE | Returns a character string consisting of blanks with length specified by the argument. |
| SQRT | Returns the square root of the argument. |
| SUBSTR | Returns a substring of a string. |
| TABLE_NAME | Returns an unqualified name of the object found after any alias chains have been resolved. |
| TABLE_SCHEMA | Returns the schema name of the object found after any alias chains have been resolved. |
| TAN | Returns the tangent of the argument, where the argument is an angle expressed in radians. |
| TANH | Returns the hyperbolic tangent of the argument, where the argument is an angle expressed in radians. |
| TIME | Returns a time from a value. |
| TIMESTAMP | Returns a timestamp from a value or a pair of values. |
| TIMESTAMP_ISO | Returns a timestamp value based on date, time or timestamp argument. |
| TIMESTAMP_FORMAT | Returns a timestamp from a character string that has been interpreted using a character template. |
| TIMESTAMPDIFF | Returns an estimated number of intervals of the type defined by the first argument, based on the difference between two timestamps. |
| TO_CHAR | Returns a character representation of a timestamp that has been formatted using a character template. TO_CHAR is a synonym for VARCHAR_FORMAT. |
| TO_DATE | Returns a timestamp from a character string that has been interpreted using a character template. TO_DATE is a synonym for TIMESTAMP_FORMAT. |
| TRANSLATE | Returns a value in which one or more characters in a string expression may have been translated into other characters. |

**Table E.2** Scalar Functions

| Function Name | Description |
|---|---|
| TRUNCATE or TRUNC | Returns expression1 truncated to expression2 places to the right of the decimal point if expression2 is positive, or to the left of the decimal point if expression2 is zero or negative. |
| TYPE_ID | Returns the internal type identifier of the dynamic data type of the argument. |
| TYPE_NAME | Returns the unqualified name of the dynamic data type of the argument. |
| TYPE_SCHEMA | Returns the schema name of the dynamic data type of the argument. |
| UCASE or UPPER | The UCASE or UPPER function is identical to the TRANSLATE function except that only the first argument is specified. |
| VALUE | Returns the first argument that is not null. |
| VARCHAR | Returns a varying-length character string representation of the argument. |
| VARCHAR_FORMAT | Returns a character representation of a timestamp that has been formatted using a character template. |
| VARGRAPHIC | Returns a varying-length graphic string representation of the argument. |
| WEEK | Returns the week of the year of the argument as an integer value in range 1-54. The week starts with Sunday. |
| WEEK_ISO | Returns the week of the year of the argument as an integer value in the range 1-53. The week starts with Monday and always includes 7 days. Week 1 is the first week of the year to contain a Thursday, which is equivalent to the first week containing January 4. It is therefore possible to have up to 3 days at the beginning of a year appear in the last week of the previous year. Conversely, up to 3 days at the end of a year may appear in the first week of the next year. |
| YEAR | Returns the year part of a value. |

## E.3 Table Functions

A table function returns the equivalent of a table and can be used only in the FROM clause of a statement. Table functions are listed in Table E.3.

**Table E.3** Table Functions

| Function Name | Description |
|---|---|
| MQREADALL | Returns a table containing the messages and message metadata from the MQSeries location specified by receive-service, using the quality of service policy service-policy. Performing this operation does not remove the messages from the queue associated with receive-service. The MSG column in the table is VARCHAR(4000). |
| MQREADALLCLOB | Returns a table containing the messages and message metadata from the MQSeries location specified by receive-service, using the quality of service policy service-policy. Performing this operation does not remove the messages from the queue associated with receive-service. The MSG column in the table is CLOB. |
| MQRECEIVEALL | Returns a table containing the messages and message metadata from the MQSeries location specified by receive-service, using the quality of service policy service-policy. Performing this operation removes the messages from the queue associated with receive-service. The MSG column in the table is VARCHAR(4000). |
| MQRECEIVEALLCLOB | Returns a table containing the messages and message metadata from the MQSeries location specified by receive-service, using the quality of service policy service-policy. Performing this operation removes the messages from the queue associated with receive-service. The MSG column in the table is CLOB. |
| SNAPSHOT_AGENT | Returns information about agents from an application snapshot. |
| SNAPSHOT_APPL | Returns general information from an application snapshot. |
| SNAPSHOT_BP | Returns information from a buffer pool snapshot. |
| SNAPSHOT_CONTAINER | Returns container configuration information from a tablespace snapshot. |
| SNAPSHOT_DATABASE | Returns information from a database snapshot. |
| SNAPSHOT_DBM | Returns information from a snapshot of the DB2 database manager. |
| SNAPSHOT_DYN_SQL | Returns information from a dynamic SQL snapshot. |
| SNAPSHOT_FCM | Returns database manager level information regarding the fast communication manager (FCM). |

**Table E.3** Table Functions

| Function Name | Description |
|---|---|
| SNAPSHOT_FCMNODE | Returns information from a snapshot of the fast communication manager in the database manager. |
| SNAPSHOT_LOCK | Returns information from a lock snapshot. |
| SNAPSHOT_LOCKWAIT | Returns lock wait information from an application snapshot. |
| SNAPSHOT_QUIESCERS | Returns information on tablespace quiescers. |
| SNAPSHOT_RANGES | Returns range information on DMS tablespaces. |
| SNAPSHOT_STATEMENT | Returns information about statements from an application snapshot. |
| SNAPSHOT_SUBJECT | Returns information about subsections of access plans from an application snapshot. |
| SNAPSHOT_SWITCHES | Returns information about the database snapshot switch state. |
| SNAPSHOT_TABLE | Returns activity information from a table snapshot. |
| SNAPSHOT_TBS | Returns activity information from a table space snapshot. |
| SNAPSHOT_TBS_CFG | Returns configuration information from a table space snapshot. |
| SQLCACHE_SNAPSHOT | Returns the results of a snapshot of the DB2 dynamic SQL statement cache. Deprecated. Use SNAPSHOT_DYN_SQL instead. |

A P P E N D I X 

# DDL

This appendix contains all the Data Definition Language (DDL) statements for the *sample* database and other database objects required to run the examples in this book. The first script is the DDL for the sample database, which can be created using the methods described below. The second section has the additional DDL required for the examples and you will have to create those objects manually.

## F.1 Creating the Sample Database

The sample database provided with DB2 can be created by two methods. You can choose to create the database from the First Steps dialog, which launches automatically after installation, or you can create the database from the command line.

The default schema used for tables in the database will be the user ID you used to login to the operating system (on Windows, this will be the user ID used to install DB2, and on UNIX, the instance user ID).

You can also create the sample database from the command line. Included with DB2 is a program called *db2sampl* that will create and populate the database for you. This program can be found in the *bin* subdirectory of the directory where db2 was installed.

You will still have to run the scripts in the second part of this appendix in order to have all the database objects required for the examples in this book. You should create these tables using the same schema used to create the sample database tables.

## Sample Database DDL: Script 1

```
------------------------------------------------
-- DDL Statements for table ORG
------------------------------------------------
CREATE TABLE ORG  (
  deptnumb SMALLINT NOT NULL,
  deptname VARCHAR(14),
  manager SMALLINT,
  division  VARCHAR(10),
  location VARCHAR(13) )
  IN USERSPACE1;

------------------------------------------------
-- DDL Statements for table STAFF
------------------------------------------------
CREATE TABLE STAFF  (
  id SMALLINT NOT NULL,
  name VARCHAR(9),
  dept SMALLINT,
  job CHAR(5),
  years SMALLINT,
  salary  DECIMAL(7,2),
  comm  DECIMAL(7,2),
  PRIMARY KEY (id))
  IN USERSPACE1;

------------------------------------------------
-- DDL Statements for table DEPARTMENT
------------------------------------------------
CREATE TABLE DEPARTMENT  (
  deptno CHAR(3) NOT NULL,
  deptname VARCHAR(29) NOT NULL,
  mgrno CHAR(6),
  admrdept CHAR(3) NOT NULL,
  location CHAR(16),
  PRIMARY KEY (deptno))
  IN USERSPACE1;

------------------------------------------------
-- DDL Statements for table EMPLOYEE
------------------------------------------------
CREATE TABLE EMPLOYEE  (
  empno CHAR(6) NOT NULL,
  firstnme VARCHAR(12) NOT NULL,
  midinit CHAR(1) NOT NULL,
  lastname VARCHAR(15) NOT NULL,
  workdept CHAR(3),
```

```
   phoneno CHAR(4),
   hiredate DATE,
   job CHAR(8),
   edlevel SMALLINT NOT NULL ,
   sex CHAR(1),
   birthdate DATE,
   salary DECIMAL(9,2),
   bonus DECIMAL(9,2),
   comm DECIMAL(9,2),
   PRIMARY KEY (empno))
   IN USERSPACE1;

------------------------------------------------
-- DDL Statements for table EMP_ACT
------------------------------------------------
CREATE TABLE EMP_ACT  (
   empno CHAR(6) NOT NULL ,
   projno CHAR(6) NOT NULL ,
   actno SMALLINT NOT NULL ,
   emptime DECIMAL(5,2) ,
   emstdate DATE ,
   emendate DATE,
   PRIMARY KEY (empno, projno))
   IN USERSPACE1;

------------------------------------------------
-- DDL Statements for table PROJECT
------------------------------------------------
CREATE TABLE PROJECT  (
   projno CHAR(6) NOT NULL ,
   projname VARCHAR(24) NOT NULL ,
   deptno CHAR(3) NOT NULL ,
   respemp CHAR(6) NOT NULL ,
   prstaff DECIMAL(5,2) ,
   prstdate DATE ,
   prendate DATE ,
   majproj CHAR(6),
   PRIMARY KEY (projno))
   IN USERSPACE1;

------------------------------------------------
-- DDL Statements for table EMP_PHOTO
------------------------------------------------
CREATE TABLE EMP_PHOTO  (
   empno CHAR(6) NOT NULL ,
   photo_format VARCHAR(10) NOT NULL ,
   picture_blob BLOB(102400) LOGGED NOT COMPACT,
   PRIMARY KEY (empno,photo_format))
   IN USERSPACE1;
```

```
------------------------------------------------
-- DDL Statements for table EMP_RESUME
------------------------------------------------
CREATE TABLE EMP_RESUME  (
   empno CHAR(6) NOT NULL ,
   resume_format VARCHAR(10) NOT NULL ,
   resume_clob CLOB(5120) LOGGED NOT COMPACT,
   PRIMARY KEY (empno,resume_format))
   IN USERSPACE1;

------------------------------------------------
-- DDL Statements for table sales
------------------------------------------------
CREATE TABLE sales  (
   sales_date DATE,
   sales_person VARCHAR(15),
   region VARCHAR(15),
   sales INTEGER )
   IN USERSPACE1;

------------------------------------------------
-- DDL Statements for table CL_SCHED
------------------------------------------------
CREATE TABLE CL_SCHED  (
   class_code CHAR(7),
   day SMALLINT,
   starting TIME,
   ending TIME )
   IN USERSPACE1;

------------------------------------------------
-- DDL Statements for table IN_TRAY
------------------------------------------------
CREATE TABLE IN_TRAY  (
   received TIMESTAMP,
   source CHAR(8),
   subject CHAR(64),
   note_text VARCHAR(3000) )
IN USERSPACE1;
```

## DDL for Additional Database Objects: Script 2

```
------------------------------------------------
-- DDL Statements for table service_rq
------------------------------------------------
CREATE TABLE service_rq(
   rqid SMALLINT NOT NULL
      CONSTRAINT rqid_pk PRIMARY KEY,
    status VARCHAR(10) NOT NULL
        WITH DEFAULT 'NEW'
        CHECK ( status IN ( 'NEW', 'ASSIGNED', 'Pending', 'CANCELLED' ) ),
    rq_desktop CHAR(1) NOT NULL
        WITH DEFAULT 'N'
```

```
        CHECK ( rq_desktop IN ( 'Y', 'N' ) ),
    rq_ipaddress CHAR(1) NOT NULL
        WITH DEFAULT 'N'
        CHECK ( rq_ipaddress IN ( 'Y', 'N' ) ),
    rq_unixid CHAR(1) NOT NULL
        WITH DEFAULT 'N'
        CHECK ( rq_unixid IN ( 'Y', 'N' ) ),
    staffid INTEGER NOT NULL,
    techid INTEGER,
    accum_rqnum INTEGER NOT NULL
        GENERATED ALWAYS AS IDENTITY
     ( START WITH 1,
     INCREMENT BY 1,
        CACHE 10 ),
  comment VARCHAR(100) );

-----------------------------------------------
-- DDL Statements for table svcrq_sw
-----------------------------------------------
CREATE TABLE svcrq_sw (
  rqid SMALLINT NOT NULL
     CONSTRAINT rqid_pk PRIMARY KEY,
  status VARCHAR(10) NOT NULL
        WITH DEFAULT 'NEW'
        CHECK (status IN ('NEW', 'ASSIGNED', 'Pending', 'CANCELLED')),
    ostype VARCHAR(50) NOT NULL
        WITH DEFAULT 'W2K',
    staffid INTEGER NOT NULL,
    techid INTEGER,
    accum_rqnum INTEGER NOT NULL
        GENERATED ALWAYS AS IDENTITY
     ( START WITH 1,
     INCREMENT BY 1,
     CACHE 10 ),
    comment VARCHAR(100) );

-----------------------------------------------
-- DDL Statements for sequence service_rq_seq
-----------------------------------------------
CREATE SEQUENCE service_rq_seq AS SMALLINT
   START WITH 1
   INCREMENT BY 1
   MAXVALUE 5000
   NO CYCLE
   CACHE 50;

-----------------------------------------------
-- DDL Statements for sequence staff_seq
-----------------------------------------------
CREATE SEQUENCE staff_seq AS INTEGER
    START WITH 360
    INCREMENT BY 10
    NO MAXVALUE
```

```
    NO CYCLE
    NO CACHE;

------------------------------------------------
-- DDL Statements for table audit
------------------------------------------------
CREATE TABLE AUDIT (
   event_time TIMESTAMP,
   desc VARCHAR(100));

------------------------------------------------
-- DDL Statements for view emp_dep_v
------------------------------------------------
CREATE VIEW emp_dep_v AS
   SELECT empno, firstnme, lastname, deptname
   FROM employee e LEFT OUTER JOIN department d
     ON e.empno=d.mgrno;

------------------------------------------------
-- DDL Statements for table atomic_test
------------------------------------------------
CREATE TABLE atomic_test(
   proc VARCHAR(20),
   res VARCHAR(20));

------------------------------------------------
-- DDL Statements for table tname
------------------------------------------------
CREATE TABLE tname(
   fullname VARCHAR(35));

------------------------------------------------
-- DDL Statements for sequence seq1
------------------------------------------------
CREATE SEQUENCE seq1;
```

APPENDIX G

# Additional Resources

There are many ways to obtain additional information pertaining to DB2 and DB2 SQL stored procedures. At the time of publication of this book, there are only DB2 v7 resources available. Nevertheless, many of these resources will be updated for DB2 v8. This appendix attempts to serve as a comprehensive list of such resources.

Note: some items are located in more than one place.

## G.1 IBM Redbooks

IBM Redbooks are developed and published by IBM's International Technical Support Organization, the ITSO. ITSO develops and delivers technical materials to technical professionals of IBM, Business Partners, customers, and to the IT marketplace.

IBM Redbooks are ITSO's core product. They typically provide positioning and value guidance, installation and implementation experiences, typical solution scenarios, and step-by-step "how-to" guidelines. They often include sample code and other support materials that are also available as downloads from this site:

*www.redbooks.ibm.com*

Redbooks are available as hardcopy books and in IBM Redbook CD-ROM collections. Refer to the "How to buy" page for order details.

The following Red Books contain information about DB2 Stored Procedures:

- *SQL Reference for Cross-Platform Development* - ftp.software.ibm.com/ps/products/db2/info/vr7/pdf/letter/ibmsqlr.pdf
- *Getting Started with DB2 Stored Procedures: Give Them a Call Through the Network*, SG24-4693-01 Redbook, published April 7, 1998 *www.redbooks.ibm.com/pubs/pdfs/redbooks/sg244693.pdf*
- *Cross-Platform DB2 Stored Procedures: Building and Debugging,* SG24-5485-01 Redbook, published May7, 2001 *www.redbooks.ibm.com/pubs/pdfs/redbooks/sg245485.pdf*
- *DB2 UDB V7.1 Porting Guide*, SG24-6128-00 Redbook, published December11, 2000 *www.redbooks.ibm.com/pubs/pdfs/redbooks/sg246128.pdf*
- *DB2 Java Stored Procedures Learning by Example*, SG24-5945-00 Redbook, published September 6, 2000 *www.redbooks.ibm.com/pubs/pdfs/redbooks/sg245945.pdf*
- *Stored Procedures and Triggers on DB2 Universal Database for iSeries*, SG24-6503-00 Redbook, published December19, 2001 *www.redbooks.ibm.com/pubs/pdfs/redbooks/sg246503.pdf*
- *DB2 UDB V7.1 Performance Tuning Guide*, SG24-6012-00 Redbook, published December17, 2000 *www.redbooks.ibm.com/pubs/pdfs/redbooks/sg246012.pdf*

## G.2 Certification

Your DB2 skill set can be validated by completing the appropriate DB2 UDB certifications. Two popular certifications include the *IBM Certified Solutions Expert—DB2 UDB V7.1 Database Administration for UNIX, Linux, Windows and OS/2* and the *IBM Certified Solutions Expert—DB2 UDB V7.1 Family Application Development*. Additional information on DB2 Certification can be obtained from both of these sites:

- *www.ibm.com/certify/certs/db_index.shtml*
- *www.ibm.com/software/data/db2/skills/cert.html.*

### G.2.1 Certification Guides

The following DB2 UDB Certification Guides can be used to prepare for the certification exams:

- *DB2 Universal Database Version 7.1 for UNIX, Linux, Windows and OS/2 Database* Administration Certification Guide, *4th Edition* by George Baklarz and Bill Wong. Published by Prentice Hall PTR, 2000. ISBN 0130913669.
- *DB2 Universal Database Version 7.1 Application Development Certification Guide, 1st Edition* by Steve Sanyal, David Martineau, and Kevin Gashyna. Published by Prentice Hall PTR, 2000. ISBN 0130913677.

### G.2.2 Tutorials

There is a series of six tutorials designed to help you prepare for the DB2 Fundamentals Certification (Exam 512). These tutorials provide a solid base for each section of the exam. However, you should not rely on these tutorials as your only preparation for the exam. Each tutorial includes a link to a free DB2 Universal Database Enterprise Edition download.

*www7b.software.ibm.com/dmdd/library/tutorials/db2cert/db2cert_tut.html*

## G.3 Education

### G.3.1 IBM Learning Services

IBM Learning Services offers a complete set of traditional classroom courses and workshops for both DB2 developers and database administrators. For additional offerings that are not listed here, please see the IBM web site at www.ibm.com/software/data/education.html. To look for class schedules in Canada, please consult the IBM Learning Services Canada site at *www.can.ibm.com/services/learning/index.html*. In the United States, consult the IBM Learning Services US DB2 site at *www.ibm.com/services/learning/spotlight/db2*, or call 1-800-426-8322 for the latest course offerings and schedule information. Information about computer-based training courses is also available from the sites.

The following lists highlights some of the traditional classroom and Computer-Based Training (CBT) courses for DB2 which are offered by IBM Learning Services:

### Application Programming

- DB2 UDB Programming Fundamentals (CF103)
- DB2 UDB Fast Path to DB2 for Experienced DBAs (CF281) - (FREE OFFER - see below)
- DB2 UDB Advanced Programming (CF113)
- DB2 UDB Programming Using Java (CG112)
- DB2 UDB Stored Procedures Programming Workshop (CF710)

### Database Administration

- DB2 UDB Database Administration Workshop for Linux (CF201)
- DB2 UDB Database Administration Workshop for UNIX (CF211)
- DB2 UDB Database Administration Workshop for Windows NT (CF231)
- DB2 UDB Programming Fastpath Course (CT10) - (FREE OFFER - see below)
- DB2 UDB EEE for UNIX Administration Workshop (CF241)
- DB2 UDB EEE for Windows NT Administration Workshop (CF261)
- DB2 UDB Database Administration Workshop for Sun Solaris (CF271)
- DB2 UDB Advanced Administration Workshop (CF451)
- DB2 UDB Advanced Admin. For Experienced Relational DBAs (CF481)
- DB2 UDB Advanced Recovery & High Availability Workshop (CF491)
- DB2 UDB EEE for DB2 UDB EE DBAs (CG241)

### Performance Tuning

- DB2 UDB Performance Tuning and Monitoring Workshop (CF411)
- DB2 UDB EEE for UNIX Performance Monitoring and Tuning Workshop (CF441)

## G.3.2 FREE Self-study Computer Based Training Courses

DB2 UDB Self-Study for Experienced Relational DBA's (CF281)

- For a limited time the Fast Path to DB2 UDB for Experienced Relational DBAs is available for free download from www.ibm.com/software/data/db2/selfstudy/. The course is targeted toward the DBA who is already proficient in one or more non-IBM relational database products, but could use some help in coming up to speed with DB2 Universal Database. This fast path course can be completed in as little as eight hours.

DB2 UDB Programming Fastpath Course (CT10)

- A new, second offering, DB2 UDB Programming Fastpath, is designed to teach experienced relational database programmers how to create applications that access data in a DB2 Universal Database system. It provides a fast path for acquiring the skills necessary to write programs against a DB2 UDB Database, and is available free for download from www.ibm.com/software/data/db2/ct10crs/.

## G.3.3 IBM Solution Partnership Centers (SPCs)

IBM SPCs provide various workshops. These are free to members of PartnerWorld for Developers. Schedules are available at the PartnerWorld for Developers website: www.developer.ibm.com.

### *Tutorials*

- DB2 Fundamentals Certification (Exam 512) Preparation: www7b.software.ibm.com/dmdd/library/tutorials/db2cert/db2cert_tut.html
- IBM DB2 Migration Series: webevents.broadcast.com/ibm/db2migrate/home.asp
- Developer Webcast on demand: webevents.broadcast.com/ibm/developer/on_demand.asp

# G.4 Printed Books

The following external DB2 publications are available from a bookstore or publisher:

- *DB2 Universal Database Version 7.1 for UNIX, Linux, Windows and OS/2 Database Administration Certification Guide, 4th Edition* by George Baklarz and Bill Wong. Published by Prentice Hall PTR, 2000. ISBN 0130913669.
- *DB2 Universal Database Version 7.1 Application Development Certification Guide, 1st Edition* by Steve Sanyal, David Martineau, and Kevin Gashyna. Published by Prentice Hall PTR, 2000. ISBN 0130913677.
- *DB2: The Complete Reference, 1st Edition* by Roman Melnyk and Paul Zikopolous Published by McGraw-Hill, 2001. ISBN 0072133449.
- *DB2 For Dummies* by Paul Zikopolous, Lili Lugomirski, Roman B. Melnyk. Published by IDG Books Worldwide, 2000. ISBN 076450696x.

- *DB2 Universal Database in Application Environments* by Tetsuya Shirai and Robert Harbus. Published by Peach Pit Press, 2000. ISBN 0130869872.
- *DB2 Developer's Guide, 4th Edition* by Craig Mullins. Published by SAMS, 2000. ISBN 0672318288.
- *DB2 Universal Database SQL Developer's Guide* by Roger Sanders. Published by OsborneMcGraw-Hill, 1999. ISBN 0071353895.

## G.5 Technical Resources

- DB2 Home Page: *www.ibm.com/software/data/db2/*
- DB2 Technical Materials Library (Books, Whitepapers, Brochures and Specs, Consultant Reports and Technology Overviews, Magazine articles and Reviews, Newsletters, and Technical Information and Manuals): *www.ibm.com/software/data/pubs/*
- DB2 Application Development: *www.ibm.com/software/data/db2/udb/ad/*
- DB2 Manuals: *www.ibm.com/software/data/db2/library/*
- DB2 WhitePapers: *www.ibm.com/software/data/pubs/papers/#dbpapers*
- IBM Database and Data Management Software Homepage: *www.ibm.com/software/data/*
- IBM Support for Data Management Products: *www.ibm.com/software/data/support*
- DB2 Developer Domain: *www.ibm.com/software/data/developer/*
- IBM PartnerWorld for Developers Home Page: *www.developer.ibm.com*
- IBM Redbooks: *www.redbooks.ibm.com*
- DB2 Professional Certification Program: *www.ibm.com/certify/certs/db_index.shtml*

### G.5.1 DB2 FixPaks and Downloads

- DB2 Maintenance Info: *www.software.ibm.com/data/db2/udb/winos2unix/support/*
- DB2 Software Product Downloads: *www.ibm.com/software/data/db2/udb/downloads.html*

### G.5.2 E-mail Services and Periodicals

- DB2 UDB News: *www.ibm.com/software/mailing-lists*, subscribe to receive notification of new FixPaks and other DB2 service news.

- DB2 Today: *www.ibm.com/software/data/db2today/*, each monthly issue will bring you our latest offers, downloads, events, web-based seminars, product news, and more. Subscribe to receive via email.
- DB2 Magazin: *www.db2mag.com*, each issue contains a variety of features on technical and business-level topics for the DB2 community, plus tips and techniques in columns on data mining, programming, system administration, content management, and more. Available in print and on the web.

## G.6 User Groups and Conferences

International DB2 User Group (IDUG): *www.idug.org/*

DB2 & Other IBM Technical Conferences: *www.ibm.com/services/learning/conf/us/index.html*

APPENDIX 

# Sample Application Code for Receiving Cursor Result Sets

This appendix provides supplementary examples for Chapter 4, "Understanding Cursors and Result Sets," which discussed returning cursors directly to an application. When a cursor has been opened by an SQL procedure for an application, the application can directly fetch data off that cursor. Here, we present examples of applications written in Java and C to show how to work with such cursors.

## H.1 Receiving Result Sets in Java Applications

Figure H.1 shows the Java application code, *TotalRaise.java*, to complete the rewrite of the *total_raise()* SQL procedure of Figure 4.3. *TotalRaise.java* relies on calling the SQL procedure *read_emp()* (Figure 4.13) to provide a cursor for data to be processed. The *TotalRaise.java* program and the *read_emp()* procedure together accomplish exactly the same task as the *total_raise()* SQL procedure, although the two approaches are fundamentally different in design. When implementing the logic inside the SQL procedure, less data is passed between the client and server which results in less network traffic and better performance. Using SQL procedures to process the logic, therefore, is more suitable for transactions involving large result sets. There are, however, advantages to processing data in the application as well:

- You can implement more complex business logic on the client side because it can be integrated better with the client's application logic.
- SQL PL is not as powerful as programming languages such as C/C++ or Java. For example, with these languages on the client side, you can issue calls to the operating system, as well as have access to information about the client environment.
- You can build applications that can be portable across different RDBMs, by using standard APIs.

**Figure H.1** TotalRaise.java - Example of Using Java to Receive a Result Set Provided by an SQL Procedure

```
import java.lang.*;
import java.util.*;
import java.io.*;
import java.sql.*;
import COM.ibm.db2.jdbc.app.*;

class TotalRaise
{
    static
    {
        try
        {
            Class.forName ("COM.ibm.db2.jdbc.app.DB2Driver").newInstance ();
        }
        catch (Exception e)
        {
            System.out.println ("\n  Error loading DB2 Driver...\n");
            System.out.println (e);
            System.exit(1);
        }
    }

    public static void main (String argv[])
    {
        double v_min, v_max;

        Connection con = null;

        if (argv.length != 2)
        {
            System.out.println("Usage: java TotalRaise MinRaise MaxRaise");
```

```
        System.exit(1);
    }

    v_min = Double.parseDouble(argv[0]);
    v_max = Double.parseDouble(argv[1]);

    try
    {
        // Connect to Sample database
        String url = "jdbc:db2:sample";
        con = DriverManager.getConnection(url);

        CallableStatement cs = con.prepareCall("CALL db2admin.read_emp()");

        cs.execute();
        ResultSet rs = cs.getResultSet();                          /*--(1)*/

        double v_total=0;
        double v_raise;
        double v_salary, v_bonus, v_comm;

        while ( rs.next() )                                        /*--(2)*/
        {
            v_raise = v_min;
            v_salary = rs.getDouble(1);                            /*--(3)*/
            v_bonus  = rs.getDouble(2);
            v_comm   = rs.getDouble(3);                            /*--(4)*/

            if ( v_bonus >= 600 ) { v_raise += 0.04; }

            if ( v_comm < 2000 )
            {
                v_raise += 0.03;
            }
            else if ( v_comm < 3000 )
            {
                v_raise += 0.02;
            }
            else
            {
                v_raise += 0.01;
            }

            if ( v_raise > v_max ) { v_raise = v_max; }

            v_total += v_salary * v_raise;
        } /* while */

        System.out.println(v_total);

        rs.close();
        cs.close ();
        con.close ();
```

```
            System.out.println("Complete(0).");
        }
        catch (Exception e)
        {
            try
            {
                if( con != null )
                {
                    con.close();
                }
            }
            catch (Exception x)
            {   //ignore this exception
            }
            System.out.println (e);
        } /* try-catch block */
    } /* main() method */
} /* class TotalRaise */
```

In Java, you need a *CallableStatement* object to invoke SQL procedures. The result sets will be returned when you invoke the *getResultSet()* method of the *Statement* interface (1). To receive the result set, you will need to also declare a *ResultSet* object to hold the retrieved data. The *ResultSet* class has many *getXXX()* methods for all regular SQL data-types. In this example, the *getDouble()* method is used at (3) and (4). By calling the *getDouble()* method, data is fetched into a local variable. The *ResultSet* class has the *next()* method to advance the cursor and fetch the next row of data. The return value from the *next()* method at (2) indicates whether the end of result set is reached. If *next()* returns *false*, the cursor has reached the end of the result set.

For better performance, and as good programming practice, close all *ResultSet*, *CallableStatement* and *Connection* objects when they are no longer needed.

There are other useful methods for the *Statement* and *ResultSet* interface. Some of them will be covered later in this appendix.

## H.2 Receiving Result Sets in C or C++ Applications

When writing a database application using C or C++ to process the result sets from SQL procedures, you have to use DB2 Call Level Interface (CLI) instead of embedded SQL. The code shown in Figure H.2 performs the equivalent data processing logic as the Java sample in Figure H.1.

**Figure H.2** TotalRaise.c - Example of Receiving sSingle Result Set from CLI Application

```
#include <stdio.h>
#include <string.h>
#include <stdlib.h>
#include <sqlcli1.h>
#include <sqlca.h>

#define MAX_SERVER_LENGTH   10
#define MAX_UID_LENGTH      10
#define MAX_PWD_LENGTH      10
#define MAX_STMT_LENGTH    200

int main(int argc, char *argv[])
{
    SQLRETURN     sqlrc = SQL_SUCCESS;
    SQLHANDLE     henv;  /* environment handle */
    SQLHANDLE     hdbc;  /* connection handle */
    SQLHANDLE     hstmt;  /* statement handle */
    SQLCHAR       server[MAX_SERVER_LENGTH + 1] ;
    SQLCHAR       uid[MAX_UID_LENGTH + 1] ;
    SQLCHAR       pwd[MAX_PWD_LENGTH + 1] ;
    SQLCHAR       stmt[MAX_STMT_LENGTH + 1];
    SQLDOUBLE     salary, bonus, comm;
    double        raise, totalRaise;
    double        min_raise, max_raise;

    /* process the input parameters */
    if ( argc != 3 )
    {
        printf("Usage: TotalRaise Min_Raise_Percentage Max_Raise_Percentage\n");
        printf("       Both percentages have to be integers.\n");
        return -1;
    }

    min_raise = atoi(argv[1])/100.0;
    max_raise = atoi(argv[2])/100.0;


    /* allocate an environment handle */
    sqlrc = SQLAllocHandle( SQL_HANDLE_ENV, SQL_NULL_HANDLE, &henv );
    if ( sqlrc != SQL_SUCCESS )
        printf( "\n--ERROR while allocating the environment handle.\n" );


    /* allocate a database connection handle */
    sqlrc = SQLAllocHandle( SQL_HANDLE_DBC, henv, &hdbc );
    if ( sqlrc != SQL_SUCCESS )
        printf( "\n--ERROR while allocating the connection handle.\n" );


    /* connect to sample database */
    strcpy( (char *)server, "sample" );
    strcpy( (char *)uid, "db2admin" );
```

```
strcpy( (char *)pwd, "db2admin" );

sqlrc = SQLConnect( hdbc,
                    server, SQL_NTS,
                    uid,    SQL_NTS,
                    pwd,    SQL_NTS
                  );
if ( sqlrc != SQL_SUCCESS )
    printf( "\n--ERROR while connecting to database.\n" );


/* allocate a statement handle */
sqlrc = SQLAllocHandle(SQL_HANDLE_STMT, hdbc, &hstmt);              /*--(1)*/
if ( sqlrc != SQL_SUCCESS )
    printf( "\n--ERROR while allocating the statement handle.\n" );


/* calling the SQL procedure */
strcpy( (char *)stmt, "CALL DB2ADMIN.READ_EMP()" );

sqlrc = SQLExecDirect( hstmt, stmt, SQL_NTS );                      /*--(2)*/
if ( sqlrc != SQL_SUCCESS )
    printf( "\n--ERROR while calling the SQL procedure.\n" );


/* bind columns to variables */
sqlrc = SQLBindCol(hstmt, 1, SQL_C_DOUBLE, &salary, 0, NULL);       /*--(3)*/
if ( sqlrc != SQL_SUCCESS )
    printf( "\n--ERROR while binding salary column.\n" );

sqlrc = SQLBindCol(hstmt, 2, SQL_C_DOUBLE, &bonus, 0, NULL);
if ( sqlrc != SQL_SUCCESS )
    printf( "\n--ERROR while binding bonus column.\n" );

sqlrc = SQLBindCol(hstmt, 3, SQL_C_DOUBLE, &comm, 0, NULL);
if ( sqlrc != SQL_SUCCESS )
    printf( "\n--ERROR while binding comm column.\n" );


/* fetch result set returned from SQL procedure */
sqlrc = SQLFetch(hstmt);                                            /*--(4)*/
if ( sqlrc != SQL_SUCCESS && sqlrc != SQL_NO_DATA_FOUND )
    printf( "\n--ERROR while fetching the result set.\n" );

totalRaise = 0;
while (sqlrc != SQL_NO_DATA_FOUND)
{
    raise = min_raise;

    /* calculate raise */
    if ( bonus >= 600 )
        raise += 0.04;
```

```
        if ( comm < 2000 )
            raise += 0.03;
        else if ( comm < 3000 )
            raise += 0.02;
        else
            raise += 0.01;

        if ( raise > max_raise )
            raise = max_raise;

        totalRaise += salary * raise;

        sqlrc = SQLFetch(hstmt);
        if ( sqlrc != SQL_SUCCESS && sqlrc != SQL_NO_DATA_FOUND )
            printf( "\n--ERROR while fetching the result set.\n" );
    }

    printf("The total cost of the raise is: %.2f\n", totalRaise);



    /* free the statement handle */
    sqlrc = SQLFreeHandle(SQL_HANDLE_STMT, hstmt);
    if ( sqlrc != SQL_SUCCESS )
        printf( "\n--ERROR while freeing the statement handle.\n" );


    /* disconnect from the database */
    sqlrc = SQLDisconnect( hdbc ) ;
    if ( sqlrc != SQL_SUCCESS )
        printf( "\n--ERROR while disconnecting from database.\n" );


    /* free the connection handle */
    sqlrc = SQLFreeHandle( SQL_HANDLE_DBC, hdbc ) ;
    if ( sqlrc != SQL_SUCCESS )
        printf( "\n--ERROR while freeing the connection handle.\n" );


    /* free the environment handle */
    sqlrc = SQLFreeHandle( SQL_HANDLE_ENV, henv );
    if ( sqlrc != SQL_SUCCESS )
        printf( "\n--ERROR while freeing the environment handle.\n" );


    printf("Completed(0).\n");
    return( 0 );
} /* main */
```

In DB2 CLI, you need to allocate a statement handle before you can invoke SQL procedures (or execute any SQL statement for that matter). The function is *SQLAllocHandle()* (1) with appropriate parameters. In this case, since the SQL procedure requires no input parameters, you can invoke the procedure by calling the *SQLExecDirect()* (2) function without going through *SQLPrepare()* and *SQLBindParameter()* calls, which would allow you to bind the host variables with input and output parameters.

After execution, the result sets are returned through the statement handle. To access the data, you need to bind the host variables to the result set columns using *SQLBindCol()* function (3). Another useful function, *SQLNumResultCols()* (which is not used in our example), allows you to check the number of columns returned by the cursor. This function would be useful if you needed to write more dynamic code to deal with cases in which the result set columns are unknown. Once the variables are bound, you can fetch one row at a time using the *SQLFetch()* function (4) in a while loop. The condition of the loop checks the return code of *SQLFetch()* against a defined constant SQL_NO_DATA_FOUND.

For more information on CLI/ODBC programming, please refer to *DB2 Call Level Interface Guide and Reference.*

When you are finished with the cursor, don't forget to free all your allocated handles.

## H.3 Receiving Multiple Result Sets in Java Applications

Receiving multiple result sets is similar to receiving a single result set. The question to ask yourself when you write your client code is whether you want to process the result sets in parallel.

Processing result sets in sequence means you access each result set one at a time. The current result set is closed before the next result set is opened. Processing result sets in parallel means you can have more than one result set open at the same time.

If the calling application is an SQL procedure, you have the option of processing the result sets in sequence or in parallel, which is covered in Chapter 7, "Nested SQL Procedures." Similarly, if the calling application is a DB2 CLI program, you have the same options. If the calling application is a Java program, however, the result sets must be processed in sequence.

In JDBC, you move to the next result set by calling the *getMoreResults()* method of the *Statement* interface. According to the JDBC standard, this method implicitly closes any existing *ResultSet* object obtained with the method *getResultSet()*.

Figure H.3 is the complete Java client code for receiving and using all three returned result sets. The program simply prints all data received from each cursor, in sequence, without saving retrieved data in local variables. The program can only process a result set after the previous result set has been processed.

**Figure H.3** PrintSalary.Java - Example of Receiving Multiple Result Sets from a Java Application

```
import java.lang.*;
import java.util.*;
import java.io.*;
import java.sql.*;
import COM.ibm.db2.jdbc.app.*;

class PrintSalary
{
    static
    {
        try
        {
            Class.forName ("COM.ibm.db2.jdbc.app.DB2Driver").newInstance ();
        }
        catch (Exception e)
        {
            System.out.println ("\n  Error loading DB2 Driver...\n");
            System.out.println (e);
            System.exit(1);
        }
    }

    public static void main (String argv[])
    {
        Connection con = null;

        try
        {
            double v_salary, v_bonus, v_comm;

            // Connect to Sample database
            String url = "jdbc:db2:sample";
            con = DriverManager.getConnection(url);

            CallableStatement cs = con.prepareCall("CALL
db2admin.read_emp_multi()");

            cs.execute();
            ResultSet rs1 = cs.getResultSet();

            while ( rs1.next() )                                        /*--(1)*/
            {
                v_salary = rs1.getDouble(1);
                System.out.println(v_salary);
            }                                                           /*--(2)*/
```

```
            cs.getMoreResults();                                          /*--(3)*/
            ResultSet rs2 = cs.getResultSet();

            while ( rs2.next() )
            {
                v_bonus = rs2.getDouble(1);
                System.out.println(v_bonus);
            }

            cs.getMoreResults();
            ResultSet rs3 = cs.getResultSet();

            while ( rs3.next() )
            {
                v_comm = rs3.getDouble(1);
                System.out.println(v_comm);
            }

            rs1.close();
            rs2.close();
            rs3.close();
            cs.close ();
            con.close ();

            System.out.println("Complete(0).");
        }
        catch (Exception e)
        {
            try
            {
                if( con != null )
                {
                    con.close();
                }
            }
            catch (Exception x)
            {   //ignore this exception
            }
            System.out.println (e);
        }
    }
}
```

Even though three different *ResultSet* object variables were declared and used for each result set, you still cannot process all result sets at the same time. If you were to move the block of code processing the first result set, between line (1) and (2), to after the invocation of the *getMoreResults()* method at (3), you would not be able to access the first result set anymore. If you wanted to work with the first and the second result set at the same time, you will have to declare an array to hold the first result set.

## H.4 Receiving Multiple Result Sets in C or C++ Applications

DB2 CLI has a similar function as the *getMoreResults()* JDBC method for sequential result set processing. The function is *SQLMoreResults()*. Additionally, DB2 CLI supports another function called *SQLNextResult()* which allows you to access and process more than one result set at the same time. Both functions are demonstrated in Figure H.4.

**Figure H.4** PrintSalary.c - Example of Receiving Multiple Result Sets from a CLI Application

```
#include <stdio.h>
#include <string.h>
#include <stdlib.h>
#include <sqlcli1.h>
#include <sqlca.h>

#define MAX_SERVER_LENGTH   10
#define MAX_UID_LENGTH      10
#define MAX_PWD_LENGTH      10
#define MAX_STMT_LENGTH    200

int main(int argc, char *argv[])
{
    SQLRETURN      sqlrc = SQL_SUCCESS;
    SQLHANDLE      henv;  /* environment handle */
    SQLHANDLE      hdbc;  /* connection handle */
    SQLHANDLE      hstmt1;  /* statement handle */
    SQLHANDLE      hstmt2;  /* statement handle */
    SQLCHAR        server[MAX_SERVER_LENGTH + 1] ;
    SQLCHAR        uid[MAX_UID_LENGTH + 1] ;
    SQLCHAR        pwd[MAX_PWD_LENGTH + 1] ;
    SQLCHAR        stmt[MAX_STMT_LENGTH + 1];
    SQLDOUBLE      salary, bonus, comm;

    /* allocate an environment handle */
    sqlrc = SQLAllocHandle( SQL_HANDLE_ENV, SQL_NULL_HANDLE, &henv );
    if ( sqlrc != SQL_SUCCESS )
        printf( "\n--ERROR while allocating the environment handle.\n" );


    /* allocate a database connection handle */
    sqlrc = SQLAllocHandle( SQL_HANDLE_DBC, henv, &hdbc );
    if ( sqlrc != SQL_SUCCESS )
        printf( "\n--ERROR while allocating the connection handle.\n" );


    /* connect to sample database */
    strcpy( (char *)server, "sample" );
    strcpy( (char *)uid, "db2admin" );
```

```
strcpy( (char *)pwd, "db2admin" );

sqlrc = SQLConnect( hdbc,
                    server, SQL_NTS,
                    uid,    SQL_NTS,
                    pwd,    SQL_NTS
                  );
if ( sqlrc != SQL_SUCCESS )
    printf( "\n--ERROR while connecting to database.\n" );


/* allocate statement handles */
sqlrc = SQLAllocHandle(SQL_HANDLE_STMT, hdbc, &hstmt1);
if ( sqlrc != SQL_SUCCESS )
    printf( "\n--ERROR while allocating the statement handle1.\n" );

sqlrc = SQLAllocHandle(SQL_HANDLE_STMT, hdbc, &hstmt2);
if ( sqlrc != SQL_SUCCESS )
    printf( "\n--ERROR while allocating the statement handle2.\n" );


/* calling the SQL procedure */
strcpy( (char *)stmt, "CALL DB2ADMIN.READ_EMP_MULTI()" );

sqlrc = SQLExecDirect( hstmt1, stmt, SQL_NTS );
if ( sqlrc != SQL_SUCCESS )
    printf( "\n--ERROR while calling the SQL procedure.\n" );


/* fetch first two result sets */
sqlrc = SQLBindCol(hstmt1, 1, SQL_C_DOUBLE, &salary, 0, NULL);
if ( sqlrc != SQL_SUCCESS )
    printf( "\n--ERROR while binding salary column.\n" );

sqlrc = SQLNextResult(hstmt1, hstmt2);                          /*--(1)*/
if ( sqlrc != SQL_SUCCESS )
    printf( "\n--ERROR while opening the second result set.\n" );

sqlrc = SQLBindCol(hstmt2, 1, SQL_C_DOUBLE, &bonus, 0, NULL);
if ( sqlrc != SQL_SUCCESS )
    printf( "\n--ERROR while binding bonus column.\n" );

sqlrc = SQLFetch(hstmt1);
if ( sqlrc != SQL_SUCCESS && sqlrc != SQL_NO_DATA_FOUND )
    printf( "\n--ERROR while fetching the result set.\n" );

sqlrc = SQLFetch(hstmt2);
if ( sqlrc != SQL_SUCCESS && sqlrc != SQL_NO_DATA_FOUND )
    printf( "\n--ERROR while fetching the result set.\n" );

while (sqlrc != SQL_NO_DATA_FOUND)
{
```

```
        printf("%.2f, %.2f\n", salary, bonus);

        sqlrc = SQLFetch(hstmt1);
        if ( sqlrc != SQL_SUCCESS && sqlrc != SQL_NO_DATA_FOUND )
            printf( "\n--ERROR while fetching the result set.\n" );

        sqlrc = SQLFetch(hstmt2);
        if ( sqlrc != SQL_SUCCESS && sqlrc != SQL_NO_DATA_FOUND )
            printf( "\n--ERROR while fetching the result set.\n" );
    }


    /* fetch the third result set */
    sqlrc = SQLMoreResults(hstmt1);                                    /*--(2)*/

    sqlrc = SQLBindCol(hstmt1, 1, SQL_C_DOUBLE, &comm, 0, NULL);
    if ( sqlrc != SQL_SUCCESS )
        printf( "\n--ERROR while binding comm column.\n" );

    sqlrc = SQLFetch(hstmt1);
    printf("\nThe comissions are:\n");
    while (sqlrc != SQL_NO_DATA_FOUND)
    {
        printf("%.2f\n", comm);

        sqlrc = SQLFetch(hstmt1);
        if ( sqlrc != SQL_SUCCESS && sqlrc != SQL_NO_DATA_FOUND )
            printf( "\n--ERROR while fetching the result set.\n" );
    }


    /* free the statement handles */
    sqlrc = SQLFreeHandle(SQL_HANDLE_STMT, hstmt1);
    if ( sqlrc != SQL_SUCCESS )
        printf( "\n--ERROR while freeing the statement handle1.\n" );

    sqlrc = SQLFreeHandle(SQL_HANDLE_STMT, hstmt2);
    if ( sqlrc != SQL_SUCCESS )
        printf( "\n--ERROR while freeing the statement handle2.\n" );


    /* disconnect from the database */
    sqlrc = SQLDisconnect( hdbc ) ;
    if ( sqlrc != SQL_SUCCESS )
        printf( "\n--ERROR while disconnecting from database.\n" );


    /* free the connection handle */
    sqlrc = SQLFreeHandle( SQL_HANDLE_DBC, hdbc ) ;
    if ( sqlrc != SQL_SUCCESS )
        printf( "\n--ERROR while freeing the connection handle.\n" );
```

```
    /* free the environment handle */
    sqlrc = SQLFreeHandle( SQL_HANDLE_ENV, henv );
    if ( sqlrc != SQL_SUCCESS )
        printf( "\n--ERROR while freeing the environment handle.\n" );


    printf("Completed(0).\n");
    return( 0 );
} /* main */
```

The C/CLI version of the *PrintSalary.c* program is similar to its Java version. However, because of the *SQLNextResult()* function, data from different result sets can be accessed at the same time. The example in Figure H.4 prints the salary and bonus columns on the same line.

In order to use *SQLNextResult()*, you need to declare and allocate an additional statement handle. With *SQLMoreResults()* (2) function, the first result set is closed to allow the next result set to be accessed. With *SQLNextResult()*function (1), the additional statement handle is associated with the next result set, without closing the first result set, allowing access to both result sets at the same time. Once the result sets are associated with different statement handles, you can fetch and use the result sets in any order you want.

*SQLMoreResults()* and *SQLNextResult()* can be used together in any order. When either function is called, a result set from the SQL procedure is transferred to a statement handle at the client and is removed from the queue of remaining result sets to be processed by that procedure, so you do not have to worry about accessing the same data twice.

APPENDIX I

# SQL PL Cross-Platform Compatibility

The SQL Procedural Language is a standard language used across the DB2 Family of products. SQL PL support is consistent for DB2 on Linux, UNIX and Windows. However, the language is not completely compatible with DB2 for OS/390 and AS/400. This appendix is derived, and reprinted with permission, from the IBM Redbook *Cross-Platform DB2 Stored Procedures: Building and Debugging*, to show SQL PL compatibility by platform.

The first column, *Supported*, indicates if the statement is available on that platform. A dash (-) means that this statement is not available/not relevant to the platform. A yes (Y) means it is supported and no (N) means it is not supported.

The second column, *Valid,* indicates if the SQL statement is valid in SQL Procedures.

SQL statements are summarized in Table I.1. SQL procedural statements are summarized in Table I.2. Table I.3 lists limits in SQL procedures.

**Table I.1** SQL Statements in SQL Procedures

| SQL Statement | UNIX, Windows, and OS/2 Supported Valid | OS/390 Supported Valid | AS/400 Supported Valid |
|---|---|---|---|
| ALLOCATE CURSOR | Y Y | Y N | - - |
| ALTER BUFFERPOOL | Y N | - - | - - |
| ALTER DATABASE | - - | Y Y | - - |
| ALTER FUNCTION | - - | Y Y in V7 | - - |
| ALTER INDEX | - - | Y Y | - - |
| ALTER NICKNAME | Y N | Y N | - - |
| ALTER NODEGROUP | Y N | - - | - - |
| ALTER PROCEDURE | - - | Y Y in V7 | - - |
| ALTER SERVER | Y N | - - | - - |
| ALTER STOGROUP | - - | Y Y | - - |
| ALTER TABLE | Y N | Y Y | Y Y |
| ALTER TABLESPACE | Y N | Y Y | - - |
| ALTER TYPE | Y N | - - | - - |
| ALTER USER MAPPING | Y N | - - | - - |
| ALTER VIEW | Y N | - - | - - |
| ASSOCIATE CURSOR | Y Y | Y N | - - |
| BEGIN DECLARE SECTION | Y N | Y N | Y N |
| CALL | Y Y (1) | Y Y (1) | Y Y |
| CLOSE | Y Y | Y Y | Y Y |
| COMMENT ON | Y Y | Y Y | Y Y |
| COMMIT | Y Y | Y N/Supported in V7 | Y Y (2) |
| COMPOUND SQL | Y Y | Y Y | Y Y |
| CONNECT | Y N | Y Y | Y Y |
| CREATE ALIAS | Y N | Y Y | Y Y |
| CREATE AUXILIARY TABLE | | Y N | - - |
| CREATE BUFFERPOOL | Y N | - - | - - |
| CREATE DATABASE | - - | Y Y | Y Y |

**Table I.1** SQL Statements in SQL Procedures (continued)

| SQL Statement | UNIX, Windows, and OS/2 Supported Valid | OS/390 Supported Valid | AS/400 Supported Valid |
|---|---|---|---|
| CREATE DISTINCT TYPE | Y N | Y Y in V7 | Y Y |
| CREATE EVENT MONITOR | Y N | - - | - - |
| CREATE FUNCTION | Y N | Y Y in V7 | Y Y(3) |
| CREATE GLOBAL TEMPORARY TABLE | - - | Y Y | - - |
| CREATE INDEX | Y Y | Y Y | Y Y |
| CREATE INDEX EXTENSION | Y N | - - | - - |
| CREATE METHOD | Y N | - - | - - |
| CREATE NICKNAME | Y N | - - | - - |
| CREATE NODEGROUP | Y N | - - | - - |
| CREATE PROCEDURE | Y N | Y Y in V7 | Y Y(4) |
| CREATE SCHEMA | Y N | - - | Y Y |
| CREATE SERVER | Y N | - - | - - |
| CREATE STOGROUP | - - | Y Y | - - |
| CREATE SYNONYM | - - | Y Y | Y Y |
| CREATE TABLE | Y Y | Y Y | Y Y |
| CREATE TABLESPACE | Y Y | Y Y | - - |
| CREATE TRANSFORM | Y N | - - | - - |
| CREATE TRIGGER | Y N | Y Y in V7 | Y N |
| CREATE TYPE | Y N | - - | Y Y |
| CREATE TYPE MAPPING | Y N | - - | - - |
| CREATE USER MAPPING | Y N | - - | - - |
| CREATE VIEW | Y Y | Y Y | Y Y |
| CREATE WRAPPER | Y N | - - | - - |
| DECLARE CURSOR | Y Y | Y Y | Y Y |
| DECLARE GLOBAL TEMPORARY TABLE | Y Y | Y Y | - - |
| DECLARE STATEMENT | Y Y | Y Y | Y N |
| DECLARE TABLE | - - | Y N | - - |
| DELETE | Y Y | Y Y(5) | Y Y |

**Table I.1** SQL Statements in SQL Procedures (continued)

| SQL Statement | UNIX, Windows, and OS/2 Supported Valid | OS/390 Supported Valid | AS/400 Supported Valid |
|---|---|---|---|
| DESCRIBE | Y N | Y N | Y N |
| DISCONNECT | Y N | - - | Y Y |
| DROP | Y Y | Y Y | Y Y |
| END DECLARE SECTION | Y N | Y N | Y N |
| EXECUTE | Y Y | Y Y | Y Y |
| EXECUTE IMMEDIATE | Y Y | Y Y | Y Y |
| EXPLAIN | Y Y | Y N | N N |
| FETCH | Y Y | Y Y | Y Y |
| FLUSH EVENT MONITOR | Y N | - - | - - |
| FREE LOCATOR | Y N | Y N | Y N |
| GRANT | Y Y | Y Y | Y Y |
| HOLD LOCATOR | - - | Y N | - - |
| INCLUDE | Y N | Y N | Y N |
| INSERT | Y Y | Y Y | Y Y |
| LABEL ON | - - | Y Y | Y Y |
| LOCK TABLE | Y Y | Y Y | Y Y |
| OPEN | Y Y | Y Y | Y Y |
| PREPARE | Y Y | Y Y | Y Y |
| REFRESH TABLE | Y N | - - | - - |
| RELEASE | Y N | Y Y | Y Y |
| RELEASE SAVEPOINT | Y Y | Y Y | N N |
| RENAME | Y N | Y Y | Y Y |
| RENAME TABLESPACE | Y N | - - | - - |
| REVOKE | Y N | Y Y | Y Y |
| ROLLBACK | Y Y | Y Y in V7 | Y Y |
| ROLLBACK SAVEPOINT | Y Y(6) | Y Y | N N |
| SAVEPOINT | Y Y | Y Y | N N |
| SELECT INTO | Y Y | Y Y | Y Y |

**Table I.1** SQL Statements in SQL Procedures (continued)

| SQL Statement | UNIX, Windows, and OS/2 Supported Valid | OS/390 Supported Valid | AS/400 Supported Valid |
|---|---|---|---|
| SET assignment | Y Y | Y Y | Y Y |
| SET CURRENT | Y Y | Y Y | Y Y(7) |
| SIGNAL SQLSTATE | Y Y | Y N | Y Y |
| UPDATE | Y Y | Y Y | Y Y |
| VALUES | Y Y | Y N | Y N |
| VALUES INTO | Y Y | Y N | Y Y |
| WHENEVER | Y N | Y N | Y N |

1. Up to 16 levels.
2. Only allowed for NOT ATOMIC procedures that are NOT invoked through DRDA.
3. Only external functions can be created in an SQL routine.
4. Static CREATE. Only external procedures can be created in an SQL routine.
5. Create procedure fails when DELETE without WHERE condition.
6. Rollback only possible to the most recent savepoint. Nested savepoints not supported. SQLCODE –20112 occurs at run-time. Build procedure works fine even if nested savepoints in procedure. Savepoints are not allowed in atomic compound statements.
7. Supported for SET CURRENT PATH.

**Table I.2** SQL PL Statements in SQL Procedures

| SQL Statement | UNIX, Windows, and OS/2 Supported Valid | OS/390 Supported Valid | AS/400 Supported Valid |
|---|---|---|---|
| ALLOCATE CURSOR | Y Y | Y N | Y Y |
| ASSIGNMENT statement | Y Y | Y Y | Y Y |
| Select statement on right hand side of SET statement | Y Y | Y N | Y Y |
| ASSOCIATE LOCATOR statement | Y Y | Y N | N N |
| CALL statement | Y Y | Y Y | Y Y |
| CASE statement | Y Y(1) | Y Y(2) | Y Y |
| COMPOUND statement | Y Y | Y Y | Y Y |

**Table I.2** SQL PL Statements in SQL Procedures *(continued)*

| SQL Statement | UNIX, Windows, and OS/2 Supported Valid | OS/390 Supported Valid | AS/400 Supported Valid |
|---|---|---|---|
| ATOMIC | Y Y | - - | Y Y |
| NOT ATOMIC | Y Y | Y Y | Y Y |
| Variable name with the same Name as column | Y Y(3) | Y Y(4) | Y Y(3) |
| CLOB data type | Y Y | Y N | Y Y |
| BIGINT data type | Y Y | - - | Y Y |
| BLOB data type | Y Y | Y N | Y Y |
| CHARACTER data type | Y Y(5) | Y Y(5) | Y Y(6) |
| DATALINK data type | Y N | - - | Y Y |
| DATE data type | Y Y | Y Y | Y Y |
| DBCLOB data type | Y Y | - - | Y Y |
| DECIMAL data type | Y Y | Y Y | Y Y |
| DOUBLE data type | Y Y | Y Y | Y Y |
| FLOAT data type | Y Y | Y Y | Y Y |
| GRAPHIC data type | Y Y | Y Y | Y Y |
| INTEGER data type | Y Y | Y Y | Y Y |
| LONGVARGRAPHIC | Y N | - - | Y N |
| REAL data type | Y Y | Y Y | Y Y |
| SMALLINT data type | Y Y | Y Y | Y Y |
| TIME data type | Y Y | Y Y | Y Y |
| TIMESTAMP data type | Y Y | Y Y | Y Y |
| User-defined data types | Y N | Y N | Y Y |
| VARCHAR data type | Y Y | Y Y | Y Y |
| VARGRAHPIC data type | Y N | Y Y | Y Y |
| CONTINUE handler | Y Y | Y Y | Y Y |
| EXIT handler | Y Y | Y Y | Y Y |
| UNDO handler | Y Y(7) | - - | Y Y |
| Nested ATOMIC compound statement | N N | - - | - - |
| Nested NOT ATOMIC coumpound statement | Y Y | - - | - - |

**Table I.2** SQL PL Statements in SQL Procedures *(continued)*

| SQL Statement | UNIX, Windows, and OS/2 Supported Valid | OS/390 Supported Valid | AS/400 Supported Valid |
|---|---|---|---|
| Specific order of statements in compound statement? | Y Y | Y Y | Y Y |
| Only compound statement in procedure body | Y Y | Y N | Y Y |
| FOR statement | Y Y | - - | Y Y |
| GET DIAGNOSTICS | Y Y | Y Y | Y Y |
| Row_count | Y Y | Y Y | Y Y |
| Return_status | Y Y | - - | Y Y |
| Message_text | N N | - - | Y |
| Message_length | N N | - - | Y Y |
| Message_octet_length | N N | - - | Y Y |
| GOTO statement | Y Y | Y Y | Y Y |
| IF statement | Y Y | Y Y | Y Y |
| ITERATE statement | Y Y | - - | - - |
| LEAVE statement | Y Y | Y Y | Y Y |
| LOOP statement | Y Y | Y Y | Y Y |
| REPEAT statement | Y Y | Y Y | Y Y |
| RESIGNAL statement | Y Y | - - | Y Y |
| RETURN statement | Y Y | - - | Y Y |
| SIGNAL statement | Y Y | - - | Y Y |
| WHILE statement | Y Y | Y Y | Y Y |

1. Allowed up to three levels for both simple and searched case statement when clause.
2. Allowed up to three levels for simple case statement when clause. Unlimited for searched case statement when clause.
3. DB2 interprets the identifier as column.
4. DB2 interprets the name as an SQL variable or parameter name. Qualify column name with table name to refer to it.
5. Max 255 bytes.
6. Max 32740 bytes.
7. ATOMIC must be specified.

**Table I.3** Limits in SQL Procedures

| SQL Statement | UNIX, Windows, and OS/2 | OS/390 | AS/400 |
|---|---|---|---|
| Max length of procedure name | 128 | 18 | 128 |
| Max length of parameter names | 128 | 18 | 30 |
| Max length of source code | 64KB | 32KB | 32KB |
| Authorization behavior with dynamic SQL statements; will use executor's authority for both DML and DDL | Supported | Supported | Supported |
| Returning result sets | Supported | Supported | Supported |
| Returning multi-rowed result sets | Supported | Supported | No |
| Stand-alone SQLCODE/SQLSTATE(1) | Supported | Supported | Supported |
| Single statement procedure(2) | Supported | Supported | Supported |
| Label on all statements (for GOTOs) | Supported | No | Supported |
| C style comment (3) | Supported | Supported | Supported |
| Overriding of PREP and compile options | Supported | Supported | Supported(3) |
| Newline stored in the catalog – consistency | Supported | (4) | (5) |
| Recognition of procedure end (for prep) | Supported | (6) | Supported |
| LOB locator | Not supported | Not supported | Supported |
| DATE arithmetic | Supported | Supported | Supported |

1. Standalone SQLSTATE/SQLCODE means: you can have a PSM variable named SQLCODE or SQLSTATE that will be updated after every SQL statement execution. You cannot have 2 of these (one global and one in a local block). They must be declared once in the main block of the SP. This function is important for people that do not want to use the handler programming model. Standalone SQLCODE/SQLSTATE are not part of SQL/PSM standard and this should be used only for applications that are migrated from other RDBMS, so the code looks nearly similar. New applications should directly code with exception handlers.
2. Single statement procedures only have one SQL statement in them. It could be a huge SELECT statement or a big CASE statement with plenty of SQL statements in it. There is no BEGIN..END block as in the following example.
3. Supported via options in Client Access. Supported on the RUNSQLSTM interface. Supported via SET OPTION in statement in V5R1.
4. Newline markers are stored in SYSIBM.SYSPSM for SPB to recover the initial "look" of the stored procedure. The debugger will display PSM source as 80 byte wide lines (a DB2 for OS/390 pre-compiler restriction).

5. Currently strip out all extra blanks and control characters. This is partially because the catalog column is VARCHAR(18432), but the procedure body can be larger than that. This will be supported in V5R1.
6. End of file indicates the end of the SQL procedure.

# INDEX

## T

## U



## V



## W

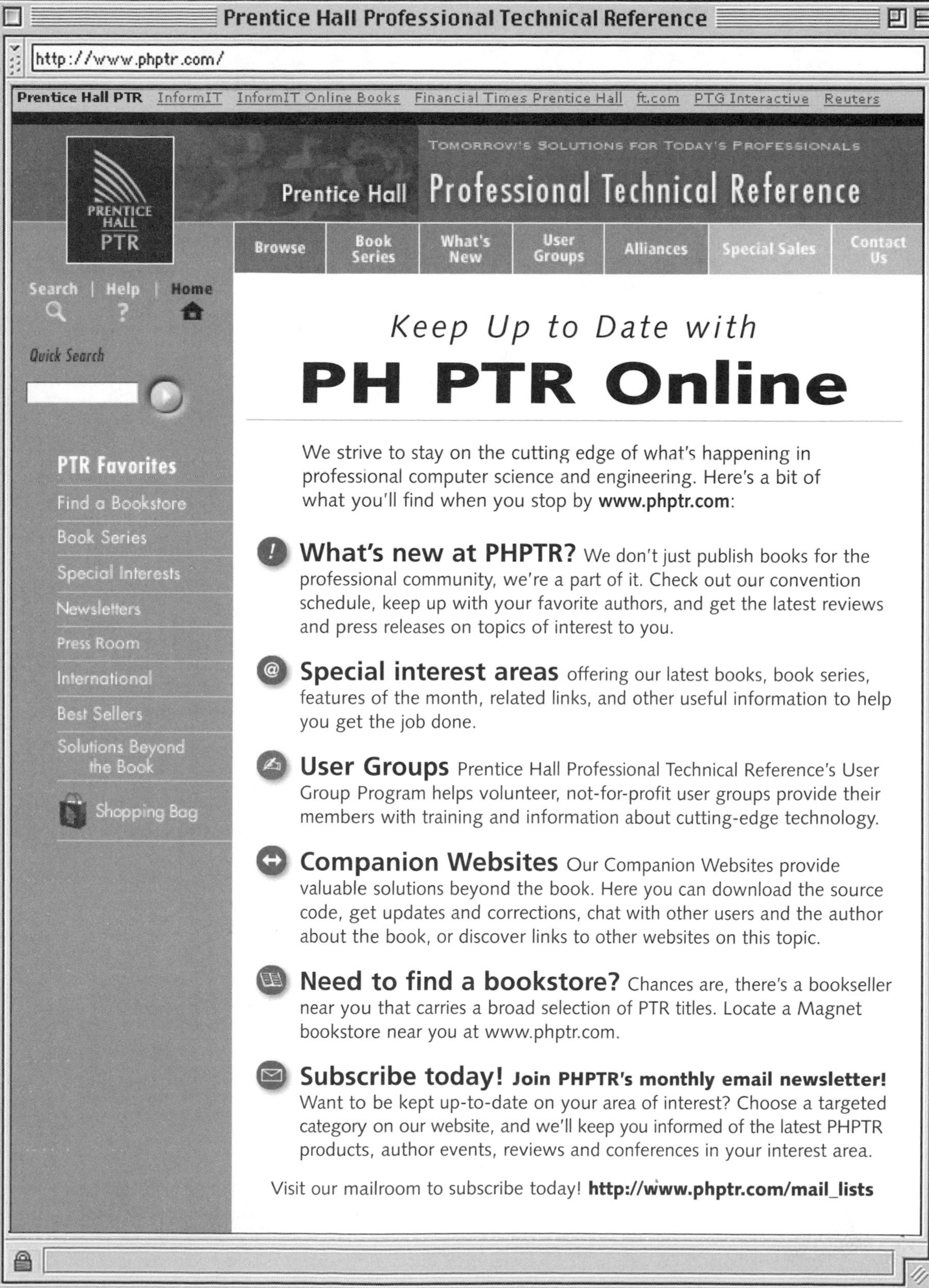
Prentice Hall Professional Technical Reference
http://www.phptr.com/
Prentice Hall PTR InformIT InformIT Online Books Financial Times Prentice Hall ft.com PTG Interactive Reuters
Tomorrow's Solutions for Today's Professionals
PRENTICE HALL PTR
Prentice Hall Professional Technical Reference
Browse
Book Series
What's New
User Groups
Alliances
Special Sales
Contact Us
Search | Help | Home
Quick Search
PTR Favorites
Find a Bookstore
Book Series
Special Interests
Newsletters
Press Room
International
Best Sellers
Solutions Beyond the Book
Shopping Bag
Keep Up to Date with
PH PTR Online
We strive to stay on the cutting edge of what's happening in professional computer science and engineering. Here's a bit of what you'll find when you stop by www.phptr.com:
What's new at PHPTR? We don't just publish books for the professional community, we're a part of it. Check out our convention schedule, keep up with your favorite authors, and get the latest reviews and press releases on topics of interest to you.
Special interest areas offering our latest books, book series, features of the month, related links, and other useful information to help you get the job done.
User Groups Prentice Hall Professional Technical Reference's User Group Program helps volunteer, not-for-profit user groups provide their members with training and information about cutting-edge technology.
Companion Websites Our Companion Websites provide valuable solutions beyond the book. Here you can download the source code, get updates and corrections, chat with other users and the author about the book, or discover links to other websites on this topic.
Need to find a bookstore? Chances are, there's a bookseller near you that carries a broad selection of PTR titles. Locate a Magnet bookstore near you at www.phptr.com.
Subscribe today! Join PHPTR's monthly email newsletter!
Want to be kept up-to-date on your area of interest? Choose a targeted category on our website, and we'll keep you informed of the latest PHPTR products, author events, reviews and conferences in your interest area.
Visit our mailroom to subscribe today! http://www.phptr.com/mail_lists

## LICENSE AGREEMENT AND LIMITED WARRANTY

READ THE FOLLOWING TERMS AND CONDITIONS CAREFULLY BEFORE OPENING THIS SOFTWARE MEDIA PACKAGE. THIS LEGAL DOCUMENT IS AN AGREEMENT BETWEEN YOU AND PRENTICE-HALL, INC. (THE "COMPANY"). BY OPENING THIS SEALED SOFTWARE MEDIA PACKAGE, YOU ARE AGREEING TO BE BOUND BY THESE TERMS AND CONDITIONS. IF YOU DO NOT AGREE WITH THESE TERMS AND CONDITIONS, DO NOT OPEN THE SOFTWARE MEDIA PACKAGE. PROMPTLY RETURN THE UNOPENED SOFTWARE MEDIA PACKAGE AND ALL ACCOMPANYING ITEMS TO THE PLACE YOU OBTAINED THEM FOR A FULL REFUND OF ANY SUMS YOU HAVE PAID.

1. **GRANT OF LICENSE:** In consideration of your payment of the license fee, which is part of the price you paid for this product, and your agreement to abide by the terms and conditions of this Agreement, the Company grants to you a nonexclusive right to use and display the copy of the enclosed software program (hereinafter the "SOFTWARE") on a single computer (i.e., with a single CPU) at a single location so long as you comply with the terms of this Agreement. The Company reserves all rights not expressly granted to you under this Agreement.

2. **OWNERSHIP OF SOFTWARE:** You own only the magnetic or physical media (the enclosed SOFTWARE) on which the SOFTWARE is recorded or fixed, but the Company retains all the rights, title, and ownership to the SOFTWARE recorded on the original SOFTWARE copy(ies) and all subsequent copies of the SOFTWARE, regardless of the form or media on which the original or other copies may exist. This license is not a sale of the original SOFTWARE or any copy to you.

3. **COPY RESTRICTIONS:** This SOFTWARE and the accompanying printed materials and user manual (the "Documentation") are the subject of copyright. You may not copy the Documentation or the SOFTWARE, except that you may make a single copy of the SOFTWARE for backup or archival purposes only. You may be held legally responsible for any copying or copyright infringement which is caused or encouraged by your failure to abide by the terms of this restriction.

4. **USE RESTRICTIONS:** You may not network the SOFTWARE or otherwise use it on more than one computer or computer terminal at the same time. You may physically transfer the SOFTWARE from one computer to another provided that the SOFTWARE is used on only one computer at a time. You may not distribute copies of the SOFTWARE or Documentation to others. You may not reverse engineer, disassemble, decompile, modify, adapt, translate, or create derivative works based on the SOFTWARE or the Documentation without the prior written consent of the Company.

5. **TRANSFER RESTRICTIONS:** The enclosed SOFTWARE is licensed only to you and may not be transferred to any one else without the prior written consent of the Company. Any unauthorized transfer of the SOFTWARE shall result in the immediate termination of this Agreement.

6. **TERMINATION:** This license is effective until terminated. This license will terminate automatically without notice from the Company and become null and void if you fail to comply with any provisions or limitations of this license. Upon termination, you shall destroy the Documentation and all copies of the SOFTWARE. All provisions of this Agreement as to warranties, limitation of liability, remedies or damages, and our ownership rights shall survive termination.

7. **MISCELLANEOUS:** This Agreement shall be construed in accordance with the laws of the United States of America and the State of New York and shall benefit the Company, its affiliates, and assignees.

8. **LIMITED WARRANTY AND DISCLAIMER OF WARRANTY:** The Company warrants that the SOFTWARE, when properly used in accordance with the Documentation, will operate in substantial conformity with the description of the SOFTWARE set forth in the Documentation. The Company does not warrant that the SOFTWARE will meet your requirements or that the operation of the SOFTWARE will be uninterrupted or error-free. The Company warrants that the

media on which the SOFTWARE is delivered shall be free from defects in materials and workmanship under normal use for a period of thirty (30) days from the date of your purchase. Your only remedy and the Company's only obligation under these limited warranties is, at the Company's option, return of the warranted item for a refund of any amounts paid by you or replacement of the item. Any replacement of SOFTWARE or media under the warranties shall not extend the original warranty period. The limited warranty set forth above shall not apply to any SOFTWARE which the Company determines in good faith has been subject to misuse, neglect, improper installation, repair, alteration, or damage by you. EXCEPT FOR THE EXPRESSED WARRANTIES SET FORTH ABOVE, THE COMPANY DISCLAIMS ALL WARRANTIES, EXPRESS OR IMPLIED, INCLUDING WITHOUT LIMITATION, THE IMPLIED WARRANTIES OF MERCHANTABILITY AND FITNESS FOR A PARTICULAR PURPOSE. EXCEPT FOR THE EXPRESS WARRANTY SET FORTH ABOVE, THE COMPANY DOES NOT WARRANT, GUARANTEE, OR MAKE ANY REPRESENTATION REGARDING THE USE OR THE RESULTS OF THE USE OF THE SOFTWARE IN TERMS OF ITS CORRECTNESS, ACCURACY, RELIABILITY, CURRENTNESS, OR OTHERWISE.

IN NO EVENT, SHALL THE COMPANY OR ITS EMPLOYEES, AGENTS, SUPPLIERS, OR CONTRACTORS BE LIABLE FOR ANY INCIDENTAL, INDIRECT, SPECIAL, OR CONSEQUENTIAL DAMAGES ARISING OUT OF OR IN CONNECTION WITH THE LICENSE GRANTED UNDER THIS AGREEMENT, OR FOR LOSS OF USE, LOSS OF DATA, LOSS OF INCOME OR PROFIT, OR OTHER LOSSES, SUSTAINED AS A RESULT OF INJURY TO ANY PERSON, OR LOSS OF OR DAMAGE TO PROPERTY, OR CLAIMS OF THIRD PARTIES, EVEN IF THE COMPANY OR AN AUTHORIZED REPRESENTATIVE OF THE COMPANY HAS BEEN ADVISED OF THE POSSIBILITY OF SUCH DAMAGES. IN NO EVENT SHALL LIABILITY OF THE COMPANY FOR DAMAGES WITH RESPECT TO THE SOFTWARE EXCEED THE AMOUNTS ACTUALLY PAID BY YOU, IF ANY, FOR THE SOFTWARE.

SOME JURISDICTIONS DO NOT ALLOW THE LIMITATION OF IMPLIED WARRANTIES OR LIABILITY FOR INCIDENTAL, INDIRECT, SPECIAL, OR CONSEQUENTIAL DAMAGES, SO THE ABOVE LIMITATIONS MAY NOT ALWAYS APPLY. THE WARRANTIES IN THIS AGREEMENT GIVE YOU SPECIFIC LEGAL RIGHTS AND YOU MAY ALSO HAVE OTHER RIGHTS WHICH VARY IN ACCORDANCE WITH LOCAL LAW.

**ACKNOWLEDGMENT**

YOU ACKNOWLEDGE THAT YOU HAVE READ THIS AGREEMENT, UNDERSTAND IT, AND AGREE TO BE BOUND BY ITS TERMS AND CONDITIONS. YOU ALSO AGREE THAT THIS AGREEMENT IS THE COMPLETE AND EXCLUSIVE STATEMENT OF THE AGREEMENT BETWEEN YOU AND THE COMPANY AND SUPERSEDES ALL PROPOSALS OR PRIOR AGREEMENTS, ORAL, OR WRITTEN, AND ANY OTHER COMMUNICATIONS BETWEEN YOU AND THE COMPANY OR ANY REPRESENTATIVE OF THE COMPANY RELATING TO THE SUBJECT MATTER OF THIS AGREEMENT.

Should you have any questions concerning this Agreement or if you wish to contact the Company for any reason, please contact in writing at the address below.

Robin Short
Prentice Hall PTR
One Lake Street
Upper Saddle River, New Jersey 07458

# About the CD-ROM

The accompanying CD-ROM contains:

- A trial version of DB2 Personal Edition for Windows
- Sample code from each chapter which can be conveniently imported into DB2 Development Center
- DB2 product documentation in HTML and PDF format
- The IBM Redbook, "Cross-Platform DB2 Stored Procedures: Building and Debugging"

## Instructions

To install DB2, run `db2v8PE\setup.exe`. After DB2 installation, see "Appendix B—Setting up the Build Environment" to configure your compiler for DB2.

For instructions on importing sample code directly into DB2 Development Center, see Appendix C.

To view the PDF documentation, open your browser to `PDFDOC\index.htm`

To view the HTML documentation, open your browser to `HTMLDOC\index.htm`

## Technical Support

Prentice Hall does not offer technical support for any of the programs on this CD-ROM. However, if there is a problem with the CD or it is damaged, you may obtain a replacement copy by sending an email describing the problem to:
`disc_exchange@prenhall.com`

For the latest information about the book, visit:
`http://ibm.com/software/data/developer/sqlplbook/`

For problems with the sample code or book content, please contact the authors at `db2sqlpl@ca.ibm.com`.